Alessandro Corsi • Filippo Barbera
Egidio Dansero • Cristiana Peano
Editors

Alternative Food Networks

An Interdisciplinary Assessment

palgrave
macmillan

Editors
Alessandro Corsi
Department of Economics and Statistics
"Cognetti de Martiis"
University of Torino
Torino, Italy

Egidio Dansero
Department of Cultures, Politics
and Society
University of Torino
Torino, Italy

Filippo Barbera
Department of Cultures, Politics
and Society
University of Torino
Torino, Italy

Collegio Carlo Alberto
Torino, Italy

Cristiana Peano
Department of Agricultural, Forest and
Food Sciences
University of Torino
Grugliasco (TO), Italy

ISBN 978-3-030-08009-9 ISBN 978-3-319-90409-2 (eBook)
https://doi.org/10.1007/978-3-319-90409-2

Cover illustration: Moment Open / Getty Images

This Palgrave Macmillan imprint is published by the registered company Springer Nature Switzerland AG
The registered company address is: Gewerbestrasse 11, 6330 Cham, Switzerland

Alternative Food Networks

Acknowledgement

Funding of this research by the University of Torino, Progetti di Ateneo [Call 3 "Strategic Research Grants", Project "Alternative Food Networks: an Interdisciplinary assessment"] is gratefully acknowledged.

We also wish to thank:

- Regione Piemonte for allowing the use of Agricultural Census data and Lorena Cora of CSI-Piemonte for very helpful assistance in using the relevant data warehouse
- The SPGs' representatives (in particular Andrea Saroldi of GAStorino) and Umberto Tresso and Mauro D'Aveni of Coldiretti for providing very helpful information, comments and suggestions and for their help in the data collection
- Vincenzo Iacomo for excellent research assistance and the interviewers who participated in the surveys
- The fruit growers who participated in our focus group
- The discussants at the Workshop on AFNs, Torino, October 26, 2016 (Maria Fonte, Giovanni Orlando, Filippo Randelli, Cristina Salvioni, Francesco Sottile) for their very helpful comments and suggestions

Contents

Part I Introductions 1

1 **Introduction** 3
Alessandro Corsi, Filippo Barbera, Egidio Dansero, and Cristiana Peano

2 **Multidisciplinary Approaches to Alternative Food Networks** 9
Alessandro Corsi, Filippo Barbera, Egidio Dansero, Giovanni Orlando, and Cristiana Peano

Part II AFNs from the Consumers' Viewpoint 47

3 **Introduction to Part II: AFNs from the Consumer's Viewpoint** 49
Filippo Barbera, Alessandro Corsi, and Cristiana Peano

4 **Determinants of Participation in AFNs and Its Value for Consumers** 57
Alessandro Corsi and Silvia Novelli

5 **Consumers' Quality Conventions in Alternative, Conventional, and High-End Food Chains** 87
Filippo Barbera, Joselle Dagnes, and Roberto Di Monaco

6 **The Environmental Quality Factors Sought by Consumers in Alternative and Conventional Market Channels** 119
Nadia Tecco and Cristiana Peano

7 **Understanding Alternative Food Networks After the Crisis: Testing Four Scenarios in Italy** 137
Giovanni Orlando

Part III AFNs from the Producers' Viewpoint 163

8 **Introduction to Part III: AFNs from the Producers' Viewpoint** 165
Alessandro Corsi, Filippo Barbera, and Silvia Novelli

9 **Determinants of Farmers' Participation in AFNs** 173
Alessandro Corsi, Silvia Novelli, and Giacomo Pettenati

10 **The Economic Viability of Solidarity Purchase Groups (*Gruppi di Acquisto Solidale*)** 197
Silvia Novelli and Alessandro Corsi

11 **Quality and Price Setting by Producers in AFNs** 215
Filippo Barbera, Joselle Dagnes, and Roberto Di Monaco

Part IV Environment, Territory, and AFNs 245

12 Introduction to Part IV: Environment, Territory, and AFNs 247
Alessandro Corsi, Egidio Dansero, and Cristiana Peano

13 Applied Environmental Sustainability of Fruit and Vegetables in Different Distribution Channels (AFNs and Large-Scale Retail) 251
Cristiana Peano, Nadia Tecco, and Vincenzo Girgenti

14 Reterritorialization, Proximity, and Urban Food Planning: Research Perspectives on AFNs 273
Egidio Dansero and Giacomo Pettenati

Part V Conclusions 303

15 Conclusions: An Interdisciplinary Assessment 305
Alessandro Corsi, Filippo Barbera, Egidio Dansero, and Cristiana Peano

Index 323

Notes on Contributors

Filippo Barbera is an Associate Professor of Economic Sociology at the Department of Cultures, Politics and Society of the University of Torino, Italy. Since 2010 he has been affiliated to the Collegio Carlo Alberto. His research interests are local development, sociology of markets and innovation and economic sociology of capitalism.

Alessandro Corsi is an Associate Professor of Agricultural Economics at the Department of Economics and Statistics "S. Cognetti de Martiis" of the University of Torino, Italy. He has been a consultant for DG/Agri of the EU Commission and for FAO. His research interests are the market of organic products and alternative food networks, wine economics, economic behaviour of family farms, agricultural labour markets and pluriactivity.

Joselle Dagnes (Ph.D., 2010, University of Torino) is a Research Fellow in Economic Sociology at the Department of Cultures, Politics and Society of the University of Torino, Italy. Her current research interests are sociology of markets, financialisation processes and social innovation.

Egidio Dansero is a Professor of Political and Economic Geography at the Department of Cultures, Politics and Society, University of Torino, Italy. His main scientific interests are in the fields of political and economic geography, development and urban studies and territorial and environmental policies.

Vincenzo Girgenti is a Temporary Research Associate at the Department of Agricultural, Forest and Food Sciences (DiSAFA) of the University of Torino, Italy. His research interests are in sustainable agriculture and Life Cycle Assessment.

Roberto Di Monaco is a Researcher and Aggregate Professor at the Department of Cultures, Politics and Society of the University of Torino, Italy, where he teaches "Organizational sociology" and "Leadership, networks and organizational processes". His research interests are innovation, competence, local development and social inequalities. From 1994 to 2007, he was a director of institutions and companies in the field of socio-economic research and counselling and he was a coordinator of many international projects.

Silvia Novelli (Ph.D., University of Torino) is an Assistant Professor (Ricercatore) of Agricultural Economics at the University of Torino (Italy), Department of Agricultural, Forest and Food Sciences (DiSAFA). Her teaching experience includes "Agro-environmental economics" and "Agricultural and Forest economics". Her main research interests focus on consumer/producer behaviour, multifunctionality in agriculture and economic evaluation of environmental goods and services.

Giovanni Orlando is currently a Marie Curie Fellow in the Department of Cultures, Politics and Society, University of Torino, Italy, where he leads the EU-funded project entitled "The value of alternative food networks after the crisis: An Italian case study". Giovanni trained as a social anthropologist at University College London (UCL) and Goldsmiths, University of London, and specialises in food studies, particularly from the angle of economic anthropology.

Cristiana Peano is an Associate Professor of Arboriculture at the Department of Agricultural, Forest and Food Sciences of the University of Torino, Italy. She has been a Scientific Advisor of several projects for the EU Commission and for FAO. Her main research interests are methods of post-harvest storage and treatments of fruits, quality evaluation and valorisation of fruits and vegetables.

Giacomo Pettenati holds a Ph.D. in Spatial Planning and Local Development. He is currently a Postdoc Researcher in Geography at the Department of Cultures, Politics and Society of the University of Torino, Italy. His main research topics are local food systems, rural and mountain development, participatory mapping and landscape heritage. He is part of the group of research working on the project Atlas of Food and the processes of definition of the urban food policies of Turin.

Nadia Tecco (Ph.D.) is a Postdoc Researcher at the Department of Cultures, Politics and Society of the University of Torino, Italy. Her present research activities are mainly focused on the analysis of agro-food supply chains and food networks and the sustainability integrated assessment of small-scale production systems (by adopting E-LCA, S-LCA, indicators).

List of Figures

Fig. 5.1	Percentage of respondents above the median value (=7) for the number of conventions regarded as important. Source: Barbera et al. (2018)	99
Fig. 5.2	Soft and hard quality in the four supply chains. Source: Barbera and Dagnes (2016)	100
Fig. 5.3	The Quality Space: Hard and Soft Quality. Note: the axis value is the percentage of consumers over the mean value of the factor by sale channels. Source: Barbera, Dagnes, and Di Monaco (2018)	108
Fig. 5.4	Positioning in the expected quality space. Note: the axis value is the percentage of consumers over the mean value of the factor by sale channels. Source: Barbera, Dagnes, and Di Monaco (2018)	111
Fig. 6.1	Graphic representation of the concept of environmental quality (according to the latent variables obtained through PCA) in the three channels. Source: Authors' calculations	129
Fig. 11.1	Map of Porta Palazzo market in Turin (farmers' market area circled in black). Source: https://scopriportapalazzo.com	223
Fig. 11.2	Two-dimensions scheme for degree of control over quality and price	238
Fig. 13.1	Generic system boundaries of fruit and vegetable life cycle with four subsystems (modified from Djekic et al., 2018)	255

Fig. 13.2 Theoretical framework for assessing environmental impacts applied to different products in our study. The framework is limited to the first three subsystems shown in Fig. 13.1 258
Fig. 14.1 Distribution of farmers' markets in the Turin metropolitan area municipalities (2016) 276
Fig. 14.2 Distribution of GASs in the Turin metropolitan area (2016) 277
Fig. 14.3 The distribution of Piedmont-based producers participating in farmers' markets and GASs in the city of Turin (2016) 280
Fig. 14.4 Dimensions of AFNs' territoriality (Dansero & Puttilli, 2013). Source: Dansero and Puttilli (2013) 285
Fig. 14.5 Interpretive framework for AFNs' territoriality (Dansero & Pettenati, 2015). Source: Dansero and Pettenati (2015) 286

List of Tables

Table 4.1	Attitudes towards the choice of market and stand	67
Table 4.2	Responses to the question about the main reasons for participating in the SPG (max 3 items)	73
Table 4.3	Reasons for staying with the SPG even with a price increase (%; $n = 85$)	75
Table 5.1	Items for quality conventions	96
Table 5.2	Consumer judgments of quality conventions in the five supply chains (scale 1–20)	97
Table 5.3	Purchasing habits by food chain	98
Table 5.4	Soft quality conventions ranking per sale channels	101
Table 5.5	Hard quality conventions ranking per sale channels	104
Table 5.6	Quality dimensions and supply chains (Anova analysis)	106
Table 5.7	Items and key words for expected quality: overall ranking	108
Table 5.8	Items and key words for expected quality: sale channels	110
Table 5.9	Positioning in the expected quality space (Anova analysis)	112
Table 6.1	Fruit and vegetables quality items	127
Table 9.1	Percentage of farms practising direct sales by type of farming	183
Table 9.2	Selected estimates of marginal effects of the determinants of on-farm and off-farm direct sales	185
Table 10.1	General information on SPGs, groups' balance, and implicit costs (IC)	206
Table 10.2	Hypotheses for balancing explicit and labour costs	207

Table 13.1 Total environmental impact (subsystems 1-2-3) for 1 kg of apples sold in different packaging formats and different markets. Production methods include integrated (PMI) and certified organic 262
Table 13.2 Total environmental impact (subsystems 1-2-3) for 250 g of strawberries sold in different packaging formats and different markets. Cultivation methods include integrated (PMI) and certified organic 263
Table 13.3 Total environmental impact (subsystems 1-2-3) for 1 kg of tomatoes sold in different packaging formats and different markets. Cultivation methods include integrated (PMI) and certified organic 264

Part I

Introductions

1

Introduction

Alessandro Corsi, Filippo Barbera, Egidio Dansero, and Cristiana Peano

A. Corsi (✉)
Department of Economics and Statistics "Cognetti de Martiis", University of Torino, Torino, Italy
e-mail: alessandro.corsi@unito.it

F. Barbera
Department of Cultures, Politics and Society, University of Torino, Torino, Italy

Collegio Carlo Alberto, Torino, Italy
e-mail: filippo.barbera@unito.it

E. Dansero
Department of Cultures, Politics and Society, University of Torino, Torino, Italy
e-mail: egidio.dansero@unito.it

C. Peano
Department of Agricultural, Forest and Food Sciences, University of Torino, Grugliasco (TO), Italy
e-mail: Cristiana.peano@unito.it

A. Corsi et al. (eds.), *Alternative Food Networks*,
https://doi.org/10.1007/978-3-319-90409-2_1

A plethora of new forms of food chains have emerged in recent decades. They include initiatives such as farmers' markets, community-supported agriculture, solidarity purchase groups, pick-up-your-product, and the like. They tend to present themselves as being different from—and often explicitly in opposition to—the "conventional" organization of the food chain. They have attracted considerable interest both in the social arena and in the academic world, where they are usually known under the heading of "Alternative Food Networks" (AFNs). On one hand, they are part of an emerging trend of consumption patterns that distance themselves from mass products and seek variety, naturalness, freshness, and authenticity in what has been called the "quality turn". On the other hand, some of them lie in a social and political stream that regards mass production with suspicion and is opposed to the existing agro-food system. Several social and political issues are connected with AFNs' existence and functioning. The most important are what could be termed the "food culture" and the environmental implications of food production and distribution. The conventional food system is faulted for its anonymity, the fungibility of food, and the lack of connection with the local area and producers, so that nothing is known about how and by whom food is produced. This, as the argument goes, has destroyed the age-old links between people and the food they eat that have arisen as a result of the coevolution between natural local resources, cooking technology, and evolving taste, thus creating a local culture of food. The conventional food system, as its critics claim, has provided cheap food at the expense of the environment, encouraging the intensification of large-scale agricultural production, the lavish use of chemical fertilizers and pesticides, the growth of huge factory farms, and global logistic chains for transporting food over long distances. Hence the emphasis on local food, seen as a way of reducing the environmental impact of long-distance transport (the "food miles" argument) and as a source of renewed cultural links that can restore meaning to food. Some authors and organizations also view AFNs as a way of supporting small farmers.

The so-called food studies have been attempting to single out AFNs' "alternativeness" with regard to sustainability, quality, and accessibility. Several definitions of AFNs have been proposed, with both descriptive and normative aims. In the last few years, a growing body of literature has underscored the need to overcome the "alternative-conventional" dichotomy, focusing instead on the multiple, overlapping worlds of food. As has been argued with regard to the topic of quality and food as "moral order", both demand and supply very rarely engage with single worlds of quality. Symbolic categories, social practices, and organizational forms are constantly blurred. However, the argument continues, this literature has rarely considered these aspects from an empirical viewpoint. We build on these studies, with a specific focus on whole food chains (demand-supply) and with a research design that considers both conventional and alternative food networks. Furthermore, we focus on a key regional context, Piedmont in northwestern Italy, which has played a leading role in the development of AFNs. Piedmont is the region where the Slow Food movement was born and also where the high-end food retailer Eataly opened its first store. It is a region where peasant agriculture in mountain and hill areas lives side by side with intensive agriculture in the flat land. Piedmont is, along with Tuscany, a key region for wine production and exports. But it is also a region where small and organic vineyards flourish. Piedmont is thus a critical case study, namely a context where AFNs have grown apace in recent years and where—for this reason—we can expect to find a sharper difference between the "worlds of food", "conventional" vs "alternative" chains. Piedmont is thus a strategic site for empirically testing whether, conversely, alternative and conventional food networks overlap. With regard to "food studics", we share their interdisciplinary perspective but differ from them in believing that the analysis of AFNs should not be separated from the major analytical concerns of the specific disciplines. AFNs are key to shedding light on general research topics, such as the interplay between intrinsic and extrinsic motivation, the sociology of markets, the urban-rural divide, environmental challenges, economic viability, and many more.

This perspective has several implications. From the analytical standpoint, unlike most of the literature, we consider the entire chain, from the producers to the end consumers. This is crucial in our view, since a chain obviously results from an interplay between different operators, connecting producers and consumers but also organizing this connection. Only by looking at the chain in its entirety and trying to analyse the different operators' behaviour and their interplay can an overall vision of how the chain functions be gained.

Second, we compare certain aspects of both alternative and conventional food chains, explicitly exploring their overlapping borders and working mechanisms. This is also important in our view, in particular with an eye to assessing the likely future prospects for AFNs. Whether the conventional chain will be able to imitate its alternative counterparts and provide consumers with desired food attributes that until now have been provided only by AFNs and which attributes will, by contrast, continue to be peculiar to AFNs are questions that can be only answered by an explicit consideration of how conventional chains operate and in particular of the concepts of quality they use in order to respond to consumers' new demands and the ways they can imitate AFNs in this respect.

Third, we adopt an interdisciplinary perspective that considers economical, sociological, geographical, anthropological, and environmental dimensions. Although there has been some interchange and overlap among different disciplines in the literature on AFNs, most studies have followed specific disciplinary approaches. We have attempted to make a more direct and explicit comparison between different disciplinary approaches and thus achieve a more comprehensive view of these chains that, by their very nature, have economic, social, geographical, and environmental implications. Economic, because even with all their possible alternative meanings, AFNs are nevertheless a form of organization that performs the economic function of delivering food from producers to consumers; social, because these transactions are deeply rooted in social relationships; geographical, because AFNs are connected with the spatial and cultural distance between producers and consumers; and environmental, because the modalities of delivering food have different environmental impacts and because consumers' and producers' beliefs and attitudes towards the environment affect these modalities.

The structure of the book follows these premises. The first Part is dedicated to the theories behind the analysis of AFNs. The discussion concerns the definition of AFNs and the criteria of "alternativeness" that are attributed to them and identifies the quality of the relationship among the participants as the main "alternative" characteristic of AFNs.

The following chapters concern the two sides of the chains, namely consumers and producers. Part II is devoted to an analysis of AFNs from the consumers' viewpoint. Corsi and Novelli discuss the issue in the light of economic theory and review the literature on consumers' motivations for participating in AFNs. They then investigate a chain that is not particularly "alternative"—farmers' stands in urban district markets—and a sample of typically "alternative" chains, namely, Solidarity Purchase

Groups (SPGs). Corsi and Novelli gauge how much the personal relationship with farmers counts in consumers' decision to buy from them directly and how much the participation in the SPG is worth for its members. Barbera, Dagnes, and Di Monaco compare consumers' concepts of quality in the intrinsic and intangible characteristics of food in alternative, conventional, and high-end food chains, arguing that high-end food retailers mimic AFNs in order to fulfil consumers' desire for "alternative" quality conventions. Tecco and Peano analyse the different mechanisms for gathering information about the environmental impact of products and how they can affect consumers' behaviour in purchasing fruit and vegetables. Orlando investigates the behaviour of a specific AFN born as a reaction to the economic crisis, especially from the point of view of consumers, concentrating on its strength and the problems it faces in conciliating political stances with the differing constraints and preferences of consumers and producers.

Part III deals with producers in AFNs. Corsi, Novelli, and Pettenati first analyse the characteristics and geographical distribution of farmers engaged in direct sales, whether on-farm or off-farm, and the determinants of their participation in these chains based on observable characteristics, highlighting the diversity of determinants, the technical constraints on engaging in direct sales, and the clustering of farms in specific areas. They then survey the subjective motivations for participation reported by a focus group of producers, who also discuss the consequences that participating in AFNs have brought about in their farms' setting and operation. Novelli and Corsi identify the voluntary work of members as the main basis for SPGs' economic viability and sustainability and thus also assess the strength of members' commitment to their SPGs. Barbera, Dagnes, and Di Monaco deal with the problem of prices and quality convention setting among small-scale producers attending a large district market, showing how producers determine their products' sales price and how different mechanisms and relationships with customers and among vendors bring about specific conflicts and compromises within and between quality conventions on the producers' side.

Part IV discusses the general implications of AFNs for the environment and the local area. Peano, Tecco, and Girgenti reflect critically on AFNs' potential and limits in reducing environmental impact and present a comparative assessment of the environmental impact of alternative and conventional chains. Dansero and Pettenati analyse the role of AFNs in the re-territorialization of food systems and locate Piedmontese AFNs in different concepts of proximity (physical, network, and cognitive).

Lastly, in Part V Corsi, Barbera, Dansero, and Peano review the main findings of theoretical and empirical research, reflect on the advantages of interdisciplinary analysis, and critically discuss AFNs' prospects for scaling up or scaling out. They stress the common finding of a strong heterogeneity across AFNs, including operators' preferences and their strength, nature of the personal relationships, and concepts of quality. As a result, they support the view that "alternativeness" lies along a continuum rather than standing in sharp, dichotomous contrast with the conventional chains. This helps in assessing the prospects for AFNs which, given the conventional food system's ability to mimic certain of their aspects and to meet demand for some food attributes that they have so far been alone in providing, are mainly dependent on the demand for attributes and modalities of exchange that conventional chains by their nature cannot offer.

2

Multidisciplinary Approaches to Alternative Food Networks

Alessandro Corsi, Filippo Barbera, Egidio Dansero, Giovanni Orlando, and Cristiana Peano

A. Corsi (✉)
Department of Economics and Statistics "Cognetti de Martiis", University of Torino, Torino, Italy
e-mail: alessandro.corsi@unito.it

F. Barbera
Department of Cultures, Politics and Society, University of Torino, Torino, Italy

Collegio Carlo Alberto, Torino, Italy
e-mail: filippo.barbera@unito.it

E. Dansero • G. Orlando
Department of Cultures, Politics and Society, University of Torino, Torino, Italy
e-mail: egidio.dansero@unito.it; giovanni.orlando@unito.it

C. Peano
Department of Agricultural, Forest and Food Sciences, University of Torino, Grugliasco (TO), Italy
e-mail: Cristiana.peano@unito.it

A. Corsi et al. (eds.), *Alternative Food Networks*,
https://doi.org/10.1007/978-3-319-90409-2_2

Alternative Definitions of Alternative Food Networks

The many examples of food chains that depart from the conventional type of organization have attracted interest not only in the social arena but also from the academic world. Such chains are generally known as Alternative Food Networks (AFNs). Alternative food networks are a wide-ranging body of practices dealing with food provisioning in a way that differs from the mainstream agro-food system (Murdoch, Marsden, & Banks, 2000). AFNs usually take the form of grassroots experiments that aim to reorganize the food system along ethical, political, moral, and health lines (Honkanen, Verplanken, & Ottar Olsen, 2006; Sassatelli, 2015; Vermeir & Verbeke, 2006). The term "alternative" seems to have been first used by geographers (Whatmore & Thorne, 1997) as "alternative geography of food", while Marsden, Banks, and Bristow (2000) more specifically cite "alternative food chains", and Renting, Marsden, and Banks (2003) introduce the term "alternative food networks", which has now become current. In spite of the extensive scientific literature on the topic, there is no shared definition of AFNs, partly because the literature focuses on different phenomena and thus uses different criteria for defining AFNs. Tregear (2011) argues that it is necessary to distinguish among different types of AFNs, rather than assigning common features to all of them. We will thus summarize the different criteria used to analyse the issue and the rationale behind them.

One of the first criteria that can be used to classify a specific food chain as "alternative" is the *length of the chain* and/or the *number of intermediaries* between producers and consumers. Several different, often interlinked, concerns underlie this criterion. The length of a chain can be considered in organizational terms, that is, the number of nodes in the chain, and from this perspective, short chains can be seen as a way of supporting farmers against intermediaries, who have market and bargaining power vis-à-vis farmers and thus benefit from rents at the expense of consumers and producers. This is especially the case when the number of intermediaries is used as a criterion of inclusion in the category of AFNs or of "short food supply chain", as it often is in official statements (Aubry & Chiffoleau, 2009). A second concern is environmental, popularized by the "food miles" concept (Paxton, 1994), where chain length is defined in terms of physical distance.

Short chains, "zero miles" initiatives, and the like are considered as tools to reduce an unnecessary waste of resources and an avoidable impact on the environment, under the assumption that the conventional chain entails several different nodes and transporting food over long distances. While this claim will be discussed in detail in Chap. 13, here we are concerned only with the rationale whereby chains are considered to be alternative.

A related criterion is the *local origin of food*. This largely overlaps with the concept of short food chain in terms of spatial distance, and the main concern is with environmental issues. Often, it shares the idea of supporting small local farmers with the criterion of the number of intermediaries, to which it adds the symbolic value of local food as a rediscovery of cultural roots. There has been much debate on this issue, both in the academic and popular literature, and a large stream of scientific literature deals with preferences for local food (often overlapping with preferences for other characteristics of AFN food, see Corsi and Novelli, Chap. 4). Consumers' preferences and the demand for policies in favour of local food have also fuelled the debate on "locavores" (e.g. Desrochers & Shimizu, 2012; for an opposing view, see Scharber & Dancs, 2016).

In the AFN literature, the production and consumption of food are closely tied together spatially, economically, and socially (Goodman & Goodman, 2009). As we argue, however, these criteria are not analytically clear and do not support a sound research perspective. Both the first and second criterion are much too close to the practical definitions of AFNs as used by lay people and practitioners. Moreover, they do not combine with each other coherently. One of the things they are lacking, for instance, "and Walmart's local food initiative is a perfect example of this, is a recognition that reduced spatial distance need not automatically result in the reduction of social distance" (Carolan, 2017, p. 219). These shortcomings have been addressed by the further criterion, popular in the academic literature, of *embeddedness*, that is, the product's connection with information on the way it is produced. In the words of Marsden et al. (2000), "It is this which enables the consumer to confidently make connections and associations with the place/space of production, *and, potentially, the values of the people involved and the production methods employed*". These values stem from the departure from the anonymous and fungible character of the undifferentiated products of the conventional chain, and it is the information content that is at the origin of the three main types of short food supply chain theorized by Marsden et al. (2000): (1) *face-to-face*, whereby authenticity and trust are directly provided by the producer-consumer interaction, possibly even through the Internet; (2) *spatial proximity*, when food is locally produced and retailed and the origin is communicated; and (3) *spatially extended*, when the information of the origin in a specific region, bearing meaning and value, is communicated to consumers elsewhere.

The embeddedness criterion has the clear merit of encompassing the different motivations for giving value to specific food and/or to specific chains under a single concept, that of information concerning the value of food. Nevertheless, it may by definition include types of food chain that are integrated in the conventional food system. This is the case for certain "spatially extended" food products. It is certainly true that products like Parmigiano Reggiano, or Champagne, derive their appeal for consumers from their regional origin. And it is certainly true, too, that the quality of these products stems from long-lasting historical practices that were originally linked to shared knowledge and skills transmitted over the centuries. Nevertheless, the relevant skills and techniques could now be easily imitated, and the economic value of reputation is legally protected by labels and appellations. More importantly, these products are often fully integrated in the conventional food chain. They are distributed by supermarkets or specialized shops, they are advertised, and from this point of view the differences with branded food are slight.

All in all, we agree with the idea that the meaning of analytical categories used by researchers is often context-dependent (see DuPuis & Goodman, 2005; Morris & Kirwan, 2011; Tregear, 2011) and that the distinctions between alternative and conventional are becoming ever more blurred.

Given this background, we thus consider a different criterion, or rather, a combination of different criteria for determining whether a food network is *alternative*. We define AFNs as those forms of marketing chain for which (1) the consumer-producer relationship is not only mediated by purely commercial operators, (2) the product has special symbolic values for consumers linked to its origin and to the type of trade, and (3) the marketing chain spans a short distance and implies personal relationships. In other words, we consider that alternativeness stems from the fact that the exchange is not purely between an anonymous and fungible commodity and money; that the benefit (or utility, in economics jargon) for consumers does not only stem from the intrinsic (physical, chemical, or organoleptic) quality of food but from the modalities themselves of the exchange; and, possibly, the utility for producers derives not only from the monetary reward but, again, from the exchange itself.[1] In our view, it is the *quality of the exchange relationship* and what is implied in the exchange that distinguishes the exchange taking place in the AFN from the exchange in the conventional chain. Exchanges in AFN bring their own rewards to individuals (De Schutter, 2017).

This approach of course encompasses several types of chain as considered above. Face-to-face exchanges are obviously included in our concept. The number of intermediaries criterion (especially when the discriminant is one intermediary between producers and consumers) does not necessarily fit in it. Even a single intermediary between the producer and the consumer might eliminate the difference in the quality of the exchange. By contrast, an organization like a Solidarity Purchasing Group (SPG), even if posited as an intermediary, does not prevent the relationship, thanks to the mechanisms of participation by members and to the trust created by reciprocal knowledge with the producers. On the other hand, this approach excludes the spatially extended food chain and, hence, Protected Designation of Origin (PDO) or Geographical Indication (GI) products when they are marketed in the conventional chain.

We hasten to add, however, that this criterion is not meant to present a binary vision of food systems. Quite the opposite, our definition calls for seeing alternative and conventional food networks as lying along a continuum where areas of overlap abound (Ponte, 2016). As argued by Tregear (2011), neat bifurcation between "alternative" and "mainstream" or between "alternative" and "oppositional" agro-food systems may often obscure the ambiguity of reality, where mixed situations and continuous rather than binary choices are frequent. Several studies (Jarosz, 2008; Murdoch & Miele, 1999; Stræte & Marsden, 2006) show that the boundaries between systems are not always clear (Sonnino & Marsden, 2006). As stated by Goodman and Goodman (2009), the interface between alternative and conventional food provisioning is an increasingly permeable and highly contested terrain.

For instance, most members of SPGs also purchase food in the conventional chain, and many farmers who supply SPGs also sell on the conventional chain. Or, among consumers' motivations for buying directly from farmers, selfish concerns coexist with altruistic motivations. Furthermore, the very idea of quality (locality, freshness, typicality) is shared among different food chains.

Even from these few brief remarks, it is clear that AFNs can be analysed from very diverse points of view, which makes different approaches and disciplinary competences necessary. Different perspectives add to the understanding of the social phenomenon, and this is a crucial goal of our work. We will now present the different disciplinary approaches to AFNs and will attempt to find a synthesis.

The Economic Approach

In a sense, the economic approach radically simplifies reality in order to bring the fundamental mechanisms behind people's and agents' behaviour into sharper focus. The basic assumption of standard economic theory is that agents try to maximize the benefit from their actions, be it personal welfare (utility) for individuals, or profits for firms. From this tenet, the trivial conclusion follows that if an AFN exists in which goods are exchanged, it is because both sides of the exchange have an interest in it. Hence, there is a demand for and a supply of goods. Understanding, and if possible quantifying, the variables affecting the demand for goods in the AFN, and doing the same for supply, is thus a primary concern of the economic approach to AFNs. A second concern is understanding the chain's functioning and organization, its efficiency, and the type of market that it represents. Third, economic activities often entail benefits or costs that do not accrue to the parties who engaged in those activities, that is, externalities (positive and negative, respectively), and this also applies to AFNs. For instance, the functioning of the chain necessarily entails an environmental impact, imposing a cost on society at large. Lastly, some economic theories deal with cases in which, by contrast with the assumptions of standard consumer theory, the exchange does not provide only personal selfish benefit, given that it also creates personal relationships, which we argue are an important component of these chains' alternativeness.

Analysis of demand tries to identify its determinants. Standard consumer theory posits that consumers maximize their utility under a budget constraint, which for homogeneous goods means that the demand for a good is a function of its price, of income, and of taste shifters. Price plays a crucial role for homogeneous goods, since it is an indicator of consumers' preferences, more specifically of their marginal willingness to pay (MWTP[2]). For goods possessing several characteristics of interest for consumers, though, both Lancaster's (1966) and Rosen's (1974) theories provide a theoretical basis for the analysis of consumers' preferences for different attributes or characteristics of a given good. As a result, there is a large literature dealing with consumers' preferences with regard to the characteristics of food. This literature will be presented in more detail in Chap. 4. Suffice here to say that it analyses which characteristics of food are sought by consumers, including different categories. Some refer to the intrinsic qualities of food, such as taste, freshness, and safety, that are of personal interest for the consumer. However, preferences (and willingness to pay) can also have altruistic motivations and concern symbolic values such as provenance from local producers, support for local farmers, environmental stewardship, and opposition to the conventional food system. Moreover, what is particular about AFNs is that, at least for some participants, utility stems not only from the exchange of goods vs. money but also from the modalities of the exchange. In other words, participating in the AFN is itself an object of preference. The economic analysis typically does not investigate the origin of preferences and takes them as a given. What is of interest in the economic analysis is which characteristics of a good are preferred and possibly to quantify their impact on demand.

Concerning the supply side, standard production theory assumes that firms are profit-maximizers. If farms are profit-maximizers, the choice of the marketing chain is simply based on a comparison between revenues and costs (including distribution costs) in the different chains (Verhaegen & Van Huylenbroeck, 2001). Nevertheless, since most firms in agriculture are family farms in which the operator's household provides a large part of the labour, a well-established stream of literature utilizes farm household models to represent family farm behaviour (Huffman, 1980; Singh, Squire, & Strauss, 1986). According to these models, farmers maximize their utility, which is a positive function of farm and off-farm income and a negative function of their labour. These models are flexible enough to allow the utility function to include any element affecting farmers' utility. Hence, along with the monetary incentive to supply the AFN chain (e.g. a price premium), the choice to engage in the AFN can depend on non-monetary motivations, such as the desire to promote the intrinsic quality value of their products (as opposed to standard/technical obligations of the conventional chain), or the pursuit of personal relationship with consumers. Again, the economic analysis is mainly interested in determining and quantifying the effect of these variables.

A third stream of economic analysis looks at the chain in itself, at how goods are exchanged in the chain, and at what the relationships along it are. In particular, a relevant issue is how distribution costs are borne by the different operators along the chain, since each stage of the chain (storage, processing, transport, retail) entails costs that are passed on to the following stage. In the conventional chain, the costs involved in the final sale to consumers, for instance, the transport costs to the selling point, are borne by supermarkets or by retailers. By contrast, these costs are borne by farmers in farmers' markets, or even by consumers for on-farm direct sales, but they still exist. That distribution costs do not vanish with shorter or even direct chains is frequently overlooked in the literature on the social aspects of AFNs. This is also because the labour used by farmers (or consumers) in AFNs is typically provided by themselves and does not entail an explicit, out-of-pocket cost, so that they often do not take its opportunity cost into consideration.

In a perfectly functioning marketing chain, in any case, the final price should be the sum of production and distribution costs. Nevertheless, some operators along the chain can have market power, so that the price may not only reflect costs but also a monopolistic or oligopolistic rent. Indeed, AFN operators and scholars often claim the market power of middlemen as a strong reason for supporting direct producer-consumer relationship. More generally, the structure and the functioning of the entire chain is of interest and how revenues, costs, and value added pertain to each participant. This must be assessed on a case-by-case basis, since there seems to be much variation in this respect, as shown, for instance, by the empirical case studies comparing the structures and the performance of local and mainstream food chains in the US reported in

King et al. (2010). These considerations could also bring to the fore the issue of the different chains' efficiency, that is, which chain entails the lowest overall cost for delivering food from the farmer to the consumer. A purely monetary comparison, though, would be inappropriate, since the benefits for participants in AFNs are not limited to revenue (for sellers) or food (for buyers), given that the exchange itself and the personal relationships provide utility, which should be deducted from the (possibly higher) costs of the AFN chain as compared to the conventional one. This is probably the reason for the lack of such comparisons in the literature, but it should not be forgotten that if AFNs are to last, a balance between (both monetary and non-monetary) benefits and costs of participation must be reached and maintained.

Indirect effects of AFNs include their economic impact and the positive and negative externalities. It is often claimed in the sociological and geographic literature that AFNs can favour the local economy (Ploeg et al., 2000; Marsden et al., 2002; Renting et al., 2003). This can happen via the multiplier effect on employment, local purchase, upstream procurement, and the like. Several studies evaluate the impacts of local or short food chains on the local economy, generally reaching the conclusion that they have a better impact than traditional chains (for a review, see Kneafsey et al., 2013). Negative externalities, according to economic theory, are a cause of market failure, that is, of inefficiency, since a larger sum of net benefits for society at large could be reached if the external costs were reduced to the level at which the marginal external cost equals the marginal abatement cost. Since virtually each consumption and production activity entails some negative externality, an immediate question is the comparison between the external costs determined by the AFN chains and those of the conventional chain. The comparison can be conducted using economic valuation techniques, but a preliminary step is the "technical" assessment of the environmental impacts of the chains. This is the objective of Chap. 13 of this book.

So far, the motivations of participants (both producers and consumers) in AFNs have been considered as independent from each other, and it was assumed that operators pursue their own interest: even when their motivations are altruistic, it can be argued that they are "purchasing moral satisfaction" (Kahneman & Knetsch, 1992). This is the standard assumption in the analysis of market functioning. Nevertheless, we argue that the alternativeness of AFNs lies in the fact that the benefit of the exchange comes from the modalities of the exchange themselves, so that the very fact of participating in an AFN brings a reward. This benefit is strictly linked to personal relationships. Personal relationships are beyond the scope of economic relationships. While one can be willing to pay to have someone sing for her, no one would pay a friend to sing together. Economic transactions are often between people, but these are fungible, anonymous, and self-interested relationships, as opposed to the idiosyncratic, reciprocal, and free nature of personal relationships like friendship, sympathy, and love. Increasingly, however, economics has dealt with various facets of human behaviour involving interpersonal relationships, leading to a growing recognition that they play a role even in economic life. The role of interpersonal relationships has been theorized as the production of relational goods (Gui, 2000; Gui & Stanca, 2010; Uhlaner, 1989). In particular, Gui (2005) views "interpersonal events as 'encounters': peculiar productive processes that employ various types of resources contributed by interacting parties (human resources, above all), and that deliver not only conventional outputs (…) but also relational outputs" (Gui & Stanca, 2010). A relational good can be created between consumers and farmers in a situation of direct interaction in alternative chains. This is the case, for instance, when a consumer buys regularly from the same vendor, becomes on friendly terms with her, and chats during the sale. For both parties, this relationship has a value, even if, by its very nature, it cannot be bought. Of course, this can also happen in a conventional chain, though less frequently. And not every transaction in an AFN creates a relational good, since attending an AFN may have only egoistic motivations.

The Sociological Approach

In sociology, AFNs are analysed in several subfields, each with its own analytical emphasis. First of all, sociological analysis looks at AFNs within the overall framework of the so-called sociology of development (Barbera, 2016). Here the sociological analysis of AFNs provides a critical appraisal of the current systems of producing and marketing food from a *political economy* standpoint. The general idea is that modern food systems are not sustainable since they have health and environmental impacts that are intertwined with strong *power imbalances* in food chains. These power imbalances stand in the way of any radical change towards a better food system (De Schutter, 2017). Malnutrition and obesity are a consequence of the top-down and profit-seeking introduction of high-processed and high-caloric food in rich countries, while hunger is the consequence of supply-side factors linked to agricultural policies and the *uneven* globalization of food chains (De Schutter, 2012). The green revolution, the spread of monocultures, and the correlated mechanization of agriculture impacted agro-biodiversity and brought about a captive value-chain with inter-firm linkages involving one-way dependency of suppliers (Gereffi, Humphrey, & Sturgeon, 2005). From the environmental viewpoint, the world agro-food system is directly implicated in the degradation of habitats and soil resilience: "Agricultural expansion has had tremendous impacts on habitats, biodiversity, carbon storage and soil conditions. In fact, worldwide agriculture has already cleared or converted 70% of the grassland, 50% of the savannah, 45% of the temperate deciduous forest, and 27% of the tropical forest biome" (Foley et al., 2011, p. 338). This line of research thus views AFNs as an antidote to the failure of the multiple crises of the "globalization project" (McMichael, 2012, chapter 8). The environmental emergency and the crisis of natural resources, the unresolved problem of hunger, the political and social crunch, and the cyclical crisis of financial capitalism have marked the path through the third millennium. As a result, there have been many attempts to rethink the very roots of global development towards a "sustainable development". But faced with collapsing ecosystems, toxic environments, soil depletion, climate chaos, disappearing species, and finite fossil fuels, does sustainability even make any sense when there is so little left to sustain? (Bullard, 2011). Accordingly, AFNs refer critically to the topic of "development", as in the case of the "degrowth" approach (Latouche, 2009). This line of thought rejects the very concept of economic growth in favour of a model founded on the quality of life, communitarian re-embeddedness of food, and conviviality.

A second take is within the framework of the "sociology of food production and consumption". Here the standpoint is that AFNs entail a different idea of quality from conventional food chains, the so-called quality turn in food production and consumption. Accordingly, the "quality conventions" perspective has gained momentum in the sociological understanding of AFNs (Ponte, 2016). The contribution of this stream of research has been summarized by Ponte (2016) in two main lines: the worlds of production framework (Salais & Storper, 1992; Storper & Salais, 1997) and the orders of worth approach (Boltanski & Thévenot, 1991, 2006).[3] The worlds of production framework was developed by Salais and Storper (1992), who distinguished between two analytical dimensions: (1) the more or less restricted community of specialists for the supply of technology, information, and skills at the production level and (2) whether demand is more or less anonymous/generic. The four possible combinations lead to a classification of "worlds of production" as follows: (1) Industrial World (production of standardized-generic products); (2) Network Market World (standardized-dedicated); (3) Marshallian Market World (specialized-dedicated); and (4) World of Innovation (specialized-generic). With regard to the orders of worth approach, Boltanski and Thévenot (1991) develop six worlds of legitimate common welfare (inspirational, domestic, opinion/fame, civic, market, and industrial worlds) that call upon orders of worth other than the neoclassical parameters of price/utility maximization. According to conventions theory, rational choice is the main component of exchange only when differences in prices directly express shared differences in quality. In this case, pure market coordination applies. When—as with AFNs—price alone cannot translate quality, actors set up other, non-market, conventions and forms of coordination (Barbera & Audifredi, 2012). In domestic coordination, uncertainty about quality is dealt with through interpersonal trust (i.e. long-term social ties between actors). In industrial coordination, uncertainty is reduced through common enforceable standards. Civic coordination works where there is a collective commitment to the welfare and/or public interest. In the opinion-based world, uncertainty about quality is solved through public celebrity, and worth derives from expert opinion. Lastly, in the inspirational world, what is worthy is what cannot be controlled, what is felt in inner experience, manifested by feelings and passions and what rejects habits and routines (Ponte, 2009). The theory of conventions has been applied to a variety of research problems, including wine production (Ponte, 2009), non-standard food production/consumption practices (Murdoch & Miele, 1999; Sassatelli & Davolio, 2010), local partnership between producers and consumers (Lamine, 2005), alternative food networks (Sage, 2003a; Goodman, 2009), the turn to quality in food production and consumption (Murdoch et al., 2000), culinary networks (Murdoch & Miele, 2004), and geographical indication (Barham, 2003). Conventional food networks would thus refer to *hard quality*, namely to certain detectable characteristics such as prices and standardized rules of production, as well as the attribution of premiums, brands, and other recognition. AFNs instead point to *soft quality*, namely to less directly perceivable qualities, which emphasize the role of stakeholders in a local context, respect for tradition, the existence of trust relations, attention for the environment, the value given to shared community spirit, and passion for farming (Barbera & Dagnes, 2017). But: "in reality, clear distinctions cannot be made between definitions of quality and (...) boundaries between categories are often blurred" (Sage, 2003b, 7). Even if soft quality is more relevant in AFNs, conventional food chains conjure up certain "alternative" ideas in the products they propose to consumers. The complexity of exchange and the overlap among different quality worlds open a window of opportunity for *camouflage* strategies by hybrid organizations whereby conventional food chains conquer specific zones of AFNs' quality space in order to fulfil consumers' desire for "alternative" quality conventions (see Barbera, Dagnes, & Di Monaco, 2018, chapter 2.2).

Lastly, in the field of rural sociology, AFNs are connected to grassroots social innovations (De Schutter, 2017), such as Community Supported Agriculture (CSA), Solidarity Purchase Groups, and new-peasants. The key topic in this stream is the relationship between food and territory. Re-thinking the agro-food chain by proposing an alternative model starting from bottom-up experience also means redefining the spatial, social, cultural, and economic relationships of each specific context (Barbera & Dagnes, 2017). AFNs are here considered from both the demand and supply side, thus overlapping the analysis with the two streams illustrated above. Community Supported Agriculture is a system in which consumers contribute to supporting local farmers by entering into direct producer-to-consumer marketing schemes. The founding idea of CSA is to: "re-establish a sense of connection to the land for urban dwellers and to foster a strong sense of community and cooperation with a decided social justice goal to provide food security for disadvantaged groups" (Adam, 2006, 2). Solidarity Purchase Groups (Grasseni, 2013) are self-organized groups buying from small producers, often although not always organic and/or in the same region or area of residence. They play a role in fighting the marginalization of small and micro-farms in the country (Grasseni, 2013; Maestripieri, 2016) and in promoting consumer's awareness and their empowerment for the impact of consumption on the food system. Lastly, the new-peasant perspective emphasizes that industrial farming is being replaced by a peasant model, both in developed countries and in developing ones (van der Ploeg, 2008). The replacement is qualitative rather than quantitative, as it points to a new model built upon ecological capital, subsistence self-provisioning, actively constructed difference, dynamic co-production, multiple resistance, extended networks, and new marketplaces (van der Ploeg, 2010). These features can translate into a variety of trajectories and development opportunities for localities where new-peasants emerge and flourish.

The Environmental Approach

In the current trend in the food market, consumers are increasingly looking for more environmental sustainable products as well for more sustainable forms of trade. The problem of the environmental impacts of the conventional food system, which until the 1990s was almost exclusively identified with pollution (water, air, soil) caused by farming and livestock production, has gradually come to be seen as much more complex and has been extended to the food supply chain's technical functions (transfer of products over time and space) and distribution features (the proximity relationship between producer and consumer, the range, the ways of provisioning, the ability to respond to specific needs, consumer behaviour).

AFNs have also gained importance as a result of their promising capacity to respond effectively to this new market demand with more environmentally friendly and small-scale production, local embedded products, and more direct systems of distribution.

This environmental sustainability has been much touted as one of the distinctive features of AFNs and their characterization (otherness and alternatively) as compared to conventional food provisioning forms. Much of this view has depended on the popular concept of food miles (Paxton, 1994), which sees AFNs as being linked to local food origin and, hence, more environmentally friendly. However, this assumption gradually came under critical scrutiny from the specialist literature (Coley, Howard, & Winter, 2009; DEFRA, 2005; Edwards-Jones et al., 2008; Van Passel, 2013), with a progressive deconstruction of the automatisms that led to belief in AFNs' intrinsic environmental sustainability (Tregear, 2011). Exemplary of this evolution was the debate about the local trap (Born & Purcell, 2006), which created the preconditions for the development of analyses and comparisons between the environmental impact assessment of alternative and conventional marketing channels.

The development of interpretative approaches for assessing the sustainability of the various organizational forms of agro-food supply chains in which the local becomes the boundary of the system and "not the intrinsic purpose of the system" (Coley et al., 2009), along with case studies that provided more insight into AFNs' actors and behaviours, relational shapes, objectives and forms of interactions in the supply chain, contributed to undermining the plausibility of a direct link between alternative networks and environmental sustainability, highlighting instances of hybridization with conventional systems of distribution.

On the one hand, almost paradoxically, the difficulty of drawing unequivocal conclusions about AFNs' environmental sustainability has challenged their own alternativeness. Consequently, even the conceptual frame based on the alternative-conventional binary opposites (Sonnino & Marsden, 2006) has been contested, legitimizing a representation of the food system (and of a possible quest for sustainability) with nuanced boundaries and where the local and global scales take the form of a continuum (Brunori et al., 2016). In practice, this continuum becomes evident with the corporate mainstreaming of the products and values conveyed by AFNs (Goodman, Goodman, & DuPuis, 2011).

On the other hand, although the literature on this matter has been extremely lucid and emphasizes that the sustainability outcomes of AFNs are unclear (Forssell & Lankoski, 2014), environmental sustainability continues to be pursued in AFNs by consumers as well as by producers and creates fertile ground for innovative social dynamics (Grasseni, 2013).

Starting from AFNs, food movements are springing up in city-regions and working with local government to address dietary health, environmental quality, and greater civic engagement.

Today, a number of questions arise spontaneously from the contradictory relationship between AFNs and environmental sustainability. These questions concern the extent to which the content on which we build AFNs' identity are shared and objective in the encounter between supply and demand, what attributes are sought, which aspects are left out but would be worth considering, and what strategies can be used to fill the information asymmetry. These are questions that have a general significance for the debate on AFNs' environmental sustainability, but can only be answered on a case-by-case basis.

To sum up, therefore, two issues are of the greatest interest from the environmental perspective. The first is the understanding of the subjective concept of environmental quality by both consumers and producers. This is relevant because it shapes consumers' purchase behaviour and farmers' production choices. The second is the objective "technical" analysis of the impact of different food chains on the environment, which responds to the question of whether the environmental quality sought by consumers and producers in AFNs is actually provided.

The Anthropological Approach

Modern anthropology is based on an empirical and deductive approach usually referred to as ethnographic fieldwork (Barnard, 2000; Barth, Gingrich, Parkin, & Silverman, 2005). Fieldwork can involve a variety of activities, but the most important one is participant observation. This method rests on the idea that to understand how different societies operate, the researcher has to take part in them, observing the society in question by participating in the daily life of the people who belong to it (Hammersley & Atkinson, 2007; Robben & Sluka, 2007). Participant observation is usually a long-term activity, lasting many months, if not years. Historically, anthropologists have studied primarily the peoples of the ex-European colonies, but since the end of the Second World War, their attention has shifted to include also their own societies. The study of AFNs can be considered part of this anthropological work carried out "at home" (Jackson, 1987; MacClancy, 2002).

From a sub-disciplinary perspective, AFNs fall broadly at the intersection between economic and political anthropology (e.g. Carrier & Luetchford, 2012; Counihan & Siniscalchi, 2013; Grasseni, 2013; Pratt & Luetchford, 2014; Rakopoulos, 2014). Two core principles may be said to underline this work. First, the questioning of Western (Euro-American) economic models that purport to have universal applicability. Through their encounters with other cultures, anthropologists have documented ways of life that do not adhere to the tenets of neoclassical economics. AFNs are often seen precisely as partial examples of these ways of life. The second principle is the acknowledgement that, even within Western societies, capitalism and market rationality, though prevalent, are not the only economic forms present (Hann & Hart, 2011; Wilk & Gliggett, 2007). Starting from these two core principles, anthropology makes use of a series of analytical distinctions to guide the study of AFNs.

First and foremost is the distinction between market and society (Hann & Hart, 2009), a deceptively simple one that cannot be taken for granted in our day and age, as Margaret Thatcher's famous comment that "there is no such thing as society" keenly testifies. The idea that capitalist markets may constitute a separate realm of reality ("the" Market) is a historical product that emerged in the UK around the eighteenth century. From the perspective of anthropology, this event marked the first time in human history when the economy became completely *disembedded* from the rest of society (Polanyi, 1944/2001). This is not to say that capitalist markets are not subject to society's influence; they are. The influence lies precisely in their being constructed—symbolically and materially—as separate from society (Pratt & Luetchford, 2014, pp. 9–10). Anthropologists have tended to document the negative consequences of this disembedding, together with people's responses to it in different times and places. AFNs may be seen as an example of this phenomenon in the world of food, where farmers, retailers, and households have become increasingly subjected to markets in the last 30 years (Heatherington, 2011).

The distinction between embedded and disembedded economies is thus also central to the anthropological approach. Neoclassical economics sees markets formally, treating them as a problem of mathematical logic. It assumes the operation of principles that are thought to have universal validity. Anthropology, on the contrary, sees markets "substantively"—as a problem of fact, not logic—treating them as one aspect of the myriad concrete ways in which human societies organize themselves to provide for their material wants. While these ways are incredibly complex, they tend to coalesce around three processes—reciprocity, redistribution, and exchange—and three social arrangements: horizontal groupings (e.g. households), central authorities (e.g. the State), and price-making markets (e.g. the international coffee market). These elements vary historically and geographically but one is usually dominant, regulating the allocation of natural resources, labour, and money and thus integrating the economy in society (Polanyi, 1957, pp. 243–250; see also pp. 90–126). The human economy, then, "is embedded and enmeshed in institutions, economic and non-economic" (Polanyi, 1957, p. 250).

By looking at AFNs through this lens, we can see how these initiatives try to combine horizontal reciprocity, market exchange, and central redistribution to achieve their goals. Most initiatives rely primarily on a combination of the first two. Within AFNs food is still exchanged in the market by using money, but this activity is subjected to a variety of moral values that temper the excesses of self-interest, making exchange more collaborative (reciprocal) and less competitive. Some initiatives also rely on redistribution (in the form of the state) to widen their appeal by getting local institutions to contribute to their costs, for example, through publicly funded allotments, food policy councils, green public procurement, electronic benefit transfers at farmer's markets, and so on.

Another important set of ideas in the anthropological study of AFNs is that the exchange of objects (including food) helps to create and maintain relationships between social beings and groups. Whereas neoclassical economics sees trade and consumption as impersonal activities that take place among anonymous individuals who try to maximize their satisfaction, anthropology recognizes the importance of forms of exchange that are based on the sociocultural identities of those involved and are inspired by moral and cosmological motives altogether different from utility maximization (Malinowski, 1922/2007; Mauss, 1925/2016; Sahlins, 1974; Strathern, 1988; Thurnwald, 1932; Weiner, 1992). These forms have been usually grouped under the umbrella term of "gift" and distinguished from commodities and commodity exchange (Carrier, 1995; Godelier, 1998; Gregory, 1982). Gifts and commodities, however, should not be rigidly opposed as simply different kinds of objects. These terms are indexes for processes that can apply, in different social contexts, places, and historical periods, to the *same* object. In other words, something may start its "life" as a commodity and end up being a gift, while a gift may be turned into a commodity by falling into the market realm (Appadurai, 1986; Gregory, 1997; Parry & Bloch, 1989).

These insights are important for the study of AFNs for two reasons. First, because many of these phenomena are represented as being—or as striving to become—social relations, rather than purely economic ones. As Pratt and Luetchford write: "The moral content of alternative [food] markets draws on non-market idioms and ideas" (2014, p. 10). Second, because they help reveal and understand the considerable overlap that exists between what is "alternative" and what is not, between the conventional food system and the initiatives that seek to set themselves apart from it. Anthropologists have thus documented the "work of appropriation" (Miller, 1987) that individuals perform by turning mass-produced commodities into objects that have more than economic value for themselves and their loved ones—effectively turning them into gifts. Eating food that is certified for its social or environmental qualities is an example of this work of appropriation (Carrier & Luetchford, 2012; Jung, Klein, & Caldwell, 2014). But anthropologists have also investigated how these "alternative" foods become again commodities, that is, how their farming systems, retail channels, and practices of consumption become more and more similar to the conventional sector they once sought to escape (DeLind, 2000; Pratt, 2009).

Finally, the anthropological approach questions the use of the terms "producer" and "consumer" that is often found in the literature on AFNs. These two terms hide the influence of neoclassical economics by suggesting that the people who take part in these initiatives are anonymous agents with only one goal in mind, selling or buying. As such, these terms reflect a disembedded view of the market as the intersection of relative scarcity (supply) and relative preference (demand). This "economistic fallacy" (Polanyi, 1977) simplifies the social and political complexity of the phenomena in question. From an anthropological perspective, "producers" are always inevitably embedded in particular historical and cultural trajectories from which their behaviour stems (Pratt, 2014). They are, in other words, small farmers from Piedmont (Black, 2012), ex-peasants from Sicily (Rakopoulos, 2017), capitalist growers from Michigan (DeLind & Bingen, 2005), banana plantation workers from Dominica (Moberg, 2016), tea pickers from Darjeeling (Besky, 2014), and so on. The same is true of "consumers", who are subjects belonging to households whose practices of food provisioning, preparation, and eating are the result of their particular life histories and that of their communities, at the local, regional, and national levels (Luetchford, 2014). Anthropologists therefore prefer speaking of families in Lombardy (Grasseni, 2013), Tuscany (Counihan, 2004), and Sicily (Orlando, 2018); of the citizens of Stockholm (Isenhour, 2010), Washington (Okura Gagné, 2011), and Lexington (Lyon, Ailshire, & Sehon, 2014); and so forth.

The Geographical Approach

AFNs are a field of study in which geographers, especially those from the US and UK, are particularly active, as they continue to play a leading role in the international debate that they do not often have in other topics, and have made a founding contribution to its "discovery" and problematization, as well as to its evolution and criticism. At the same time, geographers' contributions to this field are not restricted to their own discipline. It is significant to note that one of the geographers who has taken a pioneering part in AFN studies, Terry Marsden, has this to say of himself on his personal webpage: "I research the interdisciplinary social science and applied policy fields of rural geography, rural sociology, environmental sociology, geography and planning".

As in other fields of knowledge, the debate is also highly compartmentalized between the dominant English-speaking world and a plurality of national debates in geography (such as those in French and Italy). The latter are not always solidly anchored in this debate and indeed may have cut themselves loose, as in the case of France. Dialog is limited, or rather, reflection proceeds along parallel pathways, which is all the more significant the more the realities we investigate—the realm of AFNs and the transformations in the geographies of food—are swept by significant processes of change, as they are locally defined practices that we attempt to bring back into broader interpretative frameworks.

In one of the seminal writings (Renting et al., 2003), the authors noted that in comparison with the lagging peripheral areas, "much less reference was made to regions that were highly integrated in the global food markets like the Netherlands, and much of the United Kingdom, where the dominant discourse foresaw a continued expansion of food production systems along the lines of modernisation and within conventional market structures" (p. 395). It is probably not coincidental, then, that the most significant contributions, at least at an early stage, have come precisely from British, Irish, and Dutch geographers (or students who were trained in schools of geography in the UK), who worked together in important European research projects (such as COST actions or Food Links, SUS-CHAIN, etc.). Likewise, US and Western European literatures have differed significantly on several points—though this was limited, at least initially, to a relatively small group of scholars, as we have seen (Goodman & Goodman, 2009). The question that arises, and to which Goodman and Goodman's reflections seem to provide only a partial answer, is whether this divergence in the "respective research constituencies" which "project different sociopolitical imaginaries" is due to the phenomena being observed or the manner in which the researchers have observed them, or, as is probable, to both.

As we pointed out above, the blurred and ambiguous edges of the alternative food networks were brought into sharper focus by the work of several British geographers (and geographically trained scholars in the

Netherlands), who were the first to refer to an alternative geography of food (Whatmore & Thorne, 1997). Though these geographers apply their own discipline's approach to rural development and food studies, they are also fully engaged in the multidisciplinary debate in these macro-fields. From the disciplinary point of view (here again, however, the delimitation is somewhat forced), the theme of the AFN is part of so-called food geography, a field where rural, urban, economic, political, and social specialists break down disciplinary barriers in a lively interchange of views on critical food studies.

The reviews and discussions spearheaded by Winter (2003, 2004) and later by Cook (Cook et al., 2006, 2008, 2011) in the pages of *Progress in Human Geography* have highlighted the multitude of theoretical approaches and empirical research procedures employed by geographers in this field. In attempting to define a geographical approach to AFNs, we can thus proceed along two lines. First, by looking at how geographers have dealt with AFNs, and second, by trying to see how exquisitely geographical concepts have been deployed to interpret AFNs. Both perspectives would appear to be unsatisfactory, because in the first case it is not easy to understand what criteria should be used in deciding whether a given author is a geographer (are we to judge by current academic position, training, or the fact of writing in geography journals?), while in the second, almost all the contributions of scholars who have dealt with AFNs and who cannot be defined as geographers by any of these criteria have to do with concepts like space, place, region, and local that are explicitly spatial.

We will thus attempt to combine the two perspectives, starting from the writings of geographers (who qualify as such on the basis of at least one of the three criteria we have mentioned) that are the obligatory reference point for any study of AFNs and formulations such as Local Food Systems or short food supply chains (SFSCs) which at times are used as synonyms without much concern for the distinctions between them, and in other cases are differentiated on the basis of various considerations.[4] Lastly, we must not overlook the fundamental distinction between the perspectives of the academics and those of the practitioners, as they point out (Venn et al., 2006) and, we might add, since these reflections are incorporated into research calls and policy instruments.

The scholars—geographers for the most part, as we have said—who first began to analyse phenomena, social contexts, and actors such as direct sales, farmers' markets, organic and local food, close producer-consumer relationships, and so on and established AFNs as an analytical category were primarily interested in coming to grips with changes in rural contexts and food production by building representations that were alternative to, or at least more sophisticated than, the dominant discourses of globalization (Whatmore & Thorne, 1997) and its negative repercussions on the environmental and social levels and the actual and perceived quality of food. Initially, attention was primarily focused on the production side, while consumption and the role of consumers gained importance at a later stage.

AFNs were, at least for a certain period,[5] an umbrella under which geographers with different backgrounds, interests, and approaches took shelter: from specialists in rural development to environmentalists, scholars of development processes in the South of the world, and researchers—who in many cases were activists—interested in the analysis of social movements (Levkoe, 2006). Though the geographers who dealt with AFNs engaged mainly with economic issues (and specifically with rural and environmental concerns), they were also involved in the various "turns" that reshaped economic geography, in particular the quality and the cultural turns. On the theoretical level, geographers have approached the topic from the vantage points of political economy and institutional economy (Whatmore & Thorne, 1997), and more recently with the moral geographies of the ethics of care (Goodman, 2004; Popke, 2006), exploring combined approaches such as Latour's actor network theory and quality convention theory (Murdoch et al., 2000).

As shown by the reviews by Venn et al. (2006) and by Goodman and Goodman (2009), research approaches have been predominantly empirical, based chiefly on case studies employing ethnographic research methods, interviews, focus groups, and participant observation, in addition to traditional methods of spatial analysis (though the latter are not often used, except in some studies of local food systems, see, e.g. Kremer & DeLiberty, 2011) and comparative approaches such as that adopted by Renting et al. (2003).

The spatial dimension is central to the reflection on AFNs, where it has been variously interpreted in relation to the different research orientations. The debate on AFNs has mobilized several concepts dear to geographers, but widely used in other disciplines when scrutinizing the relationship between food, environment-territory, and quality from an analytical and political perspective. As one of the forerunners of AFN studies pointed out, "research on the emergence and development of alternative food (or agro-food) networks in recent years has highlighted the significance of quality, locality and ecology as establishing the embedded character of food derived from this sector" (Sage, 2003a, p. 47).

Obviously it is to be expected that "spatial" thinking (in the broadest sense of the term) on the part of scholars with a geographical background will be a bit more extensive and more sophisticated than that by those who use the concepts without problematizing them overmuch. Nevertheless, as Goodman and Goodman (2009) have noted "[…] major theoretical advances in human geography, notably relational conceptualizations of place, space, economy, and the politics of scale, find little reflection in AFN research, despite the critical importance attributed to the local and provenance" (p. 5). On the other hand, the same authors point out that "the AFN literature has neglected theoretical development in favour of empirically grounded, case-study analyses of alternative food production and provisioning networks, new economic forms, and institutional mechanisms of governance and policy" (p. 6).

For example, it may be instructive to consider attempts to develop spatial analysis categories such as that by Jessop, Brenner, and Jones (Jessop, Brenner, & Jones, 2008) to see how much distance lies between the theoretical depth of these concepts and their application to AFNs.

Space and place are at the centre of many authors' reflections, in observing how AFNs redefine the moments of production and consumption. The space is that of networks, a category that is generally preferred to the system, at least in the literature on AFNs, precisely in order to overturn the implicit normative and performative logic underlying the representation of the global food system. In the literature on local food systems, which originated chiefly in North America and gradually extended to involve European and international scholars, the view taken of urban food systems is implicitly critical, if not indeed explicitly radical and resistant, compared to that of the global food system (see the categorization of the scales of the food system proposed by Hinrichs, 2003).

Space also means space for social and political action. "Making spaces for alternatives" is a recurrent phrase in many writings. Some authors, drawing closely on the literature on innovation systems and the Francophone debate, reconfigure space through the concept of proximity, where AFNs redefine proximity spaces measured on different axes: physical-spatial (or Euclidean geometries), organizational, and cultural (Dansero, Pettenati, & Toldo, 2016). With respect to such advances in geographic thinking such as the conceptualization of space proposed by Harvey (2006) or Levy's systematization (1997) (to cite two leading figures from the English- and French-speaking debates), contemporary geography seeks to develop conceptual frameworks that can encompass the different configurations and measurements of space (and its various definitions) and not just physical distance in Euclidean space.

Place is an interpretative category applied above all in connection with the notions of embeddedness and re-connection between food and consumers, with quality and territories: all seen as locally specific discourses.

Much attention has been addressed to the question of the local dimension, with reference to the relations with the area of origin, as in the case of origin labelling, and the physical proximity between producer and consumer (which in Italy has been carried to extreme form in the zero kilometres rhetoric). Regarding the concept of local, the framework advanced by a non-geographer such as Brunori—a socio-economist with a keen appreciation of the territorial dimension—seems particularly significant, as it distinguishes between local and localist very clearly and effectively, considering the physical, symbolic, and relational dimensions (Brunori, 2008).

An attempt to connect the Anglophone and Francophone debates was proposed in one of the writings underlying the AFNIA project (Dansero & Puttilli, 2013), which addresses the concept of territoriality and draws on the geographer Raffestin and the recent opening to the English-speaking debate (Raffestin, 2012).

Lastly, a concept much cherished by geographers, but less used in the debate on AFNs, is that of the region, where Moya Kneafsey (2010) offers an interesting analysis on how the notion of the region is used in relation to the processes of reconnecting, re-scaling, and re-regionalizing the food system. The English geographer discusses how the concept of the region has been applied in the recent food debate in two ways. The first refers to "regional foods", in close relationship with labelling and designation schemes (PDO, IGT, IGP, etc.), that is, with efforts to link product quality with the places of production. The second can be expressed in terms of "regional food networks", which can occur when a number of elements of a food system—production, processing, retailing, and consumption of food—are organized on a regional basis in order to create a food network that is geographically distinctive and recognized as such by the actors involved. "Regional foods" may be circulated within a short and direct supply chain, but they are not limited to it (Kneafsey, 2010, p. 181).

The Approach Taken in This Book

While much of our investigation concerns issues that have already been debated in the literature, there are some points where our work departs from the received literature. The first is the intentional multidisciplinary approach. In the literature, AFNs have typically been dealt with by specific disciplinary fields (mainly sociological, anthropological, and geographic), as shown in the foregoing presentations of the approaches taken by different disciplines in addressing the issue of AFNs. However, one might conclude from these presentations that some of the approaches are incompatible. The economic approach, for instance, stresses the importance of finding common patterns and of identifying the common underlying mechanisms driving people's behaviour, so that individual and social heterogeneity are viewed as variations within a general behavioural model. By contrast, the sociological and anthropological approaches emphasize the differences and are more interested in detecting the different facets of reality from a social point of view. The environmental perspective looks for an objective measurement of the actual impact of the different chains, as well for the concept of environmental impact held by consumers and producers. The geographical approach tries to identify the networks associated with AFNs and their spatial distribution. Despite these apparent oppositions, we are convinced that analysing AFNs from these different approaches adds to the understanding of a phenomenon which by its very nature it has economic, social, geographic, and environmental implications, all of which are relevant for its understanding, and that using different approaches provides a global view of these different perspectives.

Second, adopting different disciplinary approaches helps in avoiding an ideological bias in favour of the object of inquiry. While we think it fair to state our sympathy for the AFN movement, in this research we purposely chose to adopt an a priori neutral stance. Several positive properties have been claimed for AFNs, such as embeddedness in regional and local food-culture, quality of food production, sustainability of the food supply chain, democracy of social and economic relations, and added value for the rural area and farmers. These claims have been questioned, but our interest is not to take a stand on these issues. Rather, our approach is to ask what reasons underlie the growth of AFNs, what effects they have, and what their working mechanisms are. In other words, the main objective of our research is to understand and discuss the functioning of these chains and, from this point of view, taking a neutral stand as to their desirability helps avoid the risk of ignoring weaknesses or dubious points in their operation or, conversely, of overstating their merits. In our view, only by starting from such an analysis is it also possible to make predictions about AFNs' prospects for upscaling and passing from the niche to the system level.

Third, we maintain that a comparative perspective with conventional food chains is needed in order to grasp the key features of AFNs. Such a perspective is very rarely taken, since the ideological/supportive slant of research tends to "select" case studies as "true" examples of alternativeness. By contrast, our empirical cases belong to both the alternative and the conventional worlds. Accordingly, we have compared the concepts of quality espoused by consumers who patronize different chains (supermarkets, urban district markets, farmers' markets, SPGs, high-end retailers) and investigated the modalities whereby producers and consumers match on quality and prices.

Fourth, while most of the current literature, the majority of which belongs to the sociological and economic fields, focuses on the consumer side (characteristics of the participants, motivations, etc.), our analysis embraces the entire chain. To understand AFNs' strength and resilience, it is important to analyse the motivations leading people (as consumers, as prosumers, or as concerned citizens) to attend or to participate in these chains. But at the same time, it is crucial to understand the other side of the chain, that is, producers' motivations and reactions in terms of farm setting to participation in AFNs. This is not simply because—obviously—both supply and demand are needed in order for these chains to work. It is because it is important to analyse how participation in an AFN shapes the behaviour of both consumers and producers and, more importantly, the forms of the interactions among operators in the chain. We characterize "alternativeness" in terms of the quality of the interaction that the exchange entails and, consequently, the relationship among traders, its strength, and how price-setting and the quality attributes that are demanded and produced are coordinated. By the same token, analysing the configuration of networks among producers and consumers, both spatially and culturally, helps provide a comprehensive view of the entire chain.

Notes

1. Even the use of online and social media by participants in short food supply chains only supplements existing reconnections between producers and consumers and cannot substitute for personal relationships (Bos & Owen, 2016; Fonte, 2013)
2. The MWTP is the maximum amount of money consumers would pay for an additional quantity of the good. The consumer purchases additional quantities of the good until the utility provided by them is greater than the utility foregone by paying the price of an additional quantity of the good, that is, the utility lost by giving up other goods that could have been purchased with the same money.
3. These two streams (orders of worth and worlds of production) are summarized in Lucien Karpik's perspective, where worlds of quality pair with different judgement devices that provide consumers with the knowledge to evaluate the "worth of goods" (Karpik, 2010, p. 96).

4. It is interesting to note that geographers like Renting et al. (2003), or Kneafsey (2010) now prefer the term SFSCs to AFNs and have also pointed out some distinctions between the concept of "local food system" as widely used in the early American studies. See in particular the distinctions and the choices made in the wider area of the study commissioned by the JRC (Kneafsey et al., 2013).
5. In this regard, see the distinction between the phases of the debate that we have proposed elsewhere (Dansero & Puttilli, 2013, p. 628).

References

Adam, K. L. (2006). Community Supported Agriculture, Attra. Retrieved from www.attra.ncat.org/attra-pub/csa.html; www.attra.ncat.org/attra-pub/PDF/csa.pdf

Appadurai, A. (Ed.). (1986). *The Social Life of Things: Commodities in Cultural Perspective*. Cambridge: Cambridge University Press.

Aubry, C., & Chiffoleau, Y. (2009). Le développement des circuits courts et l'agriculture péri-urbaine: histoire, évolution en cours et questions actuelles. *Innovations agronomiques, 5*, 53–67.

Audifredi, S. (2012). In Pursuit of Quality. The Institutional Change of Wine Production Market in Piedmont. *Sociologia Ruralis, 52*(3), 311–331.

Barbera, F. (2016). Development. In G. Ritzer (Ed.), *International Encyclopedia of Sociology*. London: Basil Blackwell. https://doi.org/10.1002/9781405165518.wbeos0817

Barbera, F., & Audifredi, S. (2012). In Pursuit of Quality. The Institutional Change of Wine Production Market in Piedmont. *Sociologia Ruralis, 52*(3), 311–331.

Barbera, F., & Dagnes, J. (2017). Le filiere agroalimentari alternative a Torino e in Piemonte: una questione di qualità. *Bollettino Società Geografica Italiana, Serie XIII, X*, 169–179 (English Version Available).

Barbera, F., Dagnes, J., & Di Monaco, R. (2018). Mimetic Quality: Consumer Quality Conventions and Strategic Mimicry in Food Distribution. *International Journal of Sociology of Agriculture and Food, 24*(2), 253–273.

Barham, E. (2003). Translating Terroir: The Global Challenge of French AOC Labeling. *Journal of Rural Studies, 19*, 127–138.

Barnard, A. (2000). *History and Theory in Anthropology*. Cambridge: Cambridge University Press.

Barth, F., Gingrich, A., Parkin, R., & Silverman, S. (2005). *One Discipline, Four Ways: British, German, French, and American Anthropology*. Chicago: University of Chicago Press.

Besky, S. (2014). *The Darjeeling Distinction: Labor and Justice on Fair Trade Tea Plantations in India*. Berkeley: University of California Press.

Black, R. (2012). *Porta Palazzo. The Anthropology on an Italian Market*. Philadelphia: University of Pennsylvania Press.

Boltanski, L., & Thévenot, L. (1991). *De la justification: les économies de la grandeur*. Paris: Gallimard. English Translation.

Boltanski, L., & Thévenot, L. (2006). *On Justification: Economies of Worth*. Princeton: Princeton University Press.

Born, B., & Purcell, M. (2006). Avoiding the Local Trap: Scale and Food Systems in Planning Research. *Journal of Planning Education and Research, 26*(2), 195–207.

Bos, E., & Owen, L. (2016). Virtual Reconnection: The Online Spaces of Alternative Food Networks in England. *Journal of Rural Studies, 45*, 1–14.

Brunori, G. (2008). Local Food and Alternative Food Networks: A Communication Perspective. *Anthropology of Food*, S2, March.

Brunori, G., Galli, F., Barjolle, D., van Broekhuizen, R., Colombo, L., Giampietro, M., et al. (2016). Are Local Food Chains More Sustainable than Global Food Chains? Considerations for Assessment. *Sustainability, 8*(5), 449.

Bullard, N. (2011). It's Too Late for Sustainability: What We Need Is System Change. *Development, 54*(2), 141–142.

Carolan, M. (2017). More-than-Active Food Citizens: A Longitudinal and Comparative Study of Alternative and Conventional Eaters. *Rural Sociology, 82*(2), 197–225.

Carrier, J. G. (1995). *Gifts and Commodities. Exchange and Western Capitalism Since 1700*. London: Routledge.

Carrier, J., & Luetchford, P. (Eds.). (2012). *Ethical Consumption: Social Value and Economic Practice*. New York: Berghahn.

Coley, D., Howard, M., & Winter, M. (2009). Local Food, Food Miles and Carbon Emissions: A Comparison of Farm Shop and Mass Distribution Approaches. *Food Policy, 34*(2), 150–155.

Cook, I., Hobson, K., Hallett, L., IV, Guthman, J., Murphy, A., Hulme, A., et al. (2011). Geographies of Food: 'Afters'. *Progress in Human Geography, 35*(1), 104–120.

Cook, I., et al. (2006). Geographies of Food: Following. *Progress in Human Geography, 30*(5), 655–666. http://journals.sagepub.com/doi/10.1177/0309132506070183

Cook, I., et al. (2008). Geographies of Food: Mixing. *Progress in Human Geography, 32*(6), 821–833. http://journals.sagepub.com/doi/10.1177/0309132506070183
Counihan, C. (2004). *Around the Tuscan Table. Food, Family and Gender in Twentieth Century Florence*. London: Routledge.
Counihan, C., & Siniscalchi, V. (Eds.). (2013). *Food Activism. Agency, Democracy, Economy*. London: Bloomsbury.
Dansero, E., Pettenati, G., & Toldo, A. (2016). Si proche et pourtant si loin. Etudier et construire la proximité alimentaire à Turin. In P. Mundler & J. Rouchier (Eds.), *Alimentation et proximité: jeux d'acteurs et territoires*. Educagri: Dijon.
Dansero, E., & Puttilli, M. (2013). Multiple Territorialities of Alternative Food Networks: Six Cases from Piedmont, Italy. *Local Environment, 19*(6), 626–643.
De Neve, G. P. (2008). In J. P. Luetchford & D. Wood (Eds.), *Hidden Hands in the Market: Ethnographies of Fair Trade, Ethical Consumption, and Corporate Social Responsibility*. Bingley: Emerald.
De Schutter, O. (2012). *The Adequacy of Diets and the Right to Food*. Report presented at the 19th Session of the United Nations Human Rights Council. UN doc. A/HRC/19/59.
De Schutter, O. (2017). The Political Economy of Food Systems Reform. *European Review of Agricultural Economics, 44*(3), 705–731.
DEFRA. (2005). The Validity of Food Miles as an Indicator of Sustainable Development. *Defra*, 7, p. 117.
DeLind, L., & Bingen, J. (2005). Be Careful What You Wish For: Democratic Challenges and Political Opportunities for the Michigan Organic Community. *Culture and Agriculture, 27*(2), 131–143.
DeLind, L. B. (2000). Transforming Organic Agriculture into Industrial Organic Products: Reconsidering National Organic Standards. *Human Organization, 59*(2), 198–208.
van der Ploeg, J. D. (2008). *The New Peasantries: Struggles for Autonomy and Sustainability in an Era of Empire and Globalization*. London: Earthscan.
van der Ploeg, J. D. (2010). The Peasantries of the Twenty-First Century: The Commoditisation Debate Revisited. *The Journal of Peasant Studies, 37*(1), 1–30.
Van Der Ploeg, J. D., Renting, H., Brunori, G., Knickel, K., Mannion, J., Marsden, T., et al. (2000). Rural Development: From Practices and Policies Towards Theory. *Sociologia Ruralis, 40*(4), 391–408.
Desrochers, P., & Shimizu, H. (2012). *The Locavore's Dilemma: In Praise of the 10,000-Mile Diet*. New York: Public Affairs.

DuPuis, E. M., & Goodman, D. (2005). Should We Go "Home" to Eat?: Toward a Reflexive Politics of Localism. *Journal of Rural Studies, 21*, 359–371.

Edwards-Jones, G., Milà i Canals, L., Hounsome, N., Truninger, M., Koerber, G., Hounsome, B., et al. (2008). Testing the Assertion that "Local Food Is Best": The Challenges of an Evidence-Based Approach. *Trends in Food Science and Technology, 19*(5), 265–274. https://doi.org/10.1016/j.tifs.2008.01.008

Foley, J. A., Ramankutty, N., Brauman, K. A., Cassidy, E. S., Gerber, J. S., Johnston, M., et al. (2011). Solutions for a Cultivated Planet. *Nature, 478*, 337–342.

Fonte, M. (2013). Food Consumption as Social Practice: Solidarity Purchasing Groups in Rome, Italy. *Journal of Rural Studies, 32*, 230–239.

Forssell, S., & Lankoski, L. (2014). The Sustainability Promise of Alternative Food Networks: An Examination through 'Alternative' Characteristics. *Agriculture and Human Values, 32*(1), 63–75.

Gereffi, G., Humphrey, J., & Sturgeon, T. (2005). The Governance of Global Value Chains. *Review of International Political Economy, 12*(1), 78–104.

Godelier, M. (1998). *The Enigma of the Gift*. Cambridge: Polity.

Goodman, D. (2009). *Place and Space in Alternative Food Networks: Connecting Production and Consumption, WP 21*. Environment, Politics and Development Working Paper Series, Department of Geography, King's College London.

Goodman, D., Goodman, M., & DuPuis, M. (2011). *Alternative Food Networks: Knowledge, Place and Politics*. London: Routledge.

Goodman, D., & Goodman, M. K. (2009). Food Networks, Alternative. In R. Kitchin & N. Thrift (Eds.), *International Encyclopaedia of Human Geography* (pp. 208–220). Amsterdam: Elsevier.

Goodman, M. (2004). Reading Fair Trade: Political Ecological Imaginary and the Moral Economy of Fair Trade Foods. *Political Geography, 23*(7), 891–915.

Grasseni, C. (2013). *Beyond Alternative Food Networks*. Italy's Solidarity Purchase Groups, London: Bloomsbury Academic.

Gregory, C. A. (1982). *Gifts and Commodities*. New York: Academic Press.

Gregory, C. A. (1997). *Savage Money. The Anthropology and Politics of Commodity Exchange*. Amsterdam: Harwood.

Gui, B. (2000). Beyond Transactions: On the Interpersonal Dimension of Economic Reality. *Annals of Public and Cooperative Economics, 71*(2), 139–169.

Gui, B. (2005). From Transactions to Encounters: The Joint Generation of Relational Goods and Conventional Values. In B. Gui & R. Sugden (Eds.), *Economics and Social Interactions* (pp. 23–51). Cambridge: Cambridge University Press.

Gui, B., & Stanca, L. (2010). Happiness and Relational Goods: Well-Being and Interpersonal Relations in the Economic Sphere. *International Review of Economics, 57*(2), 105–118.

Hammersley, M., & Atkinson, P. (2007). *Ethnography. Principles in Practice* (3rd ed.). London: Routledge.

Hann, C., & Hart, K. (Eds.). (2009). *Market and Society. The Great Transformation Today*. Cambridge: Cambridge University Press.

Hann, C., & Hart, K. (Eds.). (2011). *Economic Anthropology. History, Ethnography, Critique*. Cambridge: Polity.

Harvey, D. (2006). *Spaces of Global Capitalism: Towards a Theory of Uneven Geographical Development*. New York: Verso.

Heatherington, T. (2011). Introduction: Remaking Rural Landscapes in Twenty-First Century Europe, in Politicking the Farm: Transitions and Transformations in European Agriculture. *Anthropological Journal of European Cultures, 20*(1), 1–9.

Hinrichs, C. C. (2003). The Practice and Politics of Food System Localization. *Journal of Rural Studies, 19*(1), 33–45.

Honkanen, P., Verplanken, B., & Ottar Olsen, S. (2006). Ethical Values and Motives Driving Organic Food Choice. *Journal of Consumer Behaviour, 5*, 420–430.

Huffman, W. E. (1980). Farm and Off-Farm Work Decisions: Role of Human Capital. *The Review of Economics and Statistics, 62*, 14–23.

Isenhour, C. (2010). Building Sustainable Societies: A Swedish Case Study on the Limits of Reflexive Modernization. *American Ethnologist, 37*(3), 511–525.

Jackson, A. (Ed.). (1987). *Anthropology at Home*. London: Tavistock Publications.

Jarosz, L. (2008). The City in the Country: Growing Alternative Food Networks in Metropolitan Areas. *Journal of Rural Studies, 24*(3), 231–244.

Jessop, B., Brenner, N., & Jones, M. (2008). Theorizing Sociospatial Relations. *Environment and Planning D: Society and Space, 26*(3), 389–401.

Jung, Y., Klein, J. A., & Caldwell, M. L. (Eds.). (2014). *Ethical Eating in the Postsocialist and Socialist World*. Berkeley: University of California Press.

Kahneman, D., & Knetsch, J. L. (1992). Valuing Public Goods: The Purchase of Moral Satisfaction. *Journal of Environmental Economics and Management, 22*, 57–70.

Karpik, L. (2010). *Valuing the Unique: The Economics of Singularities*. Princeton: Princeton University Press.

King, R. P., Hand, M. S., DiGiacomo, G., Clancy, K., Gomez, M. I., Hardesty, S. D., et al. (2010). *Comparing the Structure, Size, and Performance of Local and Mainstream Food Supply Chains*. ERR-99, U.S. Department of Agriculture, Economic Research Service. June 2010.

Kneafsey, M. (2010). The Region in Food—Important or Irrelevant? *Cambridge Journal of Regions, Economy and Society, 3*(2), 177–190.

Kneafsey, M., Venn, L., Schmutz, U., Balazs, B., Trenchard, L., Eyden-Wood, T., et al. (2013). *short food supply chains and Local Food Systems in the E.U. A State of Play of Their Socio-Economic Characteristics* (F. Santini & S. Gomez y Paloma, Eds.). JRC Scientific and Policy Reports, Luxembourg, Publications Office of the European Union.

Kremer, P., & DeLiberty, T. L. (2011). Local Food Practices and Growing Potential: Mapping the Case of Philadelphia. *Applied Geography, 21*, 1252–1261.

Lamine, C. (2005). Settling Shared Uncertainties: Local Partnerships Between Producers and Consumers. *Sociologia Ruralis, 45*(4), 324–345.

Lancaster, K. J. (1966). A New Approach to Consumer Theory. *Journal of Political Economy., 74*(2), 132–157.

Latouche, S. (2009). *Farewell to Growth*. London: Polity.

Levkoe, C. Z. (2006). Learning Democracy Through Food Justice Movements. *Agriculture and Human Values, 23*(1), 89–98.

Lévy, J. (1997). *Europe. Une géographie*. Paris: Hachette.

Luetchford, P. (2014). Food and Consumption. In J. Pratt & P. Luetchford (Eds.), *Food for Change. The Politics and Values of Social Movements* (pp. 47–70). London: Pluto Press.

Lyon, S., Ailshire, S., & Sehon, A. (2014). Fair Trade Consumption and the Limits to Solidarity. *Human Organization, 73*(2), 141–152.

MacClancy, J. (Ed.). (2002). *Exotic No More. Anthropology on the Front Lines.* Chicago: University of Chicago Press.

Maestripieri, L. (2016). *Solidarity Purchasing Groups*. CRESSI Working Paper, 29.

Malinowski, B. (1922/2007). *Argonauts of the Western Pacific*. London: Routledge.

Marsden, T., Banks, J., & Bristow, G. (2000). Food Supply Chain Approaches: Exploring Their Role in Rural Development. *Sociologia Ruralis, 40*(4), 424–438.

Marsden, T., Banks, J., & Bristow, G. (2002). The Social Management of Rural Nature: Understanding Agrarian-Based Rural Development. *Environment and Planning A, 34*(5), 809–825.

Mauss, M. (1925/2016). *The Gift*. Selected, Annotated, and Translated by Jane I. Guyer. Chicago: University of Chicago Press.

McMichael, F. (2012). *Development and Social Change*. London: Sage.

Miller, D. (1987). *Material Culture and Mass Consumption*. Oxford: Blackwell.

Moberg, M. (2016). Market's End: Fair-Trade Social Premiums as Development in Dominica. *American Ethnologist, 43*(4), 677–690.

Morris, C., & Kirwan, J. (2011). Ecological Embeddedness: An Interrogation and Refinement of the Concept Within the Context of Alternative Food Networks in the UK. *Journal of Rural Studies, 27*(3), 322–330.

Mount, P. (2012). Growing Local Food: Scale and Local Food Systems Governance. *Agriculture and Human Values, 29*(1), 107–121. https://doi.org/10.1007/s10460-011-9331-0

Murdoch, J., Marsden, T., & Banks, J. (2000). Quality, Nature, and Embeddedness: Some Theoretical Considerations in the Context of the Food Sector. *Economic Geography, 76*(2), 107–125.

Murdoch, J., & Miele, M. (1999). "Back to Nature": Changing "Worlds of Production" in the Food Sector. *Sociologia Ruralis, 39*(4), 465–483.

Murdoch, J., & Miele, M. (2004). A New Aesthetic of Food? Relational Reflexivity in the 'Alternative' Food Movement. In M. Harvey, A. McMeekin, & A. Warde (Eds.), *Qualities of Food* (pp. 156–175). Manchester: Manchester University Press.

Okura Gagné, N. (2011). Eating Local in a U.S. City: Reconstructing "Community"—a Third Place—in a Global Neoliberal Economy. *American Ethnologist, 38*(2), 281–293.

Orlando, G. (2018). From the Risk Society to Risk Practice: Organic Food, Embodiment and Modernity in Sicily. *Food, Culture & Society, 21*(2), 144–163.

Parry, J., & Bloch, M. (Eds.). (1989). *Money and the Morality of Exchange*. Cambridge: Cambridge University Press.

Paxton, A. (1994). *The Food Miles Report*. London: Sustainable Agriculture, Food & Environment (SAFE) Alliance.

Polanyi, K. (1944/2001). *The Great Transformation. The Political and Economic Origins of Our Times*. Boston: Beacon Press.

Polanyi, K. (1957). The Economy as Instituted Process. In K. Polanyi, C. Arensberg, & H. Pearson (Eds.), *Trade and Markets in the Early Empires. Economy in History and Theory* (pp. 243–270). New York: Free Press.

Polanyi, K. (1977). *The Livelihood of Man*. New York: Academic Press.

Ponte, S. (2009). Governing through Quality: Conventions and Supply Relations in the Value Chain for South African Wine. *Sociologia Ruralis, 39*(3), 236–257.

Ponte, S. (2016). Convention Theory in the Anglophone Agro-food Literature: Past, Present and Future. *Journal of Rural Studies, 44*, 12–23.

Popke, J. (2006). Geography and Ethics: Everyday Mediations Through Care and Consumption. *Progress in Human Geography, 30*(4), 504–512.

Pratt, J. (2009). Incorporation and Resistance: Analytical Issues in the Conventionalization Debate and Alternative Food Chains. *Journal of Agrarian Change, 9*(2), 155–174.

Pratt, J. (2014). Farming and Its Values. In J. Pratt & P. Luetchford (Eds.), *Food for Change. The Politics and Values of Social Movements* (pp. 24–46). London: Pluto Press.

Pratt, J., & Luetchford, P. (2014). *Food for Change. The Politics and Values of Social Movements*. London: Pluto Press.

Raffestin, C. (2012). Space, Territory, and Territoriality. *Environment and Planning D: Society and Space, 30*(1), 121–141.

Rakopoulos, T. (2014). The Crisis Seen from Below, Within, and Against: From Solidarity Economy to Food Distribution Cooperatives in Greece. *Dialectical Anthropology, 38*, 189–207.

Rakopoulos, T. (2017). *From Clans to Co-ops. Confiscated Mafia Land in Sicily*. Oxford: Berghahn.

Renting, H., Marsden, T., & Banks, J. (2003). Understanding Alternative Food Networks: Exploring the Role of short food supply chains in Rural Development. *Environment and Planning A, 35*(3), 393–411.

Robben, A. C. G. M., & Sluka, J. A. (Eds.). (2007). *Ethnographic Fieldwork. An Anthropological Reader*. Oxford: Blackwell.

Rodgers, A., Woodward, A., Boyd, S., & Dietz, W. H. (2018). Prevalence Trends Tell Us What Did Not Precipitate the US Obesity Epidemic. *The Lancet Public Health*. Online First. Retrieved from https://www.sciencedirect.com/science/article/pii/S2468266718300021

Rosen, S. (1974). Hedonic Prices and Implicit Markets: Product Differentiation in Pure Competition. *The Journal of Political Economy, 82*(1), 34–55.

Sage, C. (2003a). Social Embeddedness and Relations of Regard: Alternative 'Good Food' Networks in South-West Ireland. *Journal of Rural Studies, 19*(1), 47–60.

Sage, C. (2003b). *Quality in Alternative Food Networks: Conventions, Regulations and Governance*. Paper presented at the International Seminar "Policies, Governance and Innovation for Rural Areas", 21–23 November 2003, Università della Calabria, Arcavacata di Rende.

Sahlins, M. (1974). *Stone Age Economics*. London: Tavistock.

Salais, R., & Storper, M. (1992). The Four 'Worlds' of Contemporary Industry. *Cambridge Journal of Economics, 16*, 169–193.

Sassatelli, R. (2015). Consumer Culture, Sustainability and a New Vision of Consumer Sovereignty. *Sociologia Ruralis, 55*(4), 483–496.

Sassatelli, R., & Davolio, F. (2010). Consumption, Pleasure and Politics. Slow Food and the Politico-aesthetic Problematization of Food. *Journal of Consumer Culture, 10*(2), 1–31.

Scharber, H., & Dancs, A. (2016). Do Locavores Have a Dilemma? Economic Discourse and the Local Food Critique. *Agriculture and Human Values, 33*(1), 121–133.

Singh, I., Squire, L., & Strauss, J. (Eds.). (1986). *Agricultural Household Models: Extensions, Applications, and Policy*. Baltimore: John Hopkins University Press.

Sonnino, R., & Marsden, T. (2006). Alternative Food Networks in the South West of England: Towards a New Agrarian Eco-Economy? In T. Marsden & J. Murdoch (Eds.), *Between the Local and the Global (Research in Rural Sociology and Development, Volume 12)* (pp. 299–322). Bingley: Emerald Group Publishing Limited.

Storper, M., & Salais, R. (1997). *Worlds of Production: The Action Frameworks of the Economy*. Cambridge, MA: Harvard University Press.

Stræte, E. P., & Marsden, T. (2006). Exploring Dimensions of Qualities in Food. In T. Marsden & J. Murdoch (Eds.), *Between the Local and the Global (Research in Rural Sociology and Development, Volume 12)* (pp. 269–297). Bingley: Emerald Group Publishing Limited.

Strathern, M. (1988). *The Gender of the Gift*. Berkeley: University of California Press.

Thurnwald, R. (1932). *Economics in Primitive Communities*. Oxford: Oxford University Press.

Tregear, A. (2011). Progressing Knowledge in Alternative and Local Food Networks: Critical Reflections and a Research Agenda. *Journal of Rural Studies, 27*(4), 419–430.

Uhlaner, C. (1989). Relational Goods and Participation: Incorporating Sociability into a Theory of Rational Action. *Public Choice, 62*, 253–285.

Van Passel, S. (2013). Food Miles to Assess Sustainability: A Revision. *Sustainable Development, 21*(1), 1–17. https://doi.org/10.1002/sd.485

Venn, L., Kneafsey, M., Holloway, L., Cox, R., Dowler, E., & Tuomainen, H. (2006). Researching European 'Alternative' Food Networks: Some Methodological Considerations. *Area, 38*(3), 248–258.

Verhaegen, I., & Van Huylenbroeck, G. (2001). Costs and Benefits for Farmers Participating in Innovative Marketing Channels for Quality Food Products. *Journal of Rural Studies, 17*, 443–456.

Vermeir, I., & Verbeke, W. (2006). Sustainable Food Consumption: Exploring the Consumer "Attitude Behavior Intention" Gap. *Journal of Agriculture and Environmental Ethics, 19*(2), 169–194.

Watts, D. C., Ilbery, B., & Maye, D. (2005). Making Reconnections in Agro-food Geography: Alternative Systems of Food Provision. *Progress in Human Geography, 29*(1), 22–40.

Weiner, A. (1992). *Inalienable Possessions. The Paradox of Keeping While Giving.* Berkeley: University of California Press.

Whatmore, S., & Thorne, L. (1997). Nourishing Networks. Alternative Geographies of Food. In D. Goodman, M. Watts, & M. J. Watts (Eds.), *Globalising Food: Agrarian Questions and Global Restructuring* (pp. 211–224). London: Routledge.

Wilk, R. R., & Gliggett, L. (2007). *Economies and Cultures. Foundations of Economic Anthropology* (2nd ed.). Boulder: Westview Press.

Winter, M. (2003). Geographies of Food: Agro-food Geographies Making Reconnections. *Progress in Human Geography, 27*(4), 505–513.

Winter, M. (2004). Geographies of Food: Agro-food Geographies—Farming, Food and Politics. *Progress in Human Geography, 28*(5), 664–670.

Part II

AFNs from the Consumers' Viewpoint

3

Introduction to Part II: AFNs from the Consumer's Viewpoint

Filippo Barbera, Alessandro Corsi, and Cristiana Peano

Introduction

Food is a reality of daily life. We all need to eat (and drink) and we spend a significant portion of our budget on purchasing food. We take the availability of food for granted, and we would be surprised if we did not find it in our favourite supermarket or farmers' market. In this sense, we do

F. Barbera (✉)
Department of Cultures, Politics and Society, University of Torino, Torino, Italy

Collegio Carlo Alberto, Torino, Italy
e-mail: filippo.barbera@unito.it

A. Corsi
Department of Economics and Statistics "Cognetti de Martiis", University of Torino, Torino, Italy
e-mail: alessandro.corsi@unito.it

C. Peano
Department of Agricultural, Forest and Food Sciences, University of Torino, Grugliasco (TO), Italy
e-mail: Cristiana.peano@unito.it

A. Corsi et al. (eds.), *Alternative Food Networks*,
https://doi.org/10.1007/978-3-319-90409-2_3

not consciously *trust* the food system; rather, we have a pre-reflexive *confidence* in it. We are used to assuming food purchasing as a systemic routine, just as we assume that car drivers in UK keep to the left while in continental Europe they keep to the right. Things might get more complicated when food becomes a "contested commodity", when its production and distribution endangers the environment, when its quality is intertwined with a specific local area, or when food chains compress producers' and processors' economic margins in favour of global distributors. In all these cases, our attitudes shift from confidence to trust: we need to reflexively decide which food product or chain we trust for our purchasing choices. This decision is quite complex, since it entails many and often contradictory dimensions.

To begin with, as Chap. 4 clearly illustrates, there are varied motivations for participating in Alternative Food Networks (AFNs). Some consumers are self-interested and look for healthier food, lower prices, better quality, food freshness and taste. Others are motivated by social, political and environmental concerns. As Chap. 6 shows, consumers' environmental concerns seem to be subjectively associated with both sustainable packaging and the organic production process. These dimensions appear to be key for the purchasing choices in district markets and farmers' markets. From the objective viewpoint, on the other hand, the environmental impacts of small-scale producers/sellers and large-scale distribution are not so different. What, in the eyes of consumers, points to environmental sustainability (e.g., small-scale, informality) clashes with objective measurement. Though consumers consider short supply chains to be more environmentally sustainable, several studies have shown that AFNs are not necessarily more sustainable than conventional agro-food goods (see also Chap. 13). Moreover, preferences may concern the specific chain in itself rather than the specific good. Both chains and goods may depend on their intrinsic characteristics such as convenience, travel cost, cleanliness and trust. For instance (Chap. 5), the major reason for choosing district markets is convenience. This is not surprising, since they are widely spread in the case of Piedmont and typically attended by people living in the area. On the contrary, convenience is not so relevant for the choice of supermarkets, which are spatially clustered in specific areas of the city (Chap. 6 and Sect. 3.2).

In addition to lower environmental impact, preferences can also involve other attributes that are of general interest, such as support for local farmers, or more generally social concerns. Altruism, civicness and political beliefs drive choices in this case. From the economic viewpoint, these other-regarding motives do not cancel out the relevance of budget constraints, they simply make them relevant for "different" arguments of the utility function. Altruistic motives can be a part of consumers' preferences, as can their social and political beliefs. The so-called "willingness-to-pay" for local products is to a certain extent linked to altruistic support for local farmers. On the other hand, the anthropological approach views AFNs and consumer choices as an expression of opposition to the industrialized and globalized agro-food sector (Chap. 7). In this case, altruistic motives act more independently from budget constraints and means-end logics. The sociological approach (Chap. 5) lies midway between the others: on the one hand, it underscores the importance of intrinsically motivated choices, while on the other hand, it acknowledges the influence of situational constraints on these choices.

A key point for all the approaches is the role played by personal relationships in the decision to join AFNs. Since we assume that what specifically distinguishes AFNs is the kind of exchange they entail, personal relationships play a key role. In economic terms, food purchases are always the result of a trade-off: food is a commodity exchanged for money, and the monetary cost of food represents the loss of utility from any alternative consumption that could be achieved with that sum, in a means-end logic. However, personal relationships in AFN transactions have a different meaning. As Chap. 4 illustrates, a typical consumer would have remained with his/her favourite farmer unless the proposed discount was over 12 or 10 per cent, and a typical member of a Solidarity Purchase Group (SPGs) would have continued to stay with it even with an almost two-thirds increase in prices. This willingness-to-pay, nevertheless, is just a measure of preferences, not the result of a trade-off, since it is not possible to buy the farmer's friendship or the pleasure of participating in an SPG without spoiling its benefit. The sociological and anthropological approaches treat interpersonal ties as "prisms", whereby social actors mirror their identity and their sense of self through a logic of appropriateness to the situation they are in. Here food is less an "alternative commodity" than an "alternative *to* commodity" which resists a mere reduction to its "exchange value" through prices. District markets, farmers' markets and SPGs share the importance assigned to the seller, showing high-quality expectations linked to this relationship. In district markets, the centrality of the personal relationship with the seller and the irrelevance of all the other dimensions embodies consumers' generic quality expectation. In farmers' markets, by contrast, the seller is perceived as an intermediary and a guarantor of a specific kind of quality relating to "soft" (intangible) elements. In Solidarity Purchase Groups, there is a somewhat negative attitude towards hard quality supported by face-to-face interaction with the seller (or the group's organizer). In SPGs, interpersonal relationships are far more important than in all the other chains, including farmers' markets.

As Chap. 7 states, AFNs might be interpreted as one example in which the principle of social protection, including the protection of nature, is applied in concrete experiments to try to contain the market principle by employing food as a "new commons" against the power of global food players. Food, like tourism, is a key global industry: there are 29 supermarkets in the world's top 100 chains by turnover, with Walmart, Carrefour and Tesco all in the list of the 5 largest global retail chains.[1] The Italian case is much more fragmented and the three biggest food distributors control only one-third of the market. Nonetheless, the National Antitrust Authority has identified several critical issues in the development of supermarkets in Italy that would weaken consumers and producers, subordinating them to the strongest chains. These are local concentration and non-competition "agreements", the lack of control in the supply chain, buyer power and the financialization of the cooperative movement. Moreover, food frauds have increased in recent years, creating a drop in food sales at large retail outlets and reinforcing consumers' distrust of supermarkets. Food quality in itself is not a driver of purchasing choices in large-scale distribution (Chaps. 5 and 7). The "broken promises" of large-scale distributors open a window of opportunity for AFNs, but taking advantage of it is not easy. On the one hand, both large-scale supermarkets and high-end retailers are adapting to the concerns for quality, local origin, preferences for organic food, health and environmental safety. On the other hand, prices, logistics and budget constraints seem to prevent AFNs from meeting this demand. It is interesting to note that AFNs as alternatives to dominant socioeconomic and cultural practices might change the sequential choice of purchasing: in the economic view, consumers choose where to buy and, once this decision is made, what to buy. By contrast, consumers choosing to join a Solidarity Purchase Group also decide to a large extent what to buy, since SPGs offer a certain basket of goods. Therefore, the attribute of the short chain which is of interest to consumers is also an attribute of the food they believe they can find there.

A point shared by the different approaches illustrated in the subchapters is that AFNs sell "credence goods" endowed with symbolic or intangible characteristics. "Alternativeness" is not an experience good that can be assessed after consumption: consumers need to trust or believe in the intangible characteristics of the food they purchase. At the same time, for sociological and anthropological approaches, a general reference to "credence goods" is not enough, since it simply shifts the problem. Credence is a symbolic dimension whose explanatory power needs to be accounted for. Where do beliefs come from? How do they shape purchasing choices? Can we reduce trust and credence entirely to prices and budget constraints? Here is where the so-called "quality conventions" approach enters the picture. Quality conventions make sense of the meaning structure of the different "worlds of quality": (1) market/commercial, based on price and commercial value of goods; (2) industrial, assessing the compliance with technical standards and reliability; (3) domestic, which are related to the concepts of interpersonal trust and traditional ways of producing; (4) opinion/fame, concerning the importance assigned to trademarks, brands and expert opinion; (5) civic, which refer to the societal and community benefits of products; (6) inspirational, based on the value of the personal passion embedded in the product; and (7) ecological, relating to the environmental sustainability of the goods and the production process. For both sociology and anthropology, these "worlds of quality" are incessantly open to negotiation, compromise and conflict by the agents in the field, that is, producers, distributors and consumers. As such, the shared ideas of what food quality actually is change over time and sometimes disappear to be replaced by new ones. Thus, quality is not a static feature defined once and for all. This process is far from being deterministic: on the one hand, consumers play a key role in "nudging" markets. Consumers can shove the market by addressing specific aspects of quality, both in conventional channels and, to an even greater extent, in AFNs. We show how in the "service economy" the qualification of products *within* the purchasing process is a key concern for the organization of markets. On the other hand, quality is strongly connected to the power of the lead firm in a given value chain. Lead firms provide quality specifications to their immediate suppliers (or buyers) who in turn transmit and translate them further along the value chain (Ponte and Gibbon 2009).

The quality process is open to multiple outcomes, since consumers tend to judge multiple quality conventions positively, thus displaying varied and complex quality profiles, and sellers need to deal with this complexity by calibrating the right "quality mix". Consumers' quality positioning does not blindly reflect the "conventional-alternative" polarization. Intangible dimensions of "soft quality" (Chap. 5) (such as the role of tradition, trust relationships, respect for the environment, community values and the farmers' passion) are at work in the quality profiles of both conventional and alternative supply chains, as are the features connected to the hard quality conception (price, trademarks and awards). Overlapping is the rule, while radical diversity is the exception. Operators use differentiated strategies to manage the quality expectations expressed by consumers. Specifically, Chap. 5 argues that "hybrid organizations" such as high-end distributors strategically overcome divisions among different worlds of quality as a marketing strategy.

The mixing of quality worlds thus might be a window of opportunity for strategic marketing choices by large-scale distribution and hybrid organizations and could also provide space for the further spread of AFNs. The mixed worlds of quality thus provide an opening for a "double movement". On the one hand, conventional food chains may have potential for conquering AFNs' quality space with specific marketing strategies; on the other hand, AFNs could meet the demands of a larger number of consumers by offering more agro-food goods characterized by spatial, economic and/or social proximity between producers and consumers.

The scaling-up of AFNs must take a trade-off into account: to meet the demand for soft quality which is actually ubiquitous, AFNs must leverage on prices, logistics and distribution while continuing to channel or mirror their distinctive worth—namely intrinsic value—in interpersonal relationships. This challenge seems to be particularly demanding in the more radical forms of AFNs we analysed, for example, Solidarity Purchase Groups. In "radical AFNs", economic and cultural values attached to food are currently being reproduced and contested as part of the capitalist system as a whole (Chap. 7). AFNs are seen by consumers as a voice raised in the struggle between market and society. In Solidarity Purchase Groups, consumers find a focal point not so much in a shared appreciation of specific quality dimensions, but rather in their opposition to the conventional food system. Their identity as consumers—and their resulting purchasing choices—are shaped by the distance they actively keep from the conventional system, rather than by their similarity to it. This "distance" is strongly intertwined with the intrinsic value of the interpersonal relationships at work in Solidarity Purchase Groups.

Note

1. See: https://www.thebalance.com/largest-retail-grocery-stores-3862931

4

Determinants of Participation in AFNs and Its Value for Consumers

Alessandro Corsi and Silvia Novelli

Consumers are the demand side of Alternative Food Networks (AFNs). This chapter will discuss their preferences and motivations for participating in AFNs, first in general and theoretical terms and as analysed in the literature. Some empirical findings from a study carried out in Piedmont will then be presented.

A. Corsi (✉)
Department of Economics and Statistics "Cognetti de Martiis", University of Torino, Torino, Italy
e-mail: alessandro.corsi@unito.it

S. Novelli
Department of Agricultural, Forest and Food Sciences, University of Torino, Grugliasco (TO), Italy
e-mail: silvia.novelli@unito.it

A. Corsi et al. (eds.), *Alternative Food Networks*,
https://doi.org/10.1007/978-3-319-90409-2_4

Consumers' Food Choices: Theoretical Framework

In economic terms, food purchases are the result of a trade-off. Food is exchanged for money. The monetary cost of food represents the loss of utility from any alternative consumption that could be achieved with that sum. This is traded off with the benefits that food brings to the consumer. Though consumers do not make such comparisons consciously and rationally at each purchase, this is the implicit exchange. All in all, therefore, the purchase of a particular food, and specifically of a particular food in a particular chain like an AFN, is a matter of preference and of the value that consumers assign to the benefits and costs of their food choices. What is particular about AFNs, we argue, is that purchasing a food in an AFN is different (i.e., provides a different utility) from purchasing exactly the same good in another chain. From this point of view, then, it is interesting to discuss the benefits that consumers obtain from purchasing food in a specific AFN.

Arguably, consumers' preferences regarding the goods purchased in AFNs can be quite diverse. The choice of the chain might be conceived as sequential: consumers choose where to buy and, once this decision is made, what to buy. While this can be true in some cases, however, in others the choice of the chain and the choice of the food are made together. As an example of the first case, consumers may decide to go to a farmers' market (FM) and then decide whether and what to buy. By contrast, consumers choosing to join a Solidarity Purchase Group (SPG) also decide to a large extent what to buy, since SPGs offer a certain basket of goods.

The economics approach assumes that consumers maximise their utility from the purchase of a particular food in a particular chain based on its perceived attributes (Thilmany, Bond, & Bond, 2008), under a budget constraint. The theoretical framework can be extended, considering: (1) the determinants of the preferences for the chain; (2) consumers' general attitudes, as also determined by values, beliefs, and habits, that may influence both the choice of the chain and the choice of the food; (3) the tastes concerning specific attributes of the food to be purchased.

Often, these three aspects are inextricably mingled. This creates a problem with empirical analyses: for example, in the consumers' eyes, the food attribute "freshness" is associated with a short food chain (Hunt, 2007; Feagan & Morris, 2009; La Trobe, 2001), so the attribute of the short chain which is of interest to consumers is also an attribute of the food they believe they can find there. Nevertheless, we will discuss these three points separately.

Preferences for chains may depend on their intrinsic characteristics or attributes (we will use the two terms interchangeably) such as convenience, travel cost, cleanliness, and trust. Convenience may be a critical issue for consumers, since AFNs typically do not ensure that purchase opportunities are continuously available. For instance, farmers' markets are usually held weekly or monthly, and SPGs collect and distribute food at time intervals. Parking facilities, opening hours, and distance may be other impediments to the choice of AFNs; participation in some AFNs (e.g., FMs) is hindered by inconveniences such as difficulty in finding them or little variety of products (Conner, Colasanti, Ross, & Smalley, 2010; Khan & Prior, 2010).

The above attributes are of self-interest to the consumer. However, chain preferences can also involve attributes that are of general interest, such as a lower environmental impact, support for local farmers, or more generally social concerns. In other words, altruistic motives can be a part of consumers' preferences, as can their social and political beliefs. Empirical studies of participation in FMs have often found that environmental and social concerns are a part of the motivation for choosing AFNs. For instance, environmental and social justice have been indicated as motivations for participating in FMs (Alkon, 2008), while Toler, Briggeman, Lusk, and Adams (2009) show that willingness-to-pay (WTP) for local products is to a certain extent linked to altruistic support for local farmers. This component of preferences has been widely stressed by a set of studies drawing on a political economy perspective (Tregear, 2011). This literature—mainly belonging to the sociological, geographical, and anthropological approaches—viewed AFNs as an expression of opposition to the industrialised and globalised agro-food sector (e.g., Allen, FitzSimmons, Goodman, & Warner, 2003; Goodman, 2004).

These general beliefs and attitudes may depend, in turn, on the consumer's (observable) socio-economic characteristics such as age, gender, occupation, and the like, but also on idiosyncratic (unobservable) individual traits. Hence, a stream of literature has attempted to characterise the features of typical AFN consumers and identify specific clusters (e.g., Rocchi, Cavicchi, & Baldeschi, 2012; Weatherell, Tregear, & Allinson, 2003).

Beliefs and attributes also affect the way consumers perceive the characteristics of chains and of food. The characteristics of interest to consumers may be intrinsic to the food (such as tastiness, freshness, safety), or symbolic or intangible characteristics associated with it. It is important to note that while the intrinsic characteristics of food are an experience good (i.e., their real quality can only be assessed after consumption), the intangible characteristics are mostly credence goods, that is, their real quality cannot be assessed, or can only be assessed at a huge cost (Darby & Karni, 1973; Nelson, 1970). This is what makes the preference for an intangible characteristic of food strictly associated with the preference for a particular chain, when consumers are confident that the chain guarantees the presence of that intangible characteristic. For instance, consumers having a preference for local products may prefer to shop at a farmers' market because they have a high confidence that the lettuce they buy there is actually locally produced, something they cannot detect personally.

The strictly monetary variables—prices and income—are also relevant for consumers' choices. Since the exchange is between AFN food (with all its intrinsic and intangible characteristics) and whatever else can be bought with the same sum, the relative price dictates the rate at which AFN food can be traded with the other goods. Economic theory predicts that rational consumers with a budget constraint will increase their consumption of a good as long as the increase in utility they get from one dollar more spent on it is greater than the loss in utility due to withdrawing one dollar from the consumption of the other good. Hence, higher prices for AFN food decrease their consumption, and vice versa. Thus, if the same product is available from the alternative and the conventional chains, and consumers buy in the AFN even though the price is higher, it is because they believe the additional characteristics of food in the alternative chain are worth the higher cost. If the price in the AFN is lower, we cannot directly infer whether the choice of buying is simply due to the lower price, or whether the other characteristics also play a role. Income is relevant because it relaxes the budget constraint, allowing greater consumption. How much consumption increases with income depends on income elasticity, that is, the ratio of the relative change in consumption to the relative change in income. Food is generally income inelastic, for the simple reason that there are physiological limitations to food intake. Nevertheless, food is also a necessity and, at low-income levels, it has a high priority. All this explains the historical evolution in food consumption. Rather than resulting in higher consumption, income growth has translated into a change in food habits, with an increase in the consumption of more expensive food, first animal products and then more sophisticated and exotic products. In several respects, the birth and expansion of AFNs reflects this tendency. The search for fresh, tasty, and healthy food in alternative chains is certainly part of this trend. This obviously leaves aside the motivations linked to the intangible attributes of alternative chains and of the food they offer, for example, support for local economy and local farmers, environmental stewardship, and justice.

Previous Research on the Motivations for Attending AFNs

There is an enormous literature on the issue of consumers and AFNs. A recent review of studies on consumers' perceptions and preferences for local food (Feldmann & Hamm, 2015) considers 73 publications out of a total of 550 scientific articles identified using the search terms "local", "regional", "food", and "consumer". "Local" is not the same as "alternative", and the count would be higher if all AFNs were included. Without claiming to provide a complete review of the literature, we will limit ourselves to indicating the main streams of literature based on the above considerations.

One part of the literature investigates which characteristics of the chain are of interest to consumers. This stream often overlaps with a second one identifying the preferences for food characteristics in AFNs. A third stream aims to identify the characteristics of consumers of AFNs in terms of their socio-economic characteristics and/or of groups of consumers with different attitudes or motivations towards FMs. A fourth streams attempts to measure preferences, estimating the WTP for particular characteristics of the food and/or of the chain.

The streams of literature dealing with preferences for chains and food characteristics are not separate, since most papers do not draw clear-cut distinctions between the preferences or the WTP for the chain and for the food, and these preferences are often related to consumer characteristics. Thus, for example, in one of the first quantitative analyses of consumers' behaviour towards AFNs, Govindasamy and Nayga (1997) estimate logit models of the probability of visiting four different direct marketing facilities, including such determinants as consumers' socio-demographic characteristics and habits as well as expected quality and price relative to supermarkets.

Among the few papers listing intrinsic characteristics of the chain as determinants for chain choice, Abelló, Palma, Waller, and Anderson (2014) show that travel distance, market promotional activities such as entertainment, education, and food events were all key factors influencing the frequency of visits to farmers' markets. In a survey reported by Govindasamy, Italia, and Adelaja (2002), approximately 20% of consumers considered convenience as the most important characteristic. Among the reasons for visiting FMs, respondents to a survey in Indiana (Betz & Farmer, 2016) assigned high ratings to the convenience of the FM location and of the opening hours. Similar assessments of the convenience of market location and hours of operation were expressed in the surveys reported by Conner et al. (2010) and by Gumirakiza, Curtis, and Bosworth (2014), while the effect of various physical attributes of farmers' markets on customers' willingness to attend a particular market was estimated by Neill, Mitchell, and Williams (2014) and by Keeling, Thilmany, and Bondet (2009).

Civic concerns and food quality are far more frequently cited as reasons for attending AFNs (the majority of papers actually concern FMs). Eating quality, and especially freshness, is almost invariably the most important feature sought in FMs, normally together with support for farmers and the local economy (Archer, Sánchez, Vignali, & Chaillot, 2003; Betz & Farmer, 2016; Conner et al., 2010; Feagan & Morris, 2009; Govindasamy et al., 2002; Keeling et al., 2009; Lyon, Collie, Kvarnbrink, & Colquhoun, 2009; Onozaka, Nurse, & Thilmany McFadden, 2010; Toler et al., 2009). All these papers concern the USA, UK or Canada, but in France too (Sainte-Marie, Balle, & Kubista, 2012), the most important reason for buying local food is support for the local economy and farmers, followed by better taste, while a Eurobarometer survey indicated that 89% of EU respondents totally agree or tend to agree that there are benefits to buying products from a local farm (Eurobarometer, 2011). In Italy, Giampietri, Koemle, Yu, and Finco (2016) find a noteworthy consumer awareness of the positive influence of buying at FMs on supporting farmers' income. Hence, self-interested motivations go hand in hand with concern for public goods. In Italy, civic concern is apparently greater among patrons of specific AFNs, SPG members in particular. In one survey, 48%, 56%, and 54% of respondents indicated environmental problems, social injustice, and food safety respectively as their main concerns, and 59.3% considered the SPG to be a way of putting responsible behaviour into practice (Carbone, Gaito, & Senni, 2007).

Nevertheless, some attracting features of AFNs stem from personal exchange and sociability. Some consumers love social interactions, such as enjoying the market, talking with farmers, and making a trip to the market a family event, which significantly increases their spending at farmers' markets (Hunt, 2007). Many consumers prefer to have a farmer hand them the produce directly rather than being helped by a generic vendor or taking it from a shelf (Giampietri et al., 2016). This suggests that the modalities of the exchange themselves, and not only the specific product, are a part of consumers' preferences.

Among the papers that seek to identify the characteristics of consumers attending AFNs, some relate attendance only to socio-demographic characteristics. As regards observable characteristics, a general finding is that shoppers at AFNs are in general wealthier, older, and better educated than the general public (e.g., McGarry Wolf, Spittler, & Ahern, 2005; Onianwa, Wheelock, & Mojica, 2005). Varner and Otto (2008) also find a positive relation between sales at FMs and average income in the area.

Other studies (e.g., Zepeda & Li, 2006) include, in addition to socio-demographic variables, general attitudes towards food, the environment, and farmers, as well as personal tastes (interest in cooking), or diet habits (Govindasamy & Nayga, 1997). Other scholars identify specific groups of AFN patrons. Rocchi et al. (2012) use a cluster analysis to characterise two groups of FM shoppers, one wealthier and better educated and primarily motivated by "a positive attitude towards environmental and rural development goals and by the willingness to participate in a social event", the second motivated by the opportunity to meet producers, which they consider to be a guarantee of quality. Weatherell et al. (2003) find evidence of a homogeneous group of "concerned consumers" (58% of respondents) prioritising all food-related issues except price, strongly interested in local food, and at the same time expressing moral and health concerns. Megicks, Memery, and Angell (2012) identify four groups according to the stated reasons for buying local food, that is, "Intrinsic quality", "Local support and provenance", "Ethical sustainability", and "Shopping benefits". However, the idea that AFN participants seek high-quality credence goods and are more willing to pay for them than non-participants is challenged by Cembalo et al. (2015), who characterise AFN patrons as having values and lifestyles that are more oriented to rational shopping, sensibility to quality and taste rather than emotional involvement. On the basis of the same survey, Pascucci, Dentoni, Lombardi, and Cembalo (2016) find that SPG participants are characterised by higher levels of uncertainty on price, negotiation, and quality monitoring than non-participants and emphasise that the role of values as aggregating factors coexists with cost-economising motivations.

Nevertheless, some studies address consumers with price concerns. The probability of shopping at an FM can be significantly lower among consumers for whom cost is the most important characteristic of food (Zepeda, 2009), and "too expensive" was the most important reason indicated by respondents for not purchasing local food (Khan & Prior, 2010). Even participation in community supported agriculture (CSA) is discouraged by the price of shares (Kolodinsky & Pelch, 1997). This is evidence of the monetary constraint that consumers necessarily face and, at the same time, shows that some consumers have weak preferences for the intrinsic and intangible characteristics of AFN food relative to other consumption items.

Lastly, some papers quantify consumers' preferences in terms of willingness-to-pay for specific characteristics of food, but they deal mostly with food of local origin, which, even if related, is not necessarily the same as AFN food.[1] Burchardi, Schröder, and Thiele (2005), for instance, estimate WTP for local milk and find that it depends significantly on strong preferences for supporting farmers. Burnett, Kuethe, and Price (2011) estimate willingness to pay a price premium for "locally grown" products. Carpio and Isengildina-Massa (2009) find a higher WTP for older and female consumers who perceive local quality as higher. Darby, Batte, Ernst, and Roe (2008) estimate a higher WTP for local products than for wider provenance and find that this demand is independent of other attributes usually associated with local foods such as freshness and affiliation with "less corporate" production. Gracia, Barreiro-Hurlé, and López-Galán (2014) find that most consumers rate "local" more highly than "organic". Only one paper (Giampietri et al., 2016) finds a lower value assigned to local products. Thilmany et al. (2008) split the WTP (price premium) for local produce between different motivations (reduction of food miles, support for local farmers and economy, superior quality).

This short literature review illustrates our points that (1) motivations for attending AFNs are highly heterogeneous, (2) hedonistic and selfish motivations coexist with altruistic and social motivations, and (3) preferences may concern the intrinsic characteristics of the chains themselves or the (intrinsic or intangible) characteristics of the food available in them. One important aspect to note is that different motivations can coexist in the same individuals, who can, for example, be attracted by the tastiness of the farmers' produce and at the same time appreciate the personal interaction with them. When different motivations are compatible, they are mutually reinforced, while when they run counter to each other, the consumer must trade off the benefits against the costs. For instance, a typical trade-off is between higher prices and better expected quality at farmers' markets.

Hence, any claim to identify "the" AFN consumer can be questionable, given the high variability of desired attributes, of beliefs, and of preferences. Nevertheless, one can try to identify certain patterns shared by groups of consumers, with a higher level of confidence when considering small or compact groups. In our empirical work, we aimed at quantifying a measure of preferences in two groups of consumers, namely, consumers attending urban open-air district markets and members of SPGs.

The Choice of Purchasing at Farmers' Stands

A first part of our empirical work concerns the preferences for a particular chain. More specifically, we investigated consumers' choice to buy at farmers' stands in urban open-air district markets (Novelli & Corsi, 2015). Open-air district markets are widespread and popular in Italy. Most sellers at these markets are retailers procuring from wholesalers and selling to the public. Nevertheless, some stands are usually kept by farmers, who have a legal right to do so. Urban district markets are open daily, and farmers sell there frequently and regularly, generally three to four days per week. This contrasts with farmers' markets (typically promoted by farmers' unions in Italy) that generally take place once or twice a month. Hence, consumers in district markets differ from those at farmers' markets: they are shopping for everyday food rather than special items and are presumably not a priori self-selected for committed consumption. While consumers attending FMs have already decided to buy directly from farmers, this is not necessarily the case for those attending district markets. It is therefore interesting to investigate the motivations for choosing to purchase at farmers' vs. conventional vendors' stalls.

We hypothesised that this choice depends on (1) socio-economic characteristics of consumers (such as gender, income, education, etc.), as proxies both of cultural traits and of economic status, and (2) general attitudes towards food and chain. If consumers' predominant interest is in the quality of food, then purchasing directly from farmers is presumably due to expected better quality of their products. If expenditure is a major concern, consumers' choice between conventional and farmer vendors might be dictated by a comparison between prices. As trust in the vendor can also be a crucial criterion, the choice of vendor can thus be due to consumers' expectations about quality, taste, healthiness of what the particular vendor sells, and on the time consistency of these characteristics in repeated purchases. From this standpoint, choosing to buy from farmers depends on whether consumers consider them more trustworthy than conventional vendors. Lastly, for some consumers the main concern when shopping might be convenience, so that the location of the farmers' stands in the district market can be relevant.

A total of 1138 valid questionnaires were collected through in-person interviews in open-air markets in Torino, Cuneo, Alessandria, and Asti, four cities in Piedmont (Italy) during the spring and summer of 2014. In Torino, the regional capital of Piedmont, a two-stage random sampling procedure was used, the first stage being a random choice of district markets. In each market, consumers to be interviewed were also chosen at random.

Consumer attitudes were assessed from responses to questions about the interviewees' reasons for choosing the district market and for choosing specific market stands. The stated reasons made it possible to identify three main attitudes: convenience, price, and quality. Likewise, the criteria for choosing market stands were clustered into four categories: convenience, price, quality, and trust in the vendor.[2] Attitudes were not mutually exclusive. Table 4.1 shows the relevant percentages of consumers.

The major reason for choosing district markets is convenience. This is not surprising, since these are district markets, typically attended by people living in the area. Quality comes second, which suggests that, since the interviewees had actually chosen the district markets, they consider that the products there are better quality than those in other facilities

Table 4.1 Attitudes towards the choice of market and stand

Attitudes	%
District market—convenience	65.4
District market—price	21.4
District market—quality	41.5
Market stand—convenience	1.3
Market stand—price	57.0
Market stand—quality	70.3
Market stand—trust	29.3

such as supermarkets. By contrast, price is a relatively minor factor in the choice of district markets.

Once at the market, convenience is no longer an important consideration in choosing a stand. Quality is a major criterion (indicated by 70% of the interviewees), but price (57%) is also important. Almost 30% indicate trust in the vendor as a reason for choosing a stand.

When asked where they bought fruit or vegetables, 33% of the interviewees stated they purchased predominantly from farmers' stands, 45% stated that they sometimes bought from them, while the rest either did not buy from or were not aware of farmers' stands.

We ran a statistical analysis of the probability of purchasing at a farmer's stand (whether regularly or occasionally). An attitude towards quality seems to play a central role in the preference for farmers' stands, as inferred from both the stated reason for choosing the local market and for choosing market stands. Both variables were statistically highly significant, and the estimates suggest that choosing the local market on the basis of quality increases the probability of buying from farmers by 9.5%.[3] If the quest for quality drove the choice of market stand, consumers were 21.5% more likely to buy from farmers. This suggests that consumers generally consider farmers' products as higher quality. The attitude of seeking a trustworthy vendor was also important in driving the choice of a farmer's stand, since it increases the probability by almost 8%. This implies that farmers are considered more trustworthy than conventional vendors. By contrast, attitudes towards low prices (both in the choice of the market and of the stand) bore a negative sign but were not significant, that is, even if farmers' stands are considered more costly, prices do not seem to be relevant in the choice of farmers' stands.

Among personal characteristics, consumers who usually took care of purchasing fruit and vegetables were 24.2% more likely to buy from farmers' stands, perhaps because they are more aware of quality issues and better acquainted with the vendors. Better educated consumers were also more likely to buy from farmers, though in this case the effect was weak (every additional schooling year increases the probability of purchasing from farmers by just 1%). Males were 5% more likely to purchase from farmers than females, though the effect was only weakly significant.

Income was not significant, and the effects of professional status were unclear.

Overall, these results suggest that (1) consumers' attitudes towards the choice of the market and of the stand are highly heterogeneous; (2) the dominant attitude determining the choice of the district market is the search for convenience, along with the search for quality; (3) the dominant attitude once in the market is the search for quality, while price comes second; (4) trust in the vendor is also relevant to the choice at the market; and (5) farmers in district markets are therefore mostly appreciated for quality and trust.

The Value of the Personal Relationship with Farmers

The finding that price, though outweighed by quality and trust, is relevant in consumers' choice bears out the truism that purchasing food entails a trade-off. The cost of food represents the loss of utility from any alternative consumption that could be achieved with that sum. This is traded off with the benefits the food brings to the consumer. In addition to quality and trust, these benefits include the intangibles stemming from disinterested personal interactions. It has been shown that such personal relationships are attractive for people attending farmers' markets (Kirwan, 2006). We wanted to investigate whether patronising farmers' stands created relational goods, that is, disinterested personal relationships with the farmers in "less alternative" facilities such as district markets and—something new to the best of our knowledge—to measure their value for consumers.[4] To this end, we used a stated preference technique similar to those used for the evaluation of environmental goods (Corsi & Novelli, 2015). We submitted a specific questionnaire to a sub-sample of the participants in the survey presented above, conducting in-person interviews with randomly chosen people attending open-air district markets in Torino and other cities in Piedmont. We retained only respondents who stated they regularly shopped in that particular market and who usually bought from farmers, since we wanted to estimate the value of the direct relationship between consumer and farmer. After the preliminary filter questions on their purchasing habits, they were asked whether they would still buy the products they frequently bought from one farmer if another farmer offered exactly the same products at a lower price.[5] The wording "exactly the same" was specified in order to rule out reasons other than the relational good and the price. In particular, we sought to rule out preferences based on the expected quality of the produce, the information provision, the preference for the point of sale, and support for farmers or local products. Proposed price discounts of 10%, 20%, and 30% were randomly assigned. In each case, the absolute change for a typical expenditure was also stated. What we wanted to estimate was thus the willingness-to-accept (WTA), that is, the minimum amount of money needed to relinquish the relational good. It should be emphasised that this is only a measure of preferences, using money as a metric, and does not imply that the relational good is for sale. To be sure that the respondents really stated their WTA for the relational good, those who stated they would rather stay with the previous vendor were asked the reason. In some cases, they mentioned trust, which is not equivalent to the relational good. We experimented with two different approaches to dealing with these cases: either the responses were reclassified as an acceptance of the alternative vendor, or they were simply dropped. Two different estimation methods were employed to assess WTA, one similar to the difference-in-utility approach used in contingent valuation of environmental goods as proposed by Hanemann (1984), the second similar to the valuation function proposed by Cameron (1988) (for details, see Corsi & Novelli, 2015). The latter makes it possible to assess the effect of the respondents' socio-demographic characteristics on the probability of accepting the change of vendor. The first model was estimated on 249 observations, the second, due to some missing data for socio-economic variables, on 241 observations (212 and 205, respectively, if trust responses were dropped). The results differ according to the models, but at the most conservative estimate, they indicate that the average WTA in the sample was 12.2% or 9.6% contingent on how trust responses were treated, with a standard deviation of 2.3% and 2.6%, respectively. The median is 12.5% and 10%, respectively. In other words, a typical consumer would have remained with his/her favourite farmer unless the proposed discount was over 12% or 10%. This suggests that even in a setting which is not particularly dedicated to alternative and committed consumers, direct sales were to a non-negligible extent driven by the personal relationship created between producer and consumer, even though there was a certain variability in this respect. However, though we sought to isolate the effect of this component, some ambiguity may remain, since some motivations may be mingled. When asked to indicate their reason for staying with their favourite vendor, for instance, some respondents answered "out of habit", which is difficult to interpret in one sense or another. Habit may mean familiarity and, hence, be related to the relational good; but it can also stem from risk-averse attitudes. Similarly, trust is not the same as a relational good, but may be strictly connected. If I know and like someone, I usually tend to trust him/her, though the converse might not hold, since I can trust someone who is indifferent to me. Moreover, if relational goods are created between farmers and consumers, this does not mean that they may not also be created with conventional vendors in a facility where sales, unlike in supermarkets, are face-to-face. Rather than being a dichotomy, opportunities for personal relationships range in a continuum, from the lowest level in supermarkets up to the highest in AFNs.

Overall, the findings from the survey in district markets suggest that in such facilities as elsewhere, customers have heterogeneous and multi-faceted reasons for purchasing directly from producers, from reasons linked to intrinsic food quality (taste, freshness) to intangible attributes such as environmental friendliness and local origin, or knowing and liking the vendor.

The Value of Participating in SPGs

The following empirical investigation concerned Solidarity Purchase Groups (SPGs; in Italian, Gruppi di Acquisto Solidale or GAS). SPGs are organisations of consumers who join together to buy food and other goods collectively and directly from producers, at a price that is fair to both parties. In their statements, SPGs typically stress the use of short food chains, quality and environmentally friendly food consumption, and support for farmers' right to fair prices (Saroldi, 2001). Hence, ethical and solidarity issues, establishing trust relationships between consumers and producers (especially local ones) and getting fresh, seasonal, and healthy food figure prominently in their ideology (Novelli & Corsi, 2018, Chap. 10). In decisions to join SPGs, ethical and political motivations and social concerns are thus arguably dominant, but more selfish and monetary reasons can be nevertheless at work, since members are in any case budget-constrained.

Accordingly, we were interested in investigating SPG members' motivations and in assessing the ethical, social, and environmental reasons on the one hand and the self-interested or strictly economic reasons on the other. In addition, we wanted to measure the value members attach to their participation in the SPG. Again, money is only a metric for measuring preferences.

For this analysis (Corsi & Novelli, 2016), an in-person questionnaire was administered to 151 members of four SPGs in the city of Torino (Italy) and other neighbouring towns. The four SPGs differed in size, as they had 25, 156, 96, and 136 member families or individuals, respectively. The questionnaires were administered during the meetings held to distribute the food ordered by members. The questionnaire included a first section in which respondents were asked about their participation in the SPG, the tasks they performed in the SPG, and their motivations. The answers to the questions concerning the tasks performed for the SPG were used to construct an indicator of respondents' commitment to the SPG.[6] Then, using an approach similar to that used for patrons of urban district markets, respondents were asked whether they would still buy from the SPG if its prices were to increase by a certain percentage above what they currently pay, and the only alternative were to buy at a supermarket. Price increases of 20%, 30%, 40%, and 50% were randomly assigned to each questionnaire. Members who responded they would still buy from the SPG were then asked to indicate their reasons. The information from this question was used to estimate a WTP function and the mean and median WTP.

As regards the respondents' socio-economic characteristics, the majority (64%) were women, the mean age was 48, and the education level was quite high (the mean corresponded to some university-level education).

The majority of respondents were white-collar workers (69%), followed by professionals (14%) and self-employed (9%) while manual workers were a minority (4%), the rest being unemployed and non-labour force. The average monthly household income was about 2500 euros, and the average number of household members was 3.2, with 0.8 children under 14 years old. Interestingly, commitment averaged 12.8 points but varied widely (±7.5), so that members performed the activities needed to run the SPG quite differently. Another relevant data is that 55% of the respondents stated that the prices of fruit and vegetables purchased through the SPG were lower than in conventional supermarkets.

Table 4.2 shows the distribution of motivations for participating in the SPG (respondents could give up to three reasons). The most frequent motivation was "Support for local farmers"; this, together with the other social motivations ("Respect for the environment" and "Fighting multinationals and supermarket chains"), accounted for 39.6% of total responses.

Responses relating to the intrinsic or symbolic characteristics of food ("Quality guarantee", "Consumption of seasonal products", "Consumption of local food") added up to another 38%. Strictly monetary considerations ("Price" and "Quality/price ratio") accounted for only 12.7%. Lastly, it is interesting to note that explicit social and relational motivations ("Participation in a collective action of people with the same

Table 4.2 Responses to the question about the main reasons for participating in the SPG (max 3 items)

	N	%
Respect for the environment	23	7.2
Support for local farmers	74	23.1
Consumption of seasonal products	36	11.2
Consumption of local food	45	14.0
Fighting multinationals and supermarket chains	30	9.3
Quality guarantee	41	12.8
Price	2	0.6
Quality/price ratio	39	12.1
Participation in a collective action of people with the same ideals	14	4.4
Knowing the producers	17	5.3
	321	100.0

ideals" and "Familiarity with the producers") accounted for almost 10% of total responses.

Different statistical models were estimated for assessing members' WTP to participate in the SPG. The valuation function approach also made it possible to assess which variables affected the probability of remaining with the SPG even with the indicated price increases. The effects of some variables are rather obvious. Price had the predicted negative effect, but it was quite weak, since a 1% increase in prices reduced the probability of remaining with the SPG by only 0.7%. Members who stated that the SPG prices were lower than the supermarkets' were 14% more likely to stay with the SPG than other members. This is consistent with having a monetary incentive to participate in the SPG.

The commitment variable was statistically significant and positive. For each one-point increase in the commitment indicator (the average is 12.8, with a range from 2 to 33), the probability of staying rose by 1.3%. This means that participation provided utility to some participants regardless of the monetary incentive. Far from being a cost, work for the SPG provided a reward: the satisfaction of engaging in an ethical activity, the pleasure of socialising through the initiatives and the activities, and, more generally, a psychic reward.

Some characteristics that are typically considered as conducive to participation in AFNs, that is, higher income and upper level occupation, were not significant in our estimates. Professionals and self-employed people did not differ from the non-labour force group (the reference category), unlike white-collar and manual workers who were more likely to stay. Younger age and higher education were also factors that made respondents more willing to stay with the SPG even with higher prices. Nevertheless, the effects of these variables were weak: each additional year of age decreased the probability by 0.6%, and each additional year of education increased it by 2.4%. Lastly, having young children reduced the probability of staying with the SPG, because of the tighter income constraint faced by households with young children: with each additional child, the probability of staying dropped by 10%. Overall, socio-economic variables did not have a strong effect. One should nevertheless consider that the analysis addressed SPG members, rather than the general population, and it is not surprising that there should be a certain homogeneity among them. Most SPGs originate from small groups of friends or neighbours, and tend to draw on a pool of acquaintances even when they grow to a larger size, so it is only to be expected that members have some similarities that make it more difficult to identify socio-economic drivers because of the lack of variation.

Average and median WTP were also estimated using the statistical models. The mean WTP according to the valuation function model was 68.4% (with a standard deviation of 26%), and the median was 66.3%. The difference-in-utility model yielded a similar value, a mean and median of 77.6%. In other words, a typical member would have continued to stay with the SPG even with an almost two-thirds increase in prices. Even allowing for some hypothetical bias, these results show members' strong commitment to their SPG. We asked respondents who stated they would stay with the SPG despite the indicated price increase to provide their most important reason for doing so. Answers are shown in Table 4.3. Among the reasons, slightly over half of the respondents cite the better quality of SPG products and distrust of supermarket offerings, while support for farmers, environmental protection, and sociality total about 45%.

Though not exactly comparable with the findings from the survey of district market patrons, these results suggest a much higher preference for the specific chain, which is not surprising, given the self-selection of SPG members. Food quality remains a crucial driver of the choice, but altruistic motivations and social concerns have a greater weight. Nevertheless, the higher WTP among those SPG members who pay lower prices and the negative sign for young children suggest that purely monetary motivations cannot be ruled out.

Table 4.3 Reasons for staying with the SPG even with a price increase (%; *n* = 85)

Quality is better and/or I don't trust the quality of supermarket products	51.8
I would be sorry to stop dealing with SPG friends	4.7
For environmental protection reasons	12.9
For reasons linked to respect for farmers	27.1
Other/no response	3.5
	100.0

Conclusions

One of the first points regarding AFNs' attractiveness to consumers that arises from the literature and from our empirical analysis is that motivations are highly heterogeneous. There is no single attribute, either of the chain or of the food, that exclusively determines the decision to participate in AFNs. Different people have different motivations and, on the other hand, AFNs themselves are far from homogeneous. They certainly share the common feature (at least in our concept) of allowing personal interactions between producers and consumers, which is not possible (or possible only to a very limited extent) in a supermarket. And they make it possible to imbue food and its consumption with fresh meaning through its links with the local area and to the people who produce it. Nevertheless, it goes without saying that having this possibility does not mean that everyone takes advantage of it, nor that everyone benefits from it in the same way. Moreover, there are differences among AFNs. Some, like SPGs or CSAs, are organisations characterised by, and requiring, a strong commitment, especially when their members are bound to contribute to the group's activities. At the other extreme, farmers' direct sales in district markets, though providing a producer-consumer connection, do not require any special effort by consumers, and an inattentive consumer might not even know that the vendor is a farmer. Other forms of AFNs, like FMs and on-farm direct sales, are somewhere in the middle of a continuum.

It is not surprising that the observed determinants for choosing to purchase food through AFNs are so diverse. There are two reasons for this. On the demand side, consumers look for different attributes. On the supply side, different AFNs offer different attributes of the chain itself and of the food that consumers can purchase in it. A strong self-selection of consumers towards the different types of AFN can explain both the socio-economic characteristics found in some literature and the apparently contradictory lack of influence of these characteristics in other literature. The literature (overwhelmingly dealing with FMs) that compares the characteristics of shoppers at AFNs to non-shoppers or to the general population generally finds that typical shoppers at FMs are older, better educated, and wealthier. This is consistent with the idea that income (with which education and age are positively correlated) is a driver of this choice, because a higher income makes it possible to shop for more expensive higher quality food, where quality is seen to include all intrinsic and intangible attributes of food. Incidentally, it can also explain why AFNs were born and grew in developed countries. This is not to say that the choice of AFNs is a "radical chic" attitude. Rather, it serves to remind us that there is always a budget constraint, which is less binding for wealthier people but nevertheless has some impact on average. From this point of view, the comparison between prices in AFNs and elsewhere is important, since those who are more income-constrained are also more interested in AFNs when they offer lower prices. This comparison is nevertheless difficult, since it entails keeping all other things equal, which is in contradiction with the intangible values that AFNs in themselves bring about.

If AFNs are diverse, people are diverse as well, and so are their preferences. The intrinsic attributes of the particular chain (such as distance, convenience, variety of products, possibility of contact with farmers, etc.) may be relevant, as our finding that convenience is the major reason for choosing a district market demonstrates. Nevertheless, a desirable attribute of AFN chains is the opportunity to access desirable intangible attributes of food. People who prefer fresh produce and are convinced that FMs provide fresher food than conventional chains prefer FMs; those preferring local products choose chains they trust as regards the provenance of the produce. Among the preferred attributes of food available in AFNs, our investigation as well as the literature indicates that quality seems to be the most important. Obviously, quality covers many aspects, but the main reference is to the intrinsic characteristics of food, such as freshness, healthiness, and taste. Nevertheless, intangible attributes such as local origin, support for farmers, and environmental protection are frequently cited among the motivations. However, it is difficult to distinguish and to assess the relative weight of the different motivations, because they are frequently associated with each other, and derive from general attitudes or beliefs. For instance, people who want direct contact with farmers prefer local products (Giampietri et al., 2016). Among the characteristics of the chains, one we stress is the value of human interactions they allow, a value that is not limited to information about the products and how they are produced, nor to trust in the quality of the products themselves. It is a value stemming from the interaction among people in the chain. It can consist in farmers and consumers in the district market knowing and liking each other, or in the value that participating in SPGs has for their members, as shown by our empirical surveys. It should also be noted that this value depends on the type of chain: the value of participating in SPGs was found to be much higher than the value of direct interaction with farmers in district markets. It is quite plausible that there is a continuum of situations from this perspective as well.

In addition to the characteristics of products and of chains, prices are a relevant variable in consumers' choices, but are frequently overlooked by the literature. There are two reasons for this. One is that many surveys are conducted among people attending FMs and more generally AFNs. These individuals, as we have argued, are self-selected and in general are inclined to assign a higher value to the intrinsic and intangible attributes of AFN produce than the general public. Hence, in the trade-off between price and food attributes, their valuation for the attributes is higher, so that prices count less. The second reason is that, in developed countries, expenditure for food accounts for a relatively minor share of household budgets, so that the effect of food price changes on real income is rather limited. That said, the effect of income should not be forgotten, as suggested by our finding that the likelihood of staying with an SPG is increased by lower prices. Actually, since lower prices for SPG members and paying fair prices to producers are only possible because of the voluntary work provided by members (Novelli & Corsi, 2018, Chap. 10), it can be argued that members trade off their work for lower purchase prices and fair prices for farmers (though it is also possible that they get utility from working for the SPG). The importance of income also differs according to the specific chain. In some cases, the goal of finding lower prices becomes dominant. An example is the Collective Purchasing Groups (Gruppi d'Acquisto Collettivo—GAC), promoted by a consumers' association and supported by the Province of Torino Department for Social Policies (Movimento consumatori, 2018). Each week, the association buys the products ordered by registered members directly from local or national organic producers and distributes them. Though some of the initiative's motivations are environmental (reduction of food miles), the emphasis is on obtaining lower prices by eliminating middlemen and on enabling "everyone to access higher quality food, not just people who can afford to buy from specialised shops or from farmers who overcharge for their products at the market" (Movimento consumatori, 2018). In this case, even if it is an organisation outside the conventional chain, the "degree of alternativeness" is rather low, since personal relationships between producers and consumers are quite irrelevant, as are the links to the local area and recovering the meaning of food.

Heterogeneity of preferences across consumers goes along with diversity of preferences within individual consumers. A person may like freshness of food and at the same time be a supporter of local farmers. When preferences for different attributes are compatible, they are mutually reinforced. In some cases, though, they might be in opposition. For instance, the desire to have contact with farmers and to know how they produce would favour on-farm direct sales, which a person who is mindful of the environment could be reluctant to choose because of the environmental impact of trips to the farm.

All the above considerations help to put the nature of AFNs and their strengths and weaknesses in perspective. If we accept that people's motivations are heterogeneous and that involvement and participation lie along a continuum in different types of AFN, then the picture is one of a population of different organisational forms, covering different market segments and responding to different economic, political, and social demands. The vision of AFNs as politically and socially oriented, as suggested by the political economy approach that conceptualises "AFNs as movements in constant struggle against a threatening forces of global capitalism" (Tregear, 2011), or by the "reflexive localism" perspective (Dupuis & Goodman, 2006) that aims at "food systems [...] making for a more inclusive metropolitan regionalism promoting equitable distribution of resources and services" (Goodman, Dupuis, & Goodman, 2012), is undoubtedly true for some, but not all AFNs. In these forms, that is, in subjective intention to change the food system, it concerns some particularly committed groups of citizens, like the SPGs described by Brunori, Rossi, and Guidi (2012), Grasseni (2013), and Fonte (2013), while other forms are mainly motivated by short-sighted and selfish interests. One might ask whether these movements may nevertheless objectively have the effect of changing the conventional food system. Though the question is obviously difficult to answer, the foregoing considerations give reason to doubts that they can. From an economic perspective, if AFNs are not underpinned by an explicit and intentional strategy for creating an alternative to conventional food systems, many other motivations are simply emerging demands that the conventional chains have not yet been able to meet, but can hijack in the future. For example, the Carrefour supermarket chain (like other supermarket chains) has created a line of quality food sold under its private label ("Terre d'Italia", Lands of Italy) and advertised as being sourced from small producers in specified geographical areas. Though this is not a line of fresh produce, conventional supermarkets are marketing increasing amounts of produce with a Protected Designation of Origin, thus providing the same attributes of freshness and quality now typically offered by AFNs.

In any case, from the efficiency perspective of standard welfare economics, AFNs are particular markets matching demand and supply and hence increasing overall welfare. According to welfare economics, any voluntary transaction represents a Pareto improvement, that is, a change in which someone or everyone benefits and no one loses. From this point of view, criticisms of AFNs based on their supposed inefficiency and on the efficiency superiority of conventional chains are ill-grounded. There can be no doubt that AFNs increase their participants' welfare. This alone would be sufficient reason to welcome them, even if there were no other points in their favour.

Notes

1. Martinez et al. (2010) present the main characteristics of local food chains in the USA and add a review of papers dealing with characteristics and attitudes associated with local food purchase and willingness to purchase and with consumer characteristics associated with willingness to pay more for local foods.
2. With regard to the district markets, convenience was identified as an attitude if consumers' stated reasons for choosing a market were "Closeness

to home", "Closeness to workplace, to school, to places where their relatives live", and "Location on the way between home and workplace". Price attitude corresponded to the answer "Reasonable prices". Quality attitude was identified by the answers "Product quality", "Wide choice", and "Pleasant ambience". Attitudes towards the choice of stands were Convenience ("Location of the stands in the market"), Price ("Reasonable prices", "Quality/price ratio"), Quality ("Product quality", "Freshness", "Supply of local products", "Region of provenance of products"), and Trust in the vendor ("Personal acquaintance with the vendor"). Respondents could indicate up to three items.

3. Since in these statistical models (probit) the marginal effect of the variables on the probability of the outcome varies according to the value of the variable itself and of the other variables, the change in probability is as usual calculated at the mean values of the variables.
4. Relational goods are discussed in Chap. 2 of this book.
5. The exact wording was: "Think of farmers' stands, in particular of the stand where you most frequently buy fruit and vegetables, and think of the farmer who usually helps you and with whom you talk while buying. Now imagine that tomorrow another farmer opens a stand in this market and offers produce that is exactly the same as the produce you buy from your regular vendor: same territorial provenance, same quality guarantee, and same freshness. *The only differences would be the vendor and the price.* If the new vendor's price were X% lower than your usual vendor's price, and you wanted to buy the same quantity, from whom would you buy? Consider, for instance, that something costing 10 euros from your usual vendor would cost X euros at the new stand."
6. Respondents were assigned up to 5 points if they made purchases for their household, depending on the frequency (less than 6 times/year; every second month; every month; every 15 days; every week); up to 5 points if they also made purchases for other households; up to 5 points if they collected products from the farmers and distributed them to the other members; 5 points if they prepared the mailing list, the website, and so on; 5 points if they managed the relationship with the producers; 5 points if they handled contacts with participants and collected orders; 5 points if they were members of the SPG board; and 1 point if they participated in the SPG assembly and social initiatives. The points are obviously arbitrary, but they attempt to reflect the time devoted to each activity and, hence, the commitment to the SPG, since members are not paid for these activities.

References

Abelló, F. J., Palma, M. A., Waller, M. L., & Anderson, D. P. (2014). Evaluating the Factors Influencing the Number of Visits to Farmers' Markets. *Journal of Food Products Marketing, 20*(1), 17–35.

Allen, P., FitzSimmons, M., Goodman, M., & Warner, K. (2003). Shifting Places in the Agrifood Landscape: The Tectonics of Alternative Agrifood Initiatives in California. *Journal of Rural Studies, 19*(1), 61–75.

Alkon, A. (2008). From Value to Values: Sustainable Consumption at Farmers Markets. *Agriculture and Human Values, 25*, 487–498.

Archer, G. P., Sánchez, J. G., Vignali, G., & Chaillot, A. (2003). Latent Consumers' Attitude to Farmers' Markets in North West England. *British Food Journal, 105*(8), 487–497.

Betz, M. E., & Farmer, J. R. (2016). Farmers' Market Governance and Its Role on Consumer Motives and Outcomes. *Local Environment, 21*(11), 1420–1434.

Brunori, G., Rossi, A., & Guidi, F. (2012). On the New Social Relations Around and Beyond Food. Analysing Consumers' Role and Action in Gruppi di Acquisto Solidale (Solidarity Purchasing Groups). *Sociologia Ruralis, 52*(1), 1–30.

Burchardi, H., Schröder, C., & Thiele, H. D. (2005). *Willingness-to-Pay for Food of the Own Region: Empirical Estimates from Hypothetical and Incentive Compatible Settings*. Selected Paper prepared for presentation at the American Agricultural Economics Association Annual Meeting, Providence, Rhode Island, July 24–27.

Burnett, P., Kuethe, T. H., & Price, C. (2011). Consumer Preference for Locally Grown Produce: An Analysis of Willingness-to-Pay and Geographic Scale. *Journal of Agriculture, Food Systems, and Community Development, 2*(1), 269–278.

Cameron, T. A. (1988). A New Paradigm for Valuing Non-market Goods Using Referendum Data: Maximum Likelihood Estimation by Censored Logistic Regression. *Journal of Environmental Economics and Management, 15*, 355–379.

Carbone, A., Gaito, M., & Senni, S. (2007). *Consumers' Buying Groups in the Short Food Chains: Alternatives for Trust.* Paper presented at the 1st International European Forum on Innovation and System Dynamics in Food Networks, Innsbruck-Igls, Austria, February 15–17, 2007.

Carpio, C. E., & Isengildina-Massa, O. (2009). Consumer Willingness to Pay for Locally Grown Products: The Case of South Carolina. *Agribusiness, 25*(3), 412–426.

Cembalo, L., Lombardi, A., Pascucci, S., Dentoni, D., Migliore, G., Verneau, F., & Schifani, G. (2015). Rationally Local: Consumer Participation in Alternative Food Chains. *Agribusiness, 3*(13), 330–352.

Conner, D., Colasanti, K., Ross, R. B., & Smalley, S. B. (2010). Locally Grown Foods and Farmers Markets: Consumer Attitudes and Behaviors. *Sustainability, 2*, 742–756.

Corsi, A., & Novelli, S. (2015). *Relational Goods and Direct Purchase from Farmers: Estimating the Value of the Relationship between Consumers and Producers*. Paper presented at the International Association of Agricultural Economists Conference, August 9–14, 2015, Milan, Italy.

Corsi, A., & Novelli, S. (2016). *Alternative Food Networks and Short Food Chains: Estimating the Economic Value of the Participation in Solidarity Purchasing Groups*. Paper presented at the 149th EAAE Seminar 'Structural Change in Agri-food Chains: New Relations between Farm Sector, Food Industry and Retail Sector' Rennes, France, October 27–28, 2016. Retrieved from https://ideas.repec.org/p/ags/eaa149/244776.html

Darby, M. R., & Karni, E. (1973). Free Competition and the Optimal Amount of Fraud. *Journal of Law and Economics, 16*(1), 67–88.

Darby, K., Batte, M. T., Ernst, S., & Roe, B. (2008). Decomposing Local: A Conjoint Analysis of Locally Produced Foods. *American Journal of Agricultural Economics, 90*(2), 476–486.

Dupuis, M. E., & Goodman, D. (2006). Should We Go "Home" to Eat? Towards a Reflexive Politics of Localism. *Journal of Rural Studies, 21*, 359–371.

Eurobarometer. (2011). The Common Agricultural Policy. Special Barometer 368. Retrieved March 27, 2018, from http://ec.europa.eu/COMMFrontOffice/publicopinion/index.cfm/Survey/getSurveyDetail/instruments/SPECIAL/surveyKy/996

Feagan, R. B., & Morris, D. (2009). Consumer Quest for Embeddedness: A Case Study of the Brantford Farmers' Market. *International Journal of Consumer Studies, 33*, 235–243.

Feldmann, C., & Hamm, U. (2015). Consumers' Perceptions and Preferences for Local Food: A Review. *Food Quality and Preference, 40*, 152–164.

Fonte, M. (2013). Food Consumption as Social Practice: Solidarity Purchasing Groups in Rome, Italy. *Journal of Rural Studies, 32*, 230–239.

Giampietri, E., Koemle, D. B. A., Yu, X., & Finco, A. (2016). Consumers' Sense of Farmers' Markets: Tasting Sustainability or Just Purchasing Food? *Sustainability, 8*(11), 1157.

Goodman, D. (2004). Rural Europe Redux? Reflections on Alternative Agro-food Networks and Paradigm Change. *Sociologia Ruralis, 44*(1), 3–16.

Goodman, D., Dupuis, M. E., & Goodman, M. K. (2012). *Alternative Food Networks. Knowledge, Practice, and Politics*. Abingdon, Oxon: Routledge.

Govindasamy, R., & Nayga, R. (1997). Determinants of Farmer-to-Consumer Direct Market Visits by Type of Facility: A Logit Analysis. *Agricultural and Resource Economics Review, 26*(1), 31–38.

Govindasamy, R., Italia, J., & Adelaja, A. (2002). Farmers' Markets: Consumer Trends, Preferences, and Characteristics. *Journal of Extension, 40*(1).

Gracia, A., Barreiro-Hurlé, J., & López-Galán, B. (2014). Are Local and Organic Claims Complements or Substitutes?: A Consumer Preferences Study for Eggs. *Journal of Agricultural Economics, 65*(1), 49–67.

Grasseni, C. (2013). *Beyond Alternative Food. Italy's Solidarity Purchase Groups*. London: Bloomsbury.

Gumirakiza, J. D., Curtis, K. R., & Bosworth, R. C. (2014). Who Attends Farmers' Markets and Why? Understanding Consumers and Their Motivations. *International Food and Agribusiness Management Review, 17*(2), 65–82.

Hanemann, W. M. (1984). Welfare Evaluations in Contingent Valuation Experiments with Discrete Responses. *American Journal of Agricultural Economics, 66*, 332–341.

Hunt, A. R. (2007). Consumer Interactions and Influences on Farmers' Market Vendors. *Renewable Agriculture and Food Systems, 22*(1), 54–66.

Keeling, J. K., Thilmany, D., & Bondet, C. (2009). What Influences Consumer Choice of Fresh Produce Purchase Location? *Journal of Agricultural and Applied Economics, 41*(1), 61–74.

Khan, F., & Prior, C. (2010). Evaluating the Urban Consumer with Regard to Sourcing Local Food: A Heart of England Study. *International Journal of Consumer Studies, 34*, 161–168.

Kirwan. (2006). The Interpersonal World of Direct Marketing: Examining Conventions of Quality at UK Farmers' Markets. *Journal of Rural Studies, 22*, 301–312.

Kolodinsky, J., & Pelch, L. (1997). Factors Influencing the Decision to Join a Community Supported Agriculture (CSA) Farm. *Journal of Sustainable Agriculture, 10*(2/3), 129–141.

La Trobe, H. (2001). Farmers' Markets: Consuming Local Rural Produce. *International Journal of Consumer Studies, 25*(3), 181–192.

Lyon, P., Collie, V., Kvarnbrink, E. B., & Colquhoun, A. (2009). Shopping at the Farmers' Market: Consumers and Their Perspectives. *Journal of Foodservice, 20*, 21–30.

Martinez, S., Hand, M., Da Pra, M., Pollack, S., Ralston, K., Smith, T., et al. (2010). *Local Food Systems: Concepts, Impacts and Issues*. ERR 97, U.S. Department of Agriculture, Economic Research Service, May 2010.

McGarry Wolf, M., Spittler, A., & Ahern, J. (2005). A Profile of Farmers' Market Consumers and the Perceived Advantages of Produce Sold at Farmers' Markets. *Journal of Food Distribution Research, 36*(1), 192–201.

Megicks, P., Memery, J., & Angell, R. J. (2012). Understanding Local Food Shopping: Unpacking the Ethical Dimension. *Journal of Marketing Management, 28*(3–4), 264–289.

Movimento consumatori. (2018). *Gruppi d'Acquisto Collettivo: il Progetto*. Retrieved March 25, 2018, from http://piemonte.movimentoconsumatori.it/gac/

Neill, C. L., Mitchell, D. M., & Williams, R. B. (2014). A Look at the Variations in Consumer Preferences for Farmers' Markets Attributes. *Proceedings of the 2014 Annual Meeting of the Southern Agricultural Economics Association*, February 1–4, 2014, Dallas, Texas. Retrieved from http://ageconsearch.umn.edu/record/162445

Nelson, P. (1970). Information and Consumer Behavior. *Journal of Political Economy, 78*(2), 311–329.

Novelli, S., & Corsi, A. (2015). *Alternative Food Networks and Local Markets: Determinants of Consumers' Choices between Conventional and Farmers' Stands*. Paper presented at the 4th AIEAA Conference "Innovation, Productivity and Growth: Towards Sustainable Agri-food Production", 11–12 June, 2015, Ancona, Italy. Retrieved from https://ideas.repec.org/p/ags/aiea15/207289.html

Novelli, S., & Corsi, A. (2018). *The Economic Viability of Solidarity Purchase Groups (Gruppi di Acquisto Solidale)*. Chapter 10 of this Book.

Onianwa, O., Wheelock, G., & Mojica, M. (2005). An Analysis of the Determinants of Farmer-to-Consumer Direct-Market Shoppers. *Journal of Food Distribution Research, 36*(1), 130–134.

Onozaka, Y., Nurse, G., & Thilmany McFadden, D. (2010). Local Food Consumers: How Motivations and Perceptions Translate to Buying Behavior. *Choices, 25*(1), 1–6.

Pascucci, S., Dentoni, D., Lombardi, A., & Cembalo, L. (2016). Sharing Values or Sharing Costs? Understanding Consumer Participation in Alternative Food Networks. *NJAS – Wageningen Journal of Life Sciences, 78*, 47–60.

Rocchi, B., Cavicchi, A., & Baldeschi, M. (2012). Consumers' Attitude Towards Farmers' Markets in Tuscany. *Sviluppo Locale, 15*(1–2), 5–23.

Sainte-Marie, J., Balle, A., & Kubista, M. (2012). Les Français et les produits locaux, Sondage CSA pour Region Midi-Pyrenees. Retrieved March 27, 2018, from https://www.laregion.fr/IMG/pdf/CSA_pour_Region_Midi-Pyrenees_-_Les_Francais_et_les_produits_locaux_presentation_.pdf

Saroldi, A. (2001). *Gruppi di acquisto solidali. Guida al consumo locale*. Bologna: Edizioni EMI.

Thilmany, D., Bond, C. A., & Bond, J. K. (2008). Going Local: Exploring Consumer Behavior and Motivations for Direct Food Purchases. *American Journal of Agricultural Economics, 90*(5), 1303–1309.

Tregear, A. (2011). Progressing Knowledge in Alternative and Local Food Networks: Critical Reflections and a Research Agenda. *Journal of Rural Studies, 27*(4), 419–430.

Toler, S., Briggeman, B. C., Lusk, J. L., & Adams, D. C. (2009). Fairness, Farmers Markets, and Local Production. *American Journal of Agricultural Economics, 91*(5), 1272–1278.

Varner, T., & Otto, D. (2008). Factors Affecting Sales at Farmers' Markets: An Iowa Study. *Review of Agricultural Economics, 30*(1), 176–189.

Weatherell, C., Tregear, A., & Allinson, J. (2003). In Search of the Concerned Consumer: UK Public Perceptions of Food, Farming and Buying Local. *Journal of Rural Studies, 19*, 233–244.

Zepeda, L., & Li, J. (2006). Who Buys Local Food? *Journal of Food Distribution Research, 37*(3), 5–14.

Zepeda, L. (2009). Which Little Piggy Goes to Market? Characteristics of US Farmers' Market Shoppers. *International Journal of Consumer Studies, 33*(3), 250–257.

5

Consumers' Quality Conventions in Alternative, Conventional, and High-End Food Chains

Filippo Barbera, Joselle Dagnes, and Roberto Di Monaco

Introduction

Alternative Food Networks (AFNs) aim to provide agri-food goods to consumers with high standards of accessibility, sustainability, and quality. Accessibility refers to the ease of access and participation in AFNs. From a spatial point of view, this means that the AFNs are distributed in the local area and easily reached by consumers. How accessibility concretely occurs depends on the spatial organization of AFN supply chains (see Dansero & Pettenati, 2018, Chap. 14). A second important point is

F. Barbera (✉)
Department of Cultures, Politics and Society, University of Torino, Torino, Italy

Collegio Carlo Alberto, Torino, Italy
e-mail: filippo.barbera@unito.it

J. Dagnes • R. Di Monaco
Department of Cultures, Politics and Society, University of Torino, Torino, Italy
e-mail: joselle.dagnes@unito.it; roberto.dimonaco@unito.it

A. Corsi et al. (eds.), *Alternative Food Networks*,
https://doi.org/10.1007/978-3-319-90409-2_5

related to the sustainability of AFNs from two different perspectives: environmental and economic. From the ecological point of view, AFNs are sustainable if their polluting emissions and use of natural resources have a low impact on the natural environment. Several studies have shown that—contrary to common sense—AFNs are not necessarily more ecologically sustainable than conventional agri-food goods (see Peano, Tecco, & Girgenti, 2018, Chap. 13). AFNs' sustainability can also be understood in the economic sense. Even if the proximity between producers and consumers minimizes the intermediate stages of the distribution, it is difficult to bring AFNs' cost structure to light because of the many implicit costs carried by the actors involved in the chain (see Corsi et al., 2018, Chaps. 4 and 10). This is the case both for farmers—for example, in relation to the time dedicated to direct sales—and for consumers, considering, for instance, the time and resources involved in organizing a solidarity purchasing group. Lastly, there are no simple indicators and parameters that can be assessed for quality. This is particularly interesting to observe in AFNs, where quality conventions are not only supply-driven but also spread from consumers to producers. In these short market chains, consumers can provide quality specifications to producers, thereby shaping the governance of the value chain and its organizational structure.

In connection with accessibility, sustainability, and quality, AFNs are often classified as a kind of social innovation toward a better food system (De Schutter, 2017). The basic idea of AFNs as social innovation is that they are an engine of change rooted in alternative ways of production and consumption generated by the response to "unmet social needs". In this regard, AFNs are supposed to bring about social change thanks to their "beneficial effects" that should enhance "society's" ability to act for desirable outcomes. Accordingly, the relevance of AFNs originates from the potential of citizen-led social innovations:

> In the agrifood sector, such innovations include for instance community-supported agriculture (CSA), in which people contribute to support local farmers by entering into direct producer-to-consumer marketing schemes, although they might have access to the very same products by less expensive and more convenient means; the joint management, by members of the same neighbourhood, of collective vegetable gardens; or fair trade schemes (…). Depending on the theoretical framework used, these innovations are

> referred to as social innovations for sustainable development (…), or (in the so-called 'multi-level perspective' on transition theory) as 'niche innovations', that must be nurtured and protected in order to provide alternatives to the mainstream regime following a crisis (…). (De Schutter, 2017, p. 721)

AFNs are thus understood as forms of grassroots experiments that aim to reorganize the food system along ethical, political, moral, and health lines (Honkanen, Verplanken, & Olsen, 2006; Micheletti, Follesdal, & Stolle, 2004; Onozaka, Nurse, & McFadden, 2010; Sassatelli, 2015). As long as AFNs are assumed to be markedly different from conventional food chains, they serve at the macro-level to achieve "systemic" needs, and AFN experiences become a positive functional reaction to agro-industry failures. At the micro-level, the underlying idea is that consumption is a political act: by "eating differently", people can change the food system and the living conditions of all those who are involved. However, AFNs can take on many and diverse forms, ranging from completely isolated and self-interested experiments to extremely networked and community-oriented initiatives (Barbera & Dagnes, 2016, p. 325). Moreover, political motivations of "conscientious consumers" are blurred with health concerns and status-based practices of highbrow groups.

We do not deny that political consumerism plays a key role in AFN consumers' purchasing habits. Nor do we deny the socially innovative features of AFNs, at least in principle. Rather, we argue that the kind of social change that AFNs enact does not occur in stages between discrete entities (conventional vs. alternative), considered as "complete and coherent" wholes that replace one another over time in meeting "systemic" needs (Goldthorpe, 2015). This flawed view of social change, we maintain, is deeply rooted in the blueprint of sociology as a "science of transition" which analyzes feudal society's transition to modernity (Stark, 1996, p. 993). The recent financial crisis and the global challenges that capitalism is facing are triggering a similar situation: "transitology" is again *à la page* (Mason, 2016) and the present easily becomes the approximation of a designed *better future* (see Stark, 1996, p. 994 for the original argument). This is the case, for instance, of those "radical" perspectives on AFNs (De Schutter, 2017) that—as inspiring as they could be from the normative and political viewpoint—risk an underlying teleology driven by an end-state. Similarly, radical perspectives frame AFNs as kinds of social innovations that: "(...) move towards an economic future in which decentralised economic activity will bear the marks of a greater freedom" (Unger, 2015, p. 245). A sharper analytical view would be to see AFNs as being built not *on* the ruins of the conventional agri-food system, but *with* its ruins (see Stark, 1996 for a broader take on this perspective). For instance, supermarket retailers are trying to build on AFNs' success at making profits by promoting their own alternative products and, in some cases, AFN supply chains need to rely on the large-scale system in order to achieve their goals. Moreover, consumers very rarely buy their food in a single food chain; rather, they often mix different sale channels and buy from a variety of food chains, both conventional and alternative. In this regard, it is key to point out that what underlies AFNs as "social innovation experiences" is not the nature of the social problem to be solved (e.g., unmet needs), but the kind of *social change* they bring about (Santana, 2014, p. 44).

From these background premises, we will first set out the conceptual framework we rely on to analyze AFN consumers' purchasing habits in quality-based markets. In the second part of the chapter, we will illustrate the research design, methods, and data on five food chains in Piedmont. In the third, we will present and discuss our key empirical findings. Lastly, we will conclude by elaborating further on the interplay between alternative and conventional food networks.

Consumers' Quality Conventions in Alternative and Conventional Food Chains

The search for high standards of food quality is one of the key aims of AFNs. At the same time, however, the very definition of quality is far from univocal. In economics, quality is connected to the role of "credence goods" as key drivers for the so-called quality-based markets (Beckert & Aspers, 2011). Consumers need to trust the quality of a product, which cannot be assessed just by looking at its price or by experiencing it. For instance, fair-trade coffee is a case in point. We argue that general reference to "quality as credence goods" must be integrated with a sociological viewpoint. Credence is a symbolic dimension whose explanatory power needs to be accounted for (Beckert, 2009; Karpik, 2010). As Wolfgang Streeck observes: "A rising share of the goods that make today's capitalist economies grow would not sell if people dreamed other dreams than they do" (Streeck, 2016, p. 212). Accordingly, the quality conventions approach reveals a more complex scenario.

Boltanski and Thévenot (2006) identified seven different quality conventions that make sense of the meaning structure of the "worlds of quality": (1) market/commercial, based on price and commercial value of goods; (2) industrial, assessing the compliance with technical standards and reliability; (3) domestic, which are related to the concepts of interpersonal trust and traditional ways of producing; (4) opinion/fame, concerning the importance assigned to trademarks, brands, and expert opinion; (5) civic, which refer to the societal and community benefits of products; (6) inspirational, based on the value of the personal passion embedded in the product; and (7) ecological, relating to the environmental sustainability of the goods and the production process (Murdoch, Marsden, & Banks, 2000). These "worlds of quality" are incessantly open to negotiation, compromise, and conflict by the agents in the field, that is, producers, distributors, and consumers. As such, the shared ideas of what food quality actually is change over time and sometimes disappear to be replaced by new ones (Barbera & Audifredi, 2012). Thus, quality is not a static feature defined once and for all. Rather, quality is "fluid and malleable, and tends to shift as a good passes from one social context to another" (Murdoch & Miele, 2004, p. 159) and from one individual to another, as a result of the *process of qualification* carried out by every actor involved in the supply chain (Callon, Meadel, & Rabeharisoa, 2002; see also Murdoch & Miele, 2004, p. 159).

This standpoint allows us to develop a more apt understanding of the social change enacted by AFNs, as well as of the central role played by quality in this process. On the one hand, quality is a contested field where *top-down* strategic maneuvering takes place (Boltanski & Thévenot, 2006; Callon et al., 2002; Negro, Hannan, Rao, & Leung, 2007). Quality is strongly connected to the power of the lead firm in a given value chain. Lead firms provide quality specifications to their immediate suppliers (or buyers) who in turn transmit and translate them further along the value chain (Ponte & Gibbon, 2009). This shapes value-chain governance over and above informational and technical parameters which define the complexity of the transaction. On the other hand, consumers can nudge the market by addressing specific aspects of quality, both in conventional channels and, to an even greater extent, in AFNs. As we stated above, quality conventions also travel from consumers to buyers and suppliers.

Research Design

From the point of view of purchasing habits, AFNs are still a marginal part of Italian households' expenditure. Nonetheless, in recent years the purchase of food products related to the world of the AFNs has increased (Crea, 2017): for instance, 40% of Italians prefer organic products and 70% declare that they prefer local food (Ibid.). At the same time, the demand for pre-cooked food is growing, as well as the demand for ethnic food and gluten-free products. Purchasing habits are thus rapidly changing in different directions, and food chains are differentiating accordingly toward customized services and new food niches. In the national scenario, Piedmont is one of the Italian regions where AFNs have spread most and where the local setting is particularly favorable for the development of an "alternative food culture" (Dansero & Puttilli, 2014). The percentage of farms involved in direct sales is higher than the Italian average, as is the percentage of off-farm sales. Moreover, about 1000 open-air urban district markets are regularly held in the region, most of them on a daily basis, while nearly 90 farmers' markets take place periodically (Pettenati & Dansero, 2015). Lastly, there are no fewer than 170 solidarity-based purchasing groups operating in Piedmont. To shed light on the quality-based attitudes of consumers in the agri-food sector, we focused on a continuum between conventional and alternative forms. Accordingly, five supply chains were singled out for the empirical analysis:

1. Hypermarkets and supermarkets. Previous research has shown that the geographical distribution of large-scale retail systems is rather uneven in Italy: hypermarkets and supermarkets are more concentrated in the North than in the South, even though there are some

exceptions (see Arcidiacono, 2016). In this scenario, Piedmont stands out due to the large number (nearly 2000) of these outlets, their average floor area, higher than in the other Italian regions (309 m^2 in Piedmont compared to 279 m^2 for the country as a whole; AGCM, 2013), and, concurrently, the low market concentration. In fact, here the lead retailer controls only about 20% of the regional market, while in several other areas, this figure is close to 50% (Arcidiacono, 2016). In summary, large-scale retailers in Piedmont are both widely distributed and highly diversified.

2. High-end food retailers. Piedmont is the birthplace of Eataly, a retailer-cum-restaurant specializing in quality food. Its founder, Oscar Farinetti, opened the first store in Turin in 2007; in the following years, on the strength of this success, several other stores cropped up both in Italy and abroad (Germany, Turkey, United Arab Emirates, Japan, Korea, U.S.A., Brazil). Eataly is connected with and sponsored by Slow Food, a movement devoted to safeguarding local food cultures and traditions which was founded in the 1980s and now has more than 100,000 members in 150 countries. Even though Eataly benefits from Slow Food's *aura*, it is indeed a true for-profit company, with 400 million euros in annual revenues and a sales growth of 28% in 2015. Since 2014, a merchant bank owns 20% of the company, which will be listed on the stock exchange in 2019 with a value of two billion euros.
3. Open-air urban district markets. Though the introduction of stricter regulations and the spread of large-scale retail systems may have weakened the presence of district markets in some areas, leading to a relative decline in their numbers, the freshness of the produce they sell and a favorable quality-price ratio have encouraged local consumers to shop at them. This is especially true in Piedmont, where around 1000 traditional markets are regularly held, most of them at least on a weekly basis.[1] The city of Turin, the region's capital, has more than 40 daily district markets.
4. Farmers' markets. Following the growing interest in locally grown food, numerous initiatives have begun to promote direct sales from local, small-scale farmers. In addition to on-farm sales, these initiatives have involved farmers in traditional district markets and

established monthly, ad hoc farmers' markets, in many cases stimulated by the farmers' unions Coldiretti and *Confederazione Italiana Agricoltori* (CIA). As mentioned above, the percentage of local farms doing direct (off-farm) sales in Piedmont is higher than in Italy's other regions, and nearly 90 open-air districts markets and 11 farmers' markets take place regularly (Pettenati & Dansero, 2015).

5. Solidarity purchasing groups (SPGs). These groups are self-organized networks of individuals and families who buy food—as well as other goods—directly from producers. In general terms, they are a kind of community-supported agriculture, which appeared in Italy in the mid-1990s and then gradually spread, culminating in over 1000 cases in 2011.[2] In Piedmont there are no fewer than 170 SPGs, over 130 of which are located in the province of Turin (Ibid.).

To investigate purchasing habits, quality conventions, expected quality dimensions, and socio-economic features, a questionnaire was administered to a sample of consumers ($N = 1090$) in each of the above five supply chains. In detail, 385 questionnaires were filled out in large-scale retailers (35.3% of the total sample), 251 in high-end retailers (23%), 216 in district markets (19.8%), 87 in farmers' markets (8%), and 151 in SPGs (13.9%).[3] Data collection took place from March 2014 to June 2015 by trained interviewers supervised by the research group.[4] For the high-end retailers, data was gathered in Turin's Eataly store. For district markets, 29 daily markets attended by both traditional vendors and farmers were identified in Turin using municipal data. Starting from this list, we adopted a stratified sampling method, first dividing the 28 smaller markets into three strata based on the number of farmers' stalls, then randomly extracting four specific markets from each stratum.[5] We then added the town's major market, Porta Palazzo, which is a particular case inasmuch as it is the largest district market in Europe, with around 800 stalls in total, including about 90 farmers' stalls. We thus obtained a sample of 13 municipal markets. Lastly, we selected four different SPGs in the province of Turin, classified according to location (in the city or in the neighboring municipalities) and number of members (small-medium groups, up to 50 members, and groups with more than 50 members). After obtaining authorization from the managers of each SPG, the interviewers attended the food distribution meetings, where they asked the SPG members to fill out the questionnaire.

Empirical Findings

The final sample consisted of 483 males (44.3%) and 602 females (55.2%), with a mean age of 47.[6] Adults between 35 and 64 years old were predominant (45.8%), followed by young people (18–34 years old, 24.4%) and the elderly (15%).[7] Data about socio-economic status were available for 931 interviewees: 40.7% belonged to the employed middle class (379 cases), 13.1% to the self-employed middle class, 14.4% to the upper class, and 12.9% to the lower class. It was not possible to define the occupational class of the remaining 18.9% of respondents, as they were not employed at the time of the data collection. With respect to income level, a large proportion of respondents (41.3%) earned between 800 and 1500 euros. Among the others, 37% claimed to have a net income of less than 800 euros per month, while 21.8% stated that they had over 1500 euros per month at their disposal.

As we illustrated, the "worlds of quality" are a first key dimension of quality-based markets. In this regard, we measured the level of importance of seven quality conventions on a 1–10 Likert scale, using two different items for each convention (so that the total score varied from 0 to 20). The items thus formed two distinct groups, focusing respectively on the quality of the product and on the producer/seller, as shown in Table 5.1:

The empirical results show that consumers perceive all conventions as significant, although the market convention is the least recognized (Table 5.2). The environmental quality convention is most important, followed by the civic and opinion conventions. Market and inspiration conventions show the highest variability, meaning that the consumers showed opposite orientations in evaluating these conventions, with some assigning low scores and others giving high scores.

How do consumers combine different sale channels in their purchasing habits? Respondents' choices of supermarkets and district markets are shown in Table 5.3. As can be seen, 18.3% declare that they buy fruit and

Table 5.1 Items for quality conventions

	Product quality	Producer/distributor quality
Quality convention	Fruit and vegetables can be considered high quality when:	Who do you feel comfortable with when you buy fruit and vegetables:
Domestic	They are grown *using traditional methods*	From people I know personally and *who I trust*
Environmental	They are products that do *not damage the environment*	From people who *respect the environment* when they produce and sell
Civic	They are produced by many people *in a geographical area*	From people who not only follow their own interest but also *work for society*
Opinion/fame	They have a *solid reputation* stemming from public recognition and expert opinion	From people who deal in and recommend products which are generally *judged to be of optimum quality* (recognition, expert opinion)
Market/ commercial	They have a *high price*	Those who sell *higher cost products*
Industrial	They have *precise rules for production* and working techniques from the field to the table	Those who sell products with an industrial/*standardized production process*
Inspiration	The product *conveys the passion* of whoever made it	Those who make and *believe in their products*

vegetables from both channels (group A). A smaller group (D, 6.1%) does not purchase agri-food goods in supermarkets or district markets, preferring alternative channels such as small shops, solidarity purchasing groups, and on-sale farms. The largest group (B, 61.1%) prefers to source food regularly from district markets, while 14.4% (group C) states that they buy only from supermarkets.

To a certain extent, purchasing choices are thus far from uniform and mix different sale channels. As we argued above, AFN quality conventions also mix and overlap along a continuum with conventional food networks. As suggested by Ponte (2016), in fact, the empirical phenomena that we observed frequently cannot be categorized neatly according to quality conventions, moral orders, or stabilized compromises. A more

Table 5.2 Consumer judgments of quality convent ons ir the five supply chains (scale 1–20)

Food supply chain		Domestic	Environmental	Civic	Opinion	Inspirational	Market	Industrial
Total	Mean	15.36	16.56	15.63	15.40	12.78	8.91	12.01
	Std.dev.	3.32	3.07	3.26	3.36	4.11	4.24	3.39
	Min	2	2	2	2	1	2	2
	Max	20	20	20	20	20	20	20
	Mode	16	20	20	16	14	10	11
Hypermarkets and supermarkets	Mean	15.40	16.28	15.77	14.87	13.34	9.51	12.20
	Std.dev.	2.89	2.88	2.96	3.38	3.62	3.98	3.24
	Min	6	5	4	2	2	2	2
	Max	20	20	20	20	20	20	20
	Mode	16	20	20	16	14	10	13
High-end food retailers (Eataly)	Mean	15.81	16.64	15.74	15.62	13.83	9.52	13.12
	Std.dev.	2.79	2.98	3.19	3.08	4.06	4.42	3.51
	Min	7	6	2	7	2	2	2
	Max	20	20	20	20	20	20	20
	Mode	16	20	16	16	16	10	15
District markets	Mean	15.34	15.97	14.95	14.64	12.74	9.80	12.26
	Std.dev.	3.33	3.02	3.36	3.42	3.95	4.10	3.62
	Min	5	4	2	2	2	2	2
	Max	20	20	20	20	20	20	20
	Mode	16	20	16	14	14	10	13
Farmers' markets	Mean	16.63	17.54	16.48	16.49	12.83	8.62	11.63
	Std.dev.	2.94	2.64	3.09	2.90	3.97	4.35	3.35
	Min	6	10	8	9	2	2	3
	Max	20	20	20	20	20	19	20
	Mode	20	20	20	20	16	11	11
Solidarity purchasing groups	Mean	13.44	16.36	15.16	15.35	10.97	6.86	10.71
	Std.dev.	3.81	3.60	3.48	3.72	4.46	3.65	2.70
	Min	2	2	2	2	1	2	2
	Max	20	20	20	20	20	20	17
	Mode	14	20	15	16	13	2	11

Source: Authors' calculations

Table 5.3 Purchasing habits by food chain

Where do you regularly buy fruit and vegetables?				
		Hypermarkets and supermarkets		
		Yes	No	Total
District markets	Yes	Group A 18.3%	Group B 61.1%	79.4%
	No	Group C 14.4%	Group D 6.1%	20.6%
	Total	32.7%	67.3%	100.0%

accurate perspective would entail examining how consumers and producers simultaneously interact through multiple quality conventions (Boltanski & Thévenot, 2006), as opposed to selectively engaging in single "worlds of quality".

The Worlds of Quality

As Fig. 5.1 clearly shows, many consumers fall under a high number of quality conventions: for the relative majority of consumers, indeed, four out of seven conventions are considered to be above median importance.

Consumers of AFNs thus focused on a number of quality conventions. But how does this plurality of quality conventions that are considered to be important relate to the canonical subdivision between conventional and alternative agri-food systems? In order to explore this aspect, we performed a principal component analysis on the quality convention items. This statistical procedure identifies a smaller number of hidden factors that might help shed light on important information. Two main conceptions of quality emerged (Fig. 5.2). The first, or "soft quality", focuses on the role of tradition, trust relationships, respect for the environment, community values, and the farmers' passion, thus referring to the conditions of the actors involved and the local context. The second conception, or "hard quality", relies on easily identifiable external characteristics whereby agri-food quality can be estimated, such

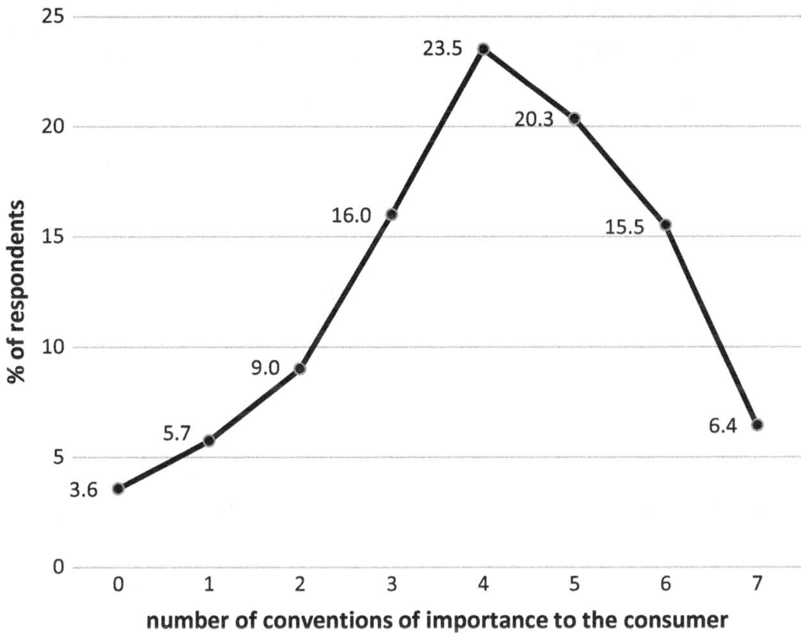

Fig. 5.1 Percentage of respondents above the median value (=7) for the number of conventions regarded as important. Source: Barbera et al. (2018)

as price, trademarks, and awards. Industrial standards such as "rules of production" and technical standards load on both components of quality.

To explore the soft and hard quality components in greater depth, we can first observe their connection with the supply chains that are the consumers' predominant place of food purchase. Looking at the different quality conventions per sale channels, a more detailed picture of "soft quality" emerges (Table 5.4). The environment nearly always ranks first in all channels and, remarkably, comes second among Eataly consumers. In farmers' markets, "passion", "trust/tradition", and the civic dimension are key for consumers' definition of quality. A similar pattern is found in district markets, albeit with lower scores. Eataly consumers give importance to "trust" in their purchasing choices and this, as we will see, opens up specific marketing strategies for high-end food chains. Supermarket

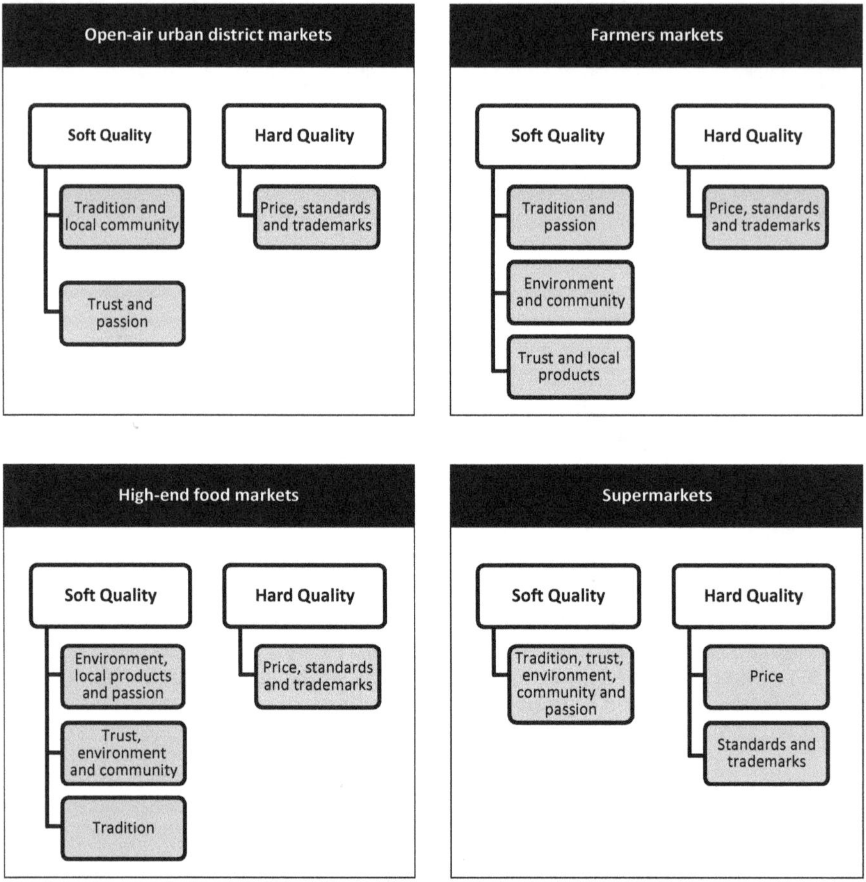

Fig. 5.2 Soft and hard quality in the four supply chains. Source: Barbera and Dagnes (2016)

consumers assign importance to the environment and to the civic dimension of soft quality. Even mass distribution channel consumers, therefore, are concerned with "alternative" quality conventions. Quite unexpectedly, solidarity purchasing group consumers consider the "rules of production" typical of the industrial convention to be important, along with environmental safety. With regard to the "hard quality" component (Table 5.5), trademarks and reputation (opinion/fame convention) are important for all consumers, with Eataly consumers assigning

Table 5.4 Soft quality conventions ranking per sale channels

Ranking	Traditional local markets	Farmers' markets	High-end food retailers (Eataly)	Hypermarkets and supermarkets	Solidarity-based purchasing groups
1		Respects the environment			
2		Does not damage the environment			
3		Transfers the passion			
4		Who I trust			
5			Who I trust		
6			Respects the environment		
7		Works for society			
8					Respects the environment
9			Does not damage the environment		
10				Does not damage the environment	
11		Within a territory			
12		According to tradition		Respects the environment	
13					Does not damage the environment
14	Does not damage the environment				
15	Who I trust				
16			Transfers the passion		

(*continued*)

Table 5.4 (continued)

Ranking	Traditional local markets	Farmers' markets	High-end food retailers (Eataly)	Hypermarkets and supermarkets	Solidarity-based purchasing groups
17			Works for society		
18		Believes in their products			
19				Works for society	
20				Who I trust	
21	Respects the environment		Precise rules for production		
22		Precise rules for production		Within a territory	
23					Precise rules for production
24					Transfers the passion
25			Within a territory		
26				Transfers the passion	
27					Works for society
28					Who I trust
29			Believes in their products		Believes in their products
30	Transfers the passion				
31	Within a territory				
32					Within a territory
33				According to tradition	

(continued)

Table 5.4 (continued)

Ranking	Traditional local markets	Farmers' markets	High-end food retailers (Eataly)	Hypermarkets and supermarkets	Solidarity-based purchasing groups
34	Works for society				
35	According to tradition		According to tradition		
36				Precise rules for production	
37	Precise rules for production				
38				Believes in their products	
39	Believes in their products				
40					According to tradition

Table 5.5 Hard quality conventions ranking per sale channels

Ranking	Traditional local markets	Farmers' markets	High-end food retailers (Eataly)	Hypermarkets and supermarkets	Solidarity-based purchasing groups
1			Judged to be of optimum quality		
2			Solid reputation		
3				Solid reputation	
4		Solid reputation			
5				Judged to be of optimum quality	
6	Solid reputation				
7	Judged to be of optimum quality				
8		Judged to be of optimum quality			
9					Solid reputation
10					Judged to be of optimum quality
11			Standardized productive process		
12	They have a high price				
13	Standardized productive process				
14				Standardized productive process	
15			They have a high price		
16				Who sells higher cost products	

(*continued*)

Table 5.5 (continued)

Ranking	Traditional local markets	Farmers' markets	High-end food retailers (Eataly)	Hypermarkets and supermarkets	Solidarity-based purchasing groups
17				They have a high price	
18	Who sells higher cost products				
19		They have a high price			
20			Who sells higher cost products		
21		Who sells higher cost products			
22		Standardized productive process			
23					They have a high price
24					Who sells higher cost products
25					Standardized productive process

the highest score. The lowest score for this convention is found among SPG consumers, who also do not regard prices as an important signal of quality. Prices are key for district market consumers, but not for consumers who attend farmers' markets.

This within-components analysis of soft and hard quality must be flanked by a between-components analysis by sale channels. In this regard, we can observe that the differences between groups are statistically significant (Table 5.6).[8] This means that the "chain effect" on soft and hard quality is stronger than the effect of individual-level attributes such as gender, age, birthplace, social class, and income, that is, the dissimilarities observed in the quality positioning of consumers who choose different supply chains are related more to the specific chain quality profile

Table 5.6 Quality dimensions and supply chains (Anova analysis)

		Sum of squares	Df	Mean square	F	Sig.
Soft quality * supply chains	Between groups	7.163	4	1.791	7.344	0.000
	Within groups	234.086	960	0.244		
	Total	241.250	964			
Hard quality * supply chains	Between groups	15.720	4	3.930	17.065	0.000
	Within groups	221.084	960	0.230		
	Total	236.804	964			

Source: Barbera, Dagnes, and Di Monaco (2018)

than to the consumers' socio-demographic characteristics. Each chain shows a specific ability to attract consumers who have a particular idea of, and demand for, quality. Both Eataly and, to a larger extent, farmers' markets are able to attract customers for whom soft quality is important. On the opposite side, supermarkets are ineffective in expressing this conception of quality. Both farmers' markets and, especially, solidarity purchasing groups have a negative effect on the hard quality component, while for Eataly and district markets the effects are not statistically significant. These results are consistent with the different chains' positioning in the quality space.

Overall, soft quality is undoubtedly more noticeable in AFNs than in conventional chains; however, it should be emphasized that supermarket consumers also express an idea and, consequently, a certain demand for soft quality, even if it is more indefinite than that of AFN consumers. The fragmentation of the soft quality conception emerging from the unconventional system, together with its existence in the mainstream chain, thus provides an opening for a "double movement". On the one hand, conventional food chains may have potential for conquering AFNs' quality space with specific marketing strategies; on the other hand, AFNs could meet the demands of a larger number of consumers by offering more agri-food goods characterized by spatial, economic, and/or social proximity between producers and consumers.

Mimetic Quality

To determine whether there are supply strategies for dealing with these overlapping quality worlds and purchasing habits, we scrutinized consumers' quality representations for the predominant chain used to source food (see Barbera et al., 2018). In fact, if consumers from different supply chains show specific quality representations that appear consistent with the chain's profile, this would indicate that operators have a certain ability to differentiate their offerings with respect to the "soft" and "hard" dimensions of quality. This is exactly what emerges from Fig. 5.3, where we see that supply operators differ greatly from one another with respect to their consumers' predominant quality profile. Attributes referring to hard quality (public reputation and prices) are prevalent among consumers who regularly shop in supermarkets and traditional local markets, with more than 60% of consumers being above the average value. Representations centering on soft quality attributes are less important, with just over 40% above average. Farmers' markets maximize the soft quality component (nearly 70% of consumers are above average), neglecting hard quality. Solidarity purchasing groups show a different positioning: they score well in the soft dimension of quality, underperforming in the hard dimension, including public reputation and prices.

Lastly, Eataly's positioning in Fig. 5.3 is distinctive, since it seems to cover both new and traditional quality conventions, thus overcoming divisions among different worlds while maintaining a consistent profile. This is a case of *mimetic strategy*, specifically implemented by the so-called hybrid organizations. In fact, Eataly leverages both dimensions of quality: it scores slightly higher than solidarity purchasing groups on the soft quality dimension, to some extent outperforming generalist supermarkets and district markets on the hard dimension.

These findings are in line with the marketing strategies implemented by the individual supply chains in the quality space. As a further step of the investigation, we measured consumers' ratings of expected quality through nine items (Table 5.7, score from 1 to 10), following a customary model for analyzing quality dimensions (Parasuraman, Zeithaml, & Berry, 1994). The aim was to shed light on the differences in expected

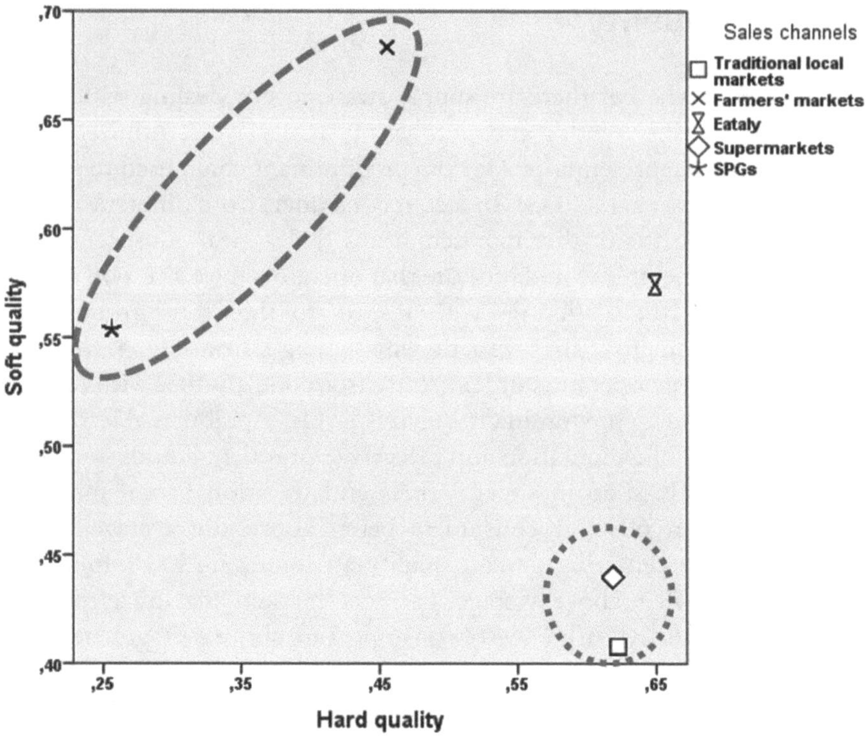

Fig. 5.3 The Quality Space: Hard and Soft Quality. Note: the axis value is the percentage of consumers over the mean value of the factor by sale channels. Source: Barbera, Dagnes, and Di Monaco (2018)

Table 5.7 Items and key words for expected quality: overall ranking

Expected quality
Ease of access
Communication on products
Competence of the seller
Courtesy of the seller
Credibility and reliability of the seller
Responsiveness of the seller
Security of products
Physical and social *appeal* of the place of sale
Knowing the customer

quality among consumers who regularly purchase in the different chains and thus determine the competitive advantage of the organizational strategies pursued by each chain. Consumers' expectations show high and homogeneous values for security, credibility, courtesy, and product communication, while greater variability and less homogeneous judgments were found for knowing the customer, ease of access, and physical and social appeal of the site (Table 5.8).

A further principal component analysis was performed on these items in order to identify organizational leverage. Here again, two clearly different dimensions emerged. The first factor emphasizes a quality expectation focusing on the personal relationship with the seller and the latter's expertise and reliability (and for this reason was labelled "the seller matters"). The second component, labelled "the retail environment matters", highlights the role of ease of access and of the physical and social appeal of the retail environment. The dimension relating to the need for personalized answers is the only one that cuts across both factors, although it performs better on the second component.

Thus, the structure of consumers' quality expectations can be summarized by referring to these two areas, which highlight different strategies put in place by supply chain operators. The first focuses on the seller, the other on the retail environment; in both cases, personalized knowledge was found to be important. We then analyzed the position of the operators in the different supply chains as regards the use of these organizational levers (Fig. 5.4).

Figure 5.4 shows that the supply chains' positioning along these two dimensions—"the seller matters" and "the sales environment matters"—highlights some differences between the organizational levers. The farmers' markets and the SPGs have the highest position on the vertical axis, with almost 80% and 70% respectively of consumers above average levels for importance assigned to the seller. In this case, the lever is thus the personal relationship with the seller. By contrast, supermarkets underperform on personal relationships, without offering a real alternative to district markets in terms of sales environment. On these dimensions as well, Eataly has a distinctive position that is consistent with the role of the organizational lever used to cope with the score for the soft dimension of quality. In fact, Eataly does not appeal to personal devices

Table 5.8 Items and key words for expected quality: sale channels

Food supply chain		Access	Communication	Competence	Courtesy	Credibility	Responsiveness	Security	Pleasantness	Knowing
Total	Mean	7.38	8.07	7.68	7.91	7.92	7.35	7.88	6.73	6.80
	Std.dev.	2.13	1.75	1.82	1.75	1.73	1.92	1.86	2.38	2.38
	Min	1	1	1	1	1	1	1	1	1
	Max	10	10	10	10	10	10	10	10	10
	Mode	8	8	8	8	8	8	8	7	8
Hypermarkets and supermarkets	Mean	7.63	7.88	7.06	7.33	7.56	7.20	7.87	6.37	6.34
	Std.dev.	1.75	1.64	1.83	1.83	1.57	1.83	1.77	2.20	2.27
	Min	1	2	1	1	3	1	1	1	1
	Max	10	10	10	10	10	10	10	10	10
	Mode	8	10	7	7	8	8	10	6	7
High-end food retailers (Eataly)	Mean	8.05	7.82	7.30	7.81	7.52	7.51	7.77	7.86	6.72
	Std.dev.	1.81	1.76	1.89	1.64	1.86	1.76	1.65	1.69	2.25
	Min	1	2	1	1	1	1	2	2	1
	Max	10	10	10	10	10	10	10	10	10
	Mode	8	8	7	8	8	8	8	8	8
Traditional local markets	Mean	7.47	8.19	7.96	8.44	8.05	7.43	8.14	6.90	7.18
	Std.dev.	2.06	1.65	1.73	1.51	1.65	1.92	1.77	2.32	2.38
	Min	1	1	1	1	1	1	1	1	1
	Max	10	10	10	10	10	10	10	10	10
	Mode	8	8	8	10	8	8	8	8	8
Farmers' markets	Mean	7.26	8.30	8.18	8.33	8.20	7.15	7.72	5.89	7.09
	Std.dev.	2.29	1.73	1.70	1.59	1.70	2.17	2.21	2.79	2.54
	Min	1	2	1	2	2	1	1	1	1
	Max	10	10	10	10	10	10	10	10	10
	Mode	8	8	9	10	8	8	10	7	8
Solidarity-based purchasing groups	Mean	6.45	8.13	7.85	7.57	8.24	7.44	7.91	6.62	6.59
	Std.dev.	2.36	1.92	1.74	1.91	1.70	1.87	1.81	2.29	2.32
	Min	1	1	2	1	1	1	1	1	1
	Max	10	10	10	10	10	10	10	10	10
	Mode	7	8	8	8	8	8	8	7	8

Source: Authors' calculations

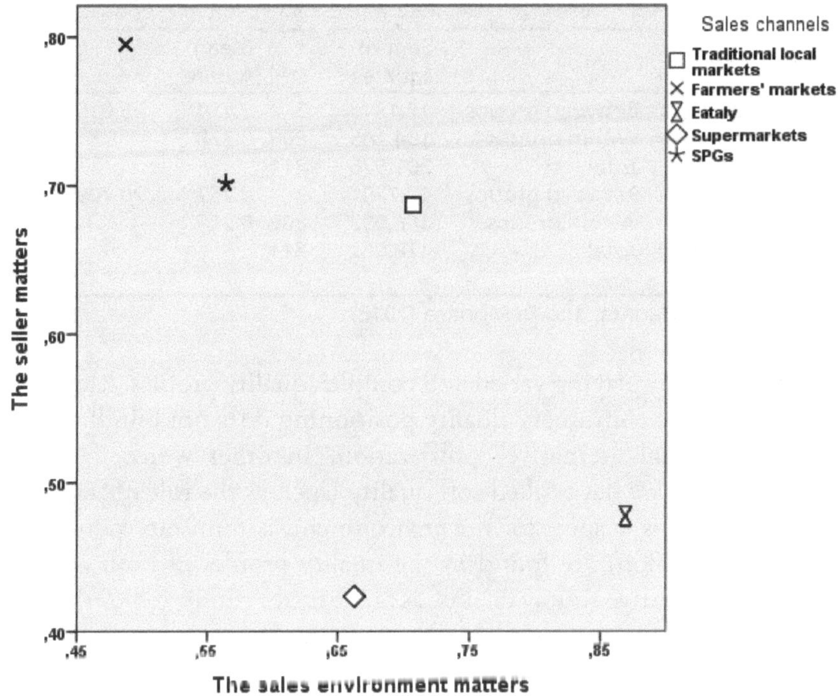

Fig. 5.4 Positioning in the expected quality space. Note: the axis value is the percentage of consumers over the mean value of the factor by sale channels. Source: Barbera, Dagnes, and Di Monaco (2018)

in order to manage the soft dimension of quality; rather, it uses more impersonal and commercial devices, referring to the sales environment. As Table 5.9 shows, these positionings are highly statistically significant even after controlling for the effect of socio-demographic characteristics. Here again, the supply chains' effect is statistically independent of individual-level attributes.

Conclusions

In this chapter, we analyzed consumer quality conventions in five different agri-food supply chains, both conventional and alternative. We first showed that consumers tend to judge multiple quality conventions

Table 5.9 Positioning in the expected quality space (Anova analysis)

		Sum of squares	Df	Mean square	F	Sig.
The seller matters × supply chains	Between groups	17.131	3	5.710	25.015	0.000
	Within groups	184.445	808	0.228		
	Total	201.576	811			
The sales environment matters × supply chains	Between groups	12.770	3	4.257	20.709	0.000
	Within groups	166.092	808	0.206		
	Total	178.862	811			

Source: Barbera, Dagnes, and Di Monaco (2018)

positively, thus displaying varied and complex quality profiles. Moreover, we observed that consumers' quality positioning does not blindly reflect the "conventional-alternative" polarization. In other words, elements relating to what we have called soft quality (such as the role of tradition, trust relationships, respect for the environment, community values, and the farmers' passion) are found in the quality profiles of both conventional and alternative supply chains, as are features connected to the hard quality conception (price, trademarks, and awards).

We then shifted attention to the food supply side, bringing out the relationship between consumers' quality representations and chain quality profiles. At this point of the analysis, two main results emerge. First, consumers maintain that the chains' quality profiles hinge on two different aspects: the role of the seller (expertise and reliability) and the role of the sales environment (ease of access and appeal). Second, there is a match between consumers' quality representations and the chains' quality profiles, that is, operators use differentiated strategies to manage the quality expectations expressed by consumers. Specifically, we showed that AFNs rely heavily on quality as a hallmark to set themselves apart from the conventional food system, but hybrid organizations such as high-end distributors strategically overcome divisions among different worlds of quality as a marketing strategy.

District markets, farmers' markets, and solidarity purchasing groups share the importance assigned to the seller, showing high quality expectations linked to this relationship. But some differences in their positioning emerge. In district markets, the centrality of the personal relationship with the seller and the irrelevance of all the other dimensions embodies consumers' generic quality expectation. In the farmers' markets, by contrast, the seller is perceived as an intermediary and a guarantor of a specific kind of quality relating to soft elements. Lastly, in solidarity purchasing groups, there is a somewhat negative attitude toward hard quality. This might be due to these consumers' low regard for market and labels/expert opinion as quality signals that are widespread in "conventional" agri-food chains. At the same time, the personal relationship with the seller is crucial for quality expectations.

In this scenario, the case of hybrid organizations such as Eataly is unique. Here, quality strategies seem to be designed to combine different worlds of quality and judgment devices. Eataly, in fact, responds to soft quality expectations by leveraging features of the retail environment. At high-end food retailers, in other words, consumers' expectations about soft quality elements are satisfied not by the relationship with a specific seller, but by creating a particular *sales atmosphere*. The retail environment is the organizational lever that Eataly relies on to generate the experience of soft quality. Eataly thus shows a specific *mimetic ability*: it makes the most of the soft dimension of quality—without relinquishing the hard dimension, that is, the visibility accorded to trademarks, awards, and formal certifications—by mimicking the trusting relationship of AFNs through *impersonal* judgment strategies where the atmosphere *substitutes* for the personal relationships with specific sellers. As Eataly's founder Oscar Farinetti has stated: "The street market has been a tremendous inspiration for me, I tried to recreate its atmosphere inside Eataly".[9] These findings support the idea that—*in the consumers' eyes*—Eataly is a new large-scale distribution retail format that offers a new food distribution paradigm inspired by concepts such as sustainability, sharing, and responsibility (Sebastiani, Montagnini, & Dalli, 2013). More generally, our analysis points to the relevance of "organizational hybrids" in the world of food, namely those organizations that respond strategically to new quality mixes and combine institutional approaches in unprecedented ways (Haigh, Walker, Bacq, & Kickul, 2015). In this sense, they are an innovation in organizational and business terms rather than in social terms.

Consumers in hybrid food chains seek artisanal quality and food safety standards, freshness, and convenience, a link with the land and variety, uniqueness, and large quantities. Hybrid models such as Eataly seem to be able to meet their consumers' demand for soft quality. At the same time, even if soft quality is more important in AFNs, customers of large-scale organized distribution chains also have their own particular idea of, and demand for, soft quality. This is a broader and less specific conception compared to ideas in the other distribution channels. However, this idea is taken seriously by large-scale distribution, as is crystal clear from the marketing strategies employed by supermarkets and hypermarkets to meet consumers' "alternative" quality conventions. The mixing of quality worlds thus might be a window of opportunity for strategic marketing choices by large-scale distribution and hybrid organizations and could also provide space for the further spread of AFNs.

Notes

1. Piedmont Region Department of Trade (see: www.regione.piemonte.it/gestione/commercio/mercati/dynIndex.php).
2. Source data: Retegas, Italian network of SPGs (see www.economiasolidale.net). Since online registration is voluntary, Retegas has estimated on the basis of several local studies that there are about twice as many unregistered solidarity purchasing groups (Grasseni, 2013).
3. The total number of questionnaires refers to valid cases for which the supply chain where the administration occurred is the predominant, or at least habitual, place of food purchase.
4. To randomize the survey, in each supply chain the interviewers contacted one consumer out of every five, regularly varied the point of administration (rotating in different locations in the markets or supermarkets), and operated on different days of the week (from Monday to Saturday) and time slots (morning, afternoon, and evening).
5. The three strata included (1) markets with 1–4 farmers' stalls, (2) markets with 5–8 farmers' stalls, and (3) markets with 9–13 farmers' stalls.
6. Minimum age 19, maximum age 86, standard deviation 16.2. Data were missing for five respondents (0.5%).
7. With regard to age, data were missing for 162 respondents (14.9%).

8. We estimated the parameters of a linear regression. In the model, the reference group is that of the large-scale system consumers, with the following social profile: working class male, over 65 years old, born in the South of Italy, and having a low income.
9. R. Fiori, *Eataly è unica come Benigni*, "La Stampa", December 21, 2014.

References

AGCM (Autorità Garante della Concorrenza e del Mercato). (2013). Indagine conoscitiva IC43 – Settore della Grande Distribuzione Organizzata. Retrieved March 20, 2018, from http://www.agcm.it/indagini-conoscitive-db/open/C12564CE0049D161/973E4D42D69C4A11C1257BC60039BBA0.html

Arcidiacono, D. (2016). La grande distribuzione alimentare. In F. Barbera, J. Dagnes, A. Salento, & F. Spina (Eds.), *Il capitale quotidiano. Un manifesto per l'economia fondamentale* (pp. 74–87). Rome: Donzelli.

Barbera, F., & Audifredi, S. (2012). In Pursuit of Quality. The Institutional Change of Wine Production Market in Piedmont. *Sociologia Ruralis, 52*(3), 311–331.

Barbera, F., & Dagnes, J. (2016). Building Alternatives from the Bottom-Up: The Case of Alternative Food Networks. *Agriculture and Agricultural Science Procedia, 8*, 324–331.

Barbera, F., Dagnes, J., & Di Monaco, R. (2018). Mimetic Quality: Consumer Quality Conventions and Strategic Mimicry in Food Distribution. *International Journal of Sociology of Agriculture and Food, 24*(2), 253–273.

Beckert, J. (2009). The Social Order of Markets. *Theory and Society, 38*(3), 245–269.

Beckert, J., & Aspers, P. (2011). *The Worth of Goods: Valuation and Pricing in the Economy*. Oxford: Oxford University Press.

Boltanski, L., & Thévenot, L. (2006). *On Justification*. Princeton, NJ: Princeton University Press.

Callon, M., Meadel, C., & Rabeharisoa, V. (2002). The Economy of Qualities. *Economy and Society, 31*(2), 194–217.

Consiglio per la ricerca in agricoltura e l'analisi dell'economia agraria. (2017). *Annuario dell'agricoltura italiana 2015*. Vol. lXiX. Roma: CREA – Centro Politiche e bioeconomia.

Dansero, E., & Pettenati, G. (2018). *Organization of the AFNs at Different Geographical Scales and Their Role in Reterritorializing the Food System*. Chapter 14 of this Book.

Dansero, E., & Puttilli, M. (2014). Multiple Territorialities of Alternative Food Networks: Six Cases from Piedmont, Italy. *Local Environment: The International Journal of Justice and Sustainability, 19*, 626–643.

De Schutter, O. (2017). The Political Economy of Food Systems Reform. *European Review of Agricultural Economics, 44*(3), 705–731.

Goldthorpe, J. H. (2015). *Sociology as a Population Science*. Cambridge: Cambridge University Press.

Grasseni, C. (2013). *Beyond Alternative Food Networks. Italy's Purchase Groups*. London: Bloomsbury Academic.

Haigh, N., Walker, J., Bacq, S., & Kickul, J. (2015). Hybrid Organizations: Origins, Strategies, Impacts, and Implications. *California Management Review, 57*(3), 5–12.

Honkanen, P., Verplanken, B., & Olsen, S. O. (2006). Ethical Values and Motives Driving Organic Food Choice. *Journal of Consumer Behaviour, 5*(5), 420–430.

Karpik, L. (2010). *Valuing the Unique: The Economics of Singularities*. Princeton: Princeton University Press.

Mason, P. (2016). *Postcapitalism: A Guide to Our Future*. London: Penguin Books.

Micheletti, M., Follesdal, A., & Stolle, D. (Eds.). (2004). *Politics, Products and Markets. Exploring Political Consumerism Past and Present*. New Brunswick: Transaction.

Murdoch, J., & Miele, M. (2004). A New Aesthetic of Food? Relational Reflexivity in the 'Alternative' Food Movement. In M. Harvey, A. McMeekin, & A. Warde (Eds.), *Qualities of Food* (pp. 156–175). Manchester: Manchester University Press.

Murdoch, J., Marsden, T., & Banks, J. (2000). Quality, Nature and Embeddedness: Some Theoretical Considerations in the Context of the Food Sector. *Economic Geography, 76*, 107–125.

Negro, G., Hannan, M. T., Rao, H., & Leung, M. D. (2007). *No Barrique, No Berlusconi: Collective Identity, Contention, and Authenticity in the Making of Barolo and Barbaresco Wines*. Research Paper, Stanford Business School.

Onozaka, Y., Nurse, G., & McFadden, D. T. (2010). Local Food Consumers: How Motivations and Perceptions Translate to Buying Behavior. *Choices, 25*(1), 1–6.

Parasuraman, A., Zeithaml, V. A., & Berry, L. L. (1994). Reassessment of Expectations as a Comparison Standard in Measuring Service Quality: Implications for Further Research. *Journal of Marketing, 58*(1), 111–124.

Peano, C., Tecco, N., & Girgenti, V. (2018). *The Environmental Sustainability of AFNs. An Honoured Promise?* Chapter 13 of this Book.

Pettenati, G., & Dansero, E. (2015). *La territorialità degli AFN: rappresentazioni, processi e politiche. I risultati della mappatura*. Research paper presented at the AFNIA workshop, Torino, Italy, 15 February.

Ponte, S. (2016). Convention Theory in the Anglophone Agri-food Literature: Past, Present and Future. *Journal of Rural Studies, 44*, 12–23.

Ponte, S., & Gibbon, P. (2009). Quality Standards, Conventions and the Governance of Global Value Chains. *Economy and Society, 34*(1), 1–31.

Santana, G. (2014). Social Innovation: Moving the Field Forward. A Conceptual Framework. *Technological Forecasting and Social Change, 82*, 42–51.

Sassatelli, R. (2015). Consumer Culture, Sustainability and a New Vision of Consumer Sovereignty. *Sociologia Ruralis, 55*(4), 483–496.

Sebastiani, R., Montagnini, F., & Dalli, D. (2013). Ethical Consumption and New Business Models in the Food Industry. Evidence from the Eataly Case. *Journal of Business Ethics, 114*(3), 473–488.

Stark, D. (1996). Recombinant Property in East European Capitalism. *American Journal of Sociology, 101*(4), 993–1027.

Streeck, W. (2016). *How Will Capitalism End?* London: Verso.

Unger, R. M. (2015). Conclusion: The Task of the Social Innovation Movement. In A. Nicholls, J. Simon, & M. Gabriel (Eds.), *New Frontiers in Social Innovation Research* (pp. 233–251). London: Palgrave Macmillan.

6

The Environmental Quality Factors Sought by Consumers in Alternative and Conventional Market Channels

Nadia Tecco and Cristiana Peano

Finding Environmental Sustainability, Finding Information

In the current food market, consumers are increasingly looking for more environmental sustainable products as well for more sustainable forms of trade.

This attitude is connected to the wider phenomena of the "quality turn" (Goodman, 2003), "concerned consumerism" (Soper, 2007), "civic environmentalism" (Wallace & Schroder, 2012), and "political consumption", all of which involve consumers who are increasingly interested in food, in how it was produced, where it comes from, and who produced it. The

N. Tecco (✉)
Department of Cultures, Politics and Society, University of Torino, Torino, Italy
e-mail: nadia.tecco@unito.it

C. Peano
Department of Agricultural, Forest and Food Sciences, University of Torino, Grugliasco (TO), Italy
e-mail: cristiana.peano@unito.it

A. Corsi et al. (eds.), *Alternative Food Networks*,
https://doi.org/10.1007/978-3-319-90409-2_6

problem of the environmental impacts of the conventional food system, which until the 1990s was almost exclusively identified with pollution (water, air, soil) caused by farming and livestock production, is now seen as much more complex. While the pervasive power of social networks combined with public and environmental health emergencies such as Bovine spongiform encephalopathy (BSE), avian influenza, and *E. coli* with their direct consequences on food choices have fuelled anxiety about the safety and quality of industrial food, they have also been able to bring consumers closer to issues that once seemed far removed from their concerns, making them much more aware of the responsibility that their choices involve and their role in the supply chain. Consumers' attention has thus gradually been extended to the food chain's technical functions (transfer of products over time and space) and distribution features (the proximity relationship between producer and consumer, the range, the ways of provisioning, the ability to respond to specific needs, and consumer behaviour).

However, there is still a notable gap between the perception of wanting more eco-friendly products and the action of actually purchasing them, as the extensive scientific evidence reminds us (Chen & Chai, 2010; Hughner, McDonagh, Prothero, Shultz, & Stanton, 2007; Vermeir & Verbeke, 2006, 2008).

Several specific studies on consumer behaviour with regard to green products indicate that there is a certain degree of inertia to change. Although this trend is less evident for food than for other goods (National Geographic Society & GlobeScan, 2014), the impediment effect of consumption determinants such as cultural and social factors, environmental and contextual influences, personal hedonistic and psychological components, and not least the presence of barriers to change (Rey & Ritzer, 2012) must be taken into account.

One of the factors that is most relevant to the economic component or physical accessibility is the lack of clear and adequate information (Connell, 2010; Padel & Foster, 2015). Information is becoming increasingly important in the global economy and all the more so in food transactions. It is not by chance that it is commonly defined as "the gold of the twenty-first century" and the right to food is also, and perhaps especially in our current society, the right to access correct, reliable information (Hassanein, 2003).

The demand for information translates into a search for guarantors, establishing a relationship of confidence with them. In building confidence in food attributes, signals embedded in food products and signals provided by sellers to reinforce quality coexist and interact (Lassoued & Hobbs, 2015).

According to a survey conducted by Nielsen in 2015, brand trust is the main driving force behind green purchases for 62% of the interviewed consumers (Nielsen, 2015).

And it is precisely in their ability to meet the need to reconvene trust between food producers and consumers (Goodman, 2003; Whatmore, Stassart, & Renting, 2003) that Alternative Food Networks (AFNs) have been able to gain ground on the market, both by filling the deficits of disembedded trust from consumers and by making consumers part of the act of purchase and not just passive recipients of products (Renting, Schermer, & Rossi, 2012).

How Does Information Matter in AFNs?

AFNs can be viewed as particular flows of food products that connect people who care about their health and the environment and are concerned with the externalities of the production/consumption practices with people who want to produce food without submitting to the market logic and hope to get better prices by managing the relationship with the consumer directly. On top of this material flow and the exchange of capital, there is also an intangible flow, involving the way information exchanges between the parties take place.

Though AFNs establish a direct relationship that narrows the geographical, social, cultural, and ecological distance between the buyer and the seller (this is one of the added values of the relationship between consumer and producer), they are not exempt from information asymmetries.

The neoclassical concept of perfect symmetry, despite the value and weight of a direct relationship between market agents, does not work in AFNs. The information asymmetry concerning the environmental attributes of fruit and vegetables (F&V), product categories at the centre of the exchange of alternative forms of food provisioning, is a sensitive issue.

This is particularly relevant for the credence attributes of fruit and vegetables, which cannot be verified even after consumption. These attributes include aspects such as the local provenance of the product, whether it is organic, and the producer's support and respect for workers' rights. In this case, the consumer's decision is based solely on how much confidence he or she has in the information on the label, the brand, or other elements that help build the product's reputation by sharing some of its extrinsic qualities. As a result, information asymmetry is reduced and the credence attribute becomes a search attribute, meaning that some information may be known to consumers before they buy, regardless of the consumption experience. It follows that the methods of finding and managing information in AFNs have a key role in the confidence building strategy, as well in whether the sources of reliability can be verified.

However, there is little scientific evidence about the mechanisms that could bridge the gap of information asymmetry for green F&V attributes in alternative and conventional sales channels. We thus decided to explore this aspect for three different distribution channels: farmers' markets (FMs), Solidarity Purchase Groups (SPGs), and supermarkets.

We focused primarily on strategies for reducing information asymmetry in the three channels and secondly on how different market circumstances affect the evaluation of the products' environmental sustainability.

For greater insight into these aspects, we examined how the relationship between consumer and producer in the three distribution channels is organized as regards information flow. We looked at the literature at the intersection between actor network theory (Murdoch, 1995, 2000) and supply chain management theory (Wilson, 1996).

We also reviewed the numerous case studies in the AFN literature that show how the consumer-producer relationship unfolds in practice.

In parallel, a questionnaire was administered in several market settings associated with the three distribution channels in Piedmont to investigate how the concept of environmental quality related to the purchase of fresh fruit and vegetables is defined in the various areas.

Confidence Building Strategies at Farmers' Markets, SPGs, and Supermarkets

Trust is widely recognized as a key relational principle in the AFN buyer-seller relationship (Tregear, 2011). While this is a common denominator between the composite set of practices that fall under the AFN umbrella concept, each has elaborated its own codes and strategies for filling the information gap concerning the environmental sustainability of the products marketed in them, with particular reference to transactions relating to fresh fruit and vegetables.

Below we will briefly illustrate the strategies adopted in FMs, SPGs, and supermarkets. As regards environmental quality, FMs start with a comparative advantage over other channels, as they are often naturally associated with environmental quality attributes such as the presence of organic, fresh, seasonal, and healthy products (Bond, Thilmany, & Bond, 2008; Holloway & Kneafsey, 2000; Moore, 2006).

In farmers' markets, information asymmetry is reduced by building a horizontal relationship based on trust and cooperation between producers and consumers. The direct marketing channel makes it possible to convey information (Brown, 2002), to enrich it with non-standardized and consumer-tailored transactions, thus consolidating interpersonal relationships between consumers and producers (Feagan & Morris, 2009). Face-to-face interaction is the means whereby producers and consumers re-aggregate the process of exchanging products and information in a new social relationship (Svenfelt & Carlsson-Kanyama, 2010; Thorne, 1996). This tie is generally characterized by direct and repeated relationships over time (in most cases) and exchange of information about the product (provenance, method of cultivation, variety) and the producers (how they manage their agricultural enterprise, their values).

FMs differ from dealers in local markets in how they display and communicate goods, which offers an immediate reference to the rural landscape, production, diversity, and the distinctive characteristics of the products and of the producer.

The challenge for the producer lies in differentiating the product from its competitors, communicating to the consumer the qualitative characteristics that distinguish his product from others in the same category. Products reach the consumer with a set of value-laden information that binds the distinctive assets of the product to the producer and to the place of production (Renting, Marsden, & Banks, 2003). However, FMs are still a type of market activity operated and initiated by producers.

In SPGs, where families who join together to buy products (not just food) from selected producers according to fundamental principles which vary from group to group, the active role is played by consumers. SPGs create and operate a new system of consumer-producer relations, in an interstitial strategy positioned between the market and civic society and where the figure of citizen-consumers emerges (Lyson, 2012). Thus, they are no longer consumers as autonomous units, but rather nodes of a system of relationships based on friendship, sociability, and reciprocity. This radically changes the meaning and content of the face-to-face relationship between consumer and producer, which is continuous and repeats itself on a more or less fixed basis at the time of delivery. In addition to expressing his own interests, the consumer becomes the spokesman of a collective interest, which regenerates and is negotiated when products are received or during the meetings where producers are selected and product pickup and delivery is organized. Beyond direct interaction, the relational context is strengthened by other communication patterns such as organizational meetings, e-mailing, events, and in some cases by on-farm visits (Brunori, Rossi, & Malandrin, 2010). Cooperating in an SPG makes it possible for people with different skills to share knowledge about the many choices concerning varieties, production methods, processing techniques, provenance and, more generally, the quality of food. Consequently, it enables effective decisions about the supply of food (and other products) to be made (Fonte, Eboli, Maietta, Pinto, & Salvioni, 2011).

Collective action is not limited in most cases to joint buying; it also concerns the participation in the SPG's organizational life, the construction of networks between the various SPGs at regional and national level, and the promotion of social or political initiatives in the local area.

The information about producers and products is collected from multiple channels, starting from personal contacts, research on the local area, and the wider network of SPGs. Producers are surrounded by a series of direct and indirect relationships that work to build their reputation and encourage them to offer a service meeting SPGs' needs (which may vary from group to group). The interweaving of the network of relationships helps reduce the asymmetry between the actors in this consumer-driven market and to redistribute knowledge among them. In most cases, the trust created in the different communication patterns replaces bargaining, so that certification for organic products is no longer necessary and transaction costs are reduced (Brunori et al. 2010).

Even now that "conventional" distribution channels sell the products marketed in AFNs and have in some cases begun to adopt communicational patterns that mimic farmer's markets (in the arrangement of products, the presence of producers, the way products are narrated, and the evidence of local origin), the mechanism for narrowing information asymmetry continues to be focused on the key role of the label and certification schemes adopted by the retailer.

From an ontological perspective, the fact that products sold in AFNs have spread to conventional distribution contributes to making the distinction between "alternative" and "conventional" questionable in practice, and to converge on a frame of analysis that mostly contemplates hybridization and cross-fertilization.

As AFNs have developed in antithesis to the conventional distribution channels, in an attempt to put a brake on business models dictated by the needs of a standardized market, so has the conventional channel gradually opened its doors to the AFNs' products, recognizing their ability to attract the consumer's interest. However, if we consider the mechanisms for finding information in each distribution channel, we cannot fail to notice that the channels differ widely in how they organize their own relational and communication patterns and that the consumer moves with a certain fluidity between them.

In supermarkets, the information gap is balanced by a vertical relationship between consumers and producers mediated by the retailer and the selected certification scheme. The relationship between producer and consumer thus becomes indirect and hinges almost exclusively on the information conveyed by labels and in-store or on-pack logos. In this case, the information content is necessarily limited and more related to single specific issues with objective and measurable characteristics (organic production, respect for selected standards). Given the competition between products that use the label as a vehicle of sustainability, the risk that emerges on the consumer front is that of generating an information overload, which creates confusion instead of bringing out the distinctive characteristics of a product (Grunert, 2011; Horne, 2009). Even on the label, there is competition between environmental attributes and other information about nutritional content and ingredients that risk neutralizing each other (Chatzidakis, Hibbert, & Smith, 2007; Grunert, Hieke, & Wills, 2014).

What Does "Environmental Quality" Mean for Fresh Fruit and Vegetables?

Environmental quality is a declared goal for many AFNs and is increasingly sought in conventional food provisioning channels. The attribute of environmental quality can be considered a sub-attribute of the broader and generally understood concept of quality, while in the theoretical frame of reference of conventions theory, ecological quality is one of the six conventions relating to the quality of food products (Boltanski & Thévenot, 1991; Murdoch, Marsden, & Banks, 2000).

In the specific case of fresh fruit and vegetables, environmental quality refers to a myriad of considerations which to be concretely understood must necessarily be put in a clear and circumscribed context.

Moreover, while environmental quality is undeniably important in the meeting of supply and demand, from the consumer's point of view, the concept also involves many nuances concerning the production method, the company's reputation, geographical origin, appearance, and price (Moser, Raffaelli, & Thilmany-McFadden, 2011). From the producers' perspective, quality—environmental and otherwise—has become a powerful lever for communication with the consumer and a fundamental factor in companies' competition and diversification. As described in the previous section, different food distribution channels have different ways of presenting and displaying (real or presumed) environmental quality, and consumers try to find their way between them. After exploring the strategies for reducing information asymmetry employed by farmers' markets, SPGs, and supermarkets, we investigated how the criteria for evaluating products' environmental sustainability are organized and negotiated in the relationships that arise in the three channels.

To date, little research has assessed how consumers weigh environmental attributes, and what relative importance is assigned to them in situations that differ in the strategies used to cope with lack of complete information about what is being exchanged.

In order to capture the "green attributes" of fresh fruit and vegetables, a survey was carried out in the three different distribution channels (farmers' markets, SPGs, and supermarkets) in several areas of Piedmont through the direct administration of a questionnaire to consumers at the moment of purchase. Farmers' markets, SPGs, and supermarkets were selected so as to be sufficiently representative of Piedmont in terms of size, composition of producers, type of consumers, location in large urban areas (Turin), and medium-small cities (Cuneo, Alessandria, Asti, Avigliana, Alpignano, Grugliasco, Collegno, Condove, Carmagnola).

In Piedmont, the short supply chain is not an entirely new phenomenon, since the regional agricultural tradition has always been characterized by close relations between producers and consumers based on direct sales at markets or wineries. What is particularly innovative about farmers' markets is how much the phenomenon has grown, attracting many new producers and consumers in the last 15 years largely through the support given by Coldiretti[1] to the *Campagna Amica* initiative.[2]

The consumers who stated that they visited the sales channel regularly and were sensitive to the environmental impacts of the fruit and vegetable supply chain were asked to rank a number of green attributes (intrinsic and extrinsic) that were relevant to their F&V purchases. Green attributes were identified through a literature survey of environmental quality signals and are listed in Table 6.1. Respondents were asked: "What signals do you use to recognize the quality of fresh fruit and vegetables? Please rate their importance on a scale of 1 to 5".

Table 6.1 Fruit and vegetables quality items

1. Provenance from Piedmont (zero kilometres)
2. Small-scale production
3. Confidence in the seller
4. Knowledge of the product's place of origin
5. Appearance
6. Presence of local F&V varieties
7. Use of environmentally friendly production methods
8. Minimized or recyclable/reusable packaging
9. Knowledge of the producer (personal or mediated)
10. Organic certification
11. Use of organic production method
12. The possibility to choose the needed quantity and avoid waste

The list of attributes and signals included intrinsic factors such as local varieties and packaging, as well as extrinsic aspects such as provenance, method of production, knowledge of the producers/vendor, knowledge of the place of origin, and the presence of brands and/or certifications. Along with these aspects, we collected data on fruit and vegetable buying habits (frequency, quantity, type of packaging, seasonality, waste).

The F&V types considered in the questionnaire included apples, strawberries, courgettes, and tomatoes. These products were chosen for several reasons. First, they are marketed by all vendors, although with different types of packaging.[3]

They are commonly consumed products that exemplify some of the features characterizing fruit and vegetables: seasonality, level of perishability and conservation, and average purchase quantity.

A total of 342 interviews were conducted (97 at farmers' markets, 135 at SPGs, and 110 at supermarkets). The percentage of regular customers was 93% in SPGs, 80% in farmers' markets, and 50% in supermarkets.

Varimax-rotated Principal Component Analysis (PCA) was performed on the data on extrinsic and intrinsic signals sought by each consumer group when buying "green F&V".

The primary purpose of the PCA was to reduce the 12 components to a smaller set of latent variables. This was accomplished through a linear transformation that projects the original variables onto a new Cartesian system where they are arranged in descending order of variance. Complexity was reduced by analysing the composition of the new latent variables (Fig. 6.1).

In the search for green signals, placeness[4] plays the key role at farmers' markets, followed by information about the method of production.[5] In this case it is significant to note that the environmental quality signals are identified from the product, and the producer is the channel for this information.

It would thus seem possible that in FMs, consumers equate environmental quality with F&V produced locally using environmentally friendly methods, which do not necessarily need to be certified. This builds loyalty to the market, rather than to the producer, and a relationship of trust with those who place themselves within the frame of the farmers' market. This interpretation would also seem to be consistent

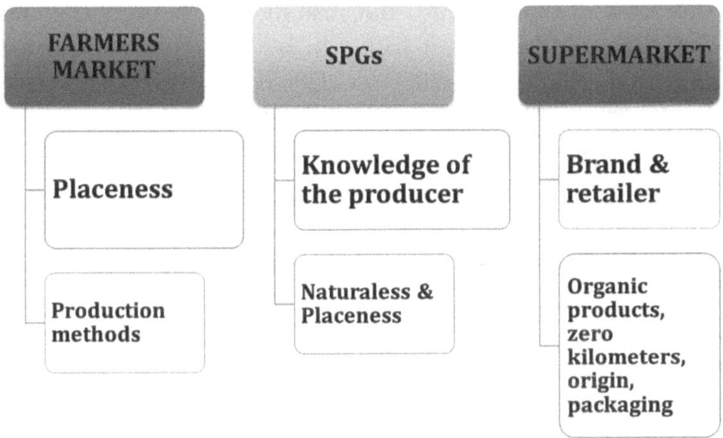

Fig. 6.1 Graphic representation of the concept of environmental quality (according to the latent variables obtained through PCA) in the three channels. Source: Authors' calculations

with the information collected from the questionnaires, which indicates a loyalty to the market, but not an exclusive relationship with a single producer, and where the purchase would also seem to be determined by the availability of the product sought or by the attractiveness of the product offered.

We could thus say that our findings show that the consumer sees the farmers' market as a source of local and organic (not necessarily certified) fruit and vegetables, where it is the context that establishes the conditions for a relationship of trust which can be transferred to different producers. This representation also seems consistent with the messaging conveyed by the producers present in the FMs we analysed.

In fact, all the case studies dealt with farmers' markets organized by the *Coldiretti Campagna Amica* initiative, which, although located in different urban contexts, share common values and visual identity.

Given the uncertainty about the environmental quality of the fruit and vegetables offered at the farmers' market, the ability to supply the expected level of quality is guaranteed by the farmers' market as such and by Coldiretti, who is the *super-partes* guarantor of this quality.

By contrast with the literature, our case study of farmers' markets indicated that the most important factor in building trust is not face-face mediation, but the guarantee provided by the markets' distinctive signals.

In SPGs, recognition of environmental quality focuses on the producer, who is in turn the guarantor of the environmental quality of the products he sells. This is particularly relevant for the attributes of product naturalness and placeness, which include signals concerning product origin, production method and company size, and which can be inferred from the product's appearance. The selection process lays the groundwork for creating a trust base that leads to a constantly renewed confidence and renegotiation through peer control in a dynamic negotiation between individual producers and the consumer network.

As the literature also indicates, organic certification appears to be superfluous, since information about the production method is already conveyed through other means and there is no need for further reinforcement. The creation of the trust relationship between the producers and the SPGs is a barrier to entry on the part of producers outside the network. The barrier comes down only if this relationship of trust between existing producers and SPG members weakens.

For purchasers of fruit and vegetables at supermarkets, the case studies confirmed that the attributes that are recognized as guaranteeing environmental quality are the label and knowledge of/confidence in the retailer. The search for environmental quality focuses on aspects that can be certified or declared on the label, such as the organic production method, product origin, and regional provenance. Packaging is another attribute that connotes environmental quality at the supermarket, by contrast with farmers' markets and SPGs.

On the one hand, this could be due to the different packaging solutions that the retailer offers for the same category of fruit and vegetable product (tray, bag, basket). However, it should be noted that the packaging not only serves to protect/preserve the product, but is also the physical medium whereby information about the product is conveyed. In the case of supermarkets, the survey also shows a more varied picture as regards consumers' socio-demographic characteristics.

The fact that farmers' markets are held in certain time slots in the morning or afternoon and, for SPGs, the delivery schedules, the time and effort that members must commit to the organization, and the type of products and criteria involved all mean that the respondents who patronize these channels are more homogeneous by gender composition (mainly women), by age group (35–50), and by income (medium-high) than supermarket shoppers.

Socially Embedded Environmental Quality

This chapter has provided empirical insights into the drivers and outcomes of consumer trust in food, exploring the environmental attributes orienting fruit and vegetable purchases in different distribution channels. The varying representations of environmental quality in these channels shed light on the process of social construction of the relationship between the parties and the behavioural strategies used to fill the information gap relating to fruit and vegetables.

This mediation leads to an ecological/environmental quality embedded in the complex web of the consumer's social relations and interactions.

In other words, for the environmental/ecological convention, our empirical analysis has identified specific norms and interactions for the different forms of food provisioning. What consumers seek in terms of green F&V attributes seems to be consistent with the different relational shape and types of interaction characterizing each channel: the latent attributes we identified are in line with the forms of quality communication that have been developed to differentiate products in each distribution segment. Farmers' markets, SPGs, and supermarkets are different institutional settings where people apply different evaluation criteria to choices.

These findings encourage us to consider the importance of evaluating the relationship between environmental sustainability and the distribution channel from both the technical-economic and the social vantage points. For environmental sustainability, on the one hand, it is important to consider the distribution channel as a technical-economic path that the product follows as it moves from the producer to the final consumer, evaluating the efficiency, the value redistribution mechanisms, and the environmental impacts of organizational/logistical processes.

On the other hand, the distribution channel is a relational-contextual path whose forms of interaction contribute to different interpretations[6] of environmental quality which do not necessarily take into account the technical-economic aspects of supply chain organization, and where environmental quality is socially defined by the distribution channel, with the risk of overshadowing the real environmental content of the marketed product.

These multiple perspectives provide a more nuanced perception of each distribution channels' environmental performance and point to the need to combine objective assessments of the various channels (see an analysis of this type in Chap. 9) with a reflection on the mechanisms for verifying the reliability of information sources.

Despite this more nuanced perception, however, it will continue to be difficult for consumers to evaluate the complex consequences stemming from the products they purchase and the repercussions of their food consumption choices.

Notes

1. Coldiretti is one of the largest farmers' unions in Italy.
2. The Campagna Amica initiative sponsored by Coldiretti promotes direct sales by creating farmers' markets. These markets are governed by an internal regulation that establishes the conditions and types of products that can be sold; the companies participating in them undertake to comply with market regulations, subjecting themselves to internal control and external control by a third party.
3. As the evaluation of the environmental impact of different fruit and vegetable products sold through the various distribution channels presented in Chap. 9 indicates, packaging (together with production) is one of the most significant variables in determining differences between channels.
4. Factor identified by the explanatory variables "Provenance from Piedmont" and "Knowledge of the product's place of origin".

5. Factor identified by the explanatory variables "Use of environmentally friendly production methods", "Possession of organic product certification/organic farming", "Use of organic production method".
6. In the sense of both explanation and performance.

References

Boltanski, L., & Thévenot, L. (1991). The Six Worlds. In *On Justification: Economies of Worth* (pp. 159–211).

Bond, C. A., Thilmany, D., & Bond, J. K. (2008). Understanding Consumer Interest in Product and Process-Based Attributes for Fresh Produce. *Agribusiness, 24*(2), 231–252 https://doi.org/10.1002/agr.20157

Brown, A. (2002). Farmers' Market Research 1940–2000: An Inventory and Review. *American Journal of Alternative Agriculture, 17*(4), 167–176 https://doi.org/10.1079/AJAA2002167

Brunori, G., Rossi, A., & Malandrin, V. (2010). Co-producing Transition: Innovation Processes in Farms Adhering to Solidarity-Based Purchase Groups (GAS) in Tuscany, Italy. *International Journal of Sociology of Agriculture and Food, 18*(1), 28–53.

Chatzidakis, A., Hibbert, S., & Smith, A. P. (2007). Why People Don't Take Their Concerns About Fair Trade to the Supermarket: The Role of Neutralisation. *Journal of Business Ethics, 74*(1), 89–100 https://doi.org/10.1007/s10551-006-9222-2

Chen, T. B., & Chai, L. T. (2010). Attitude Towards the Environment and Green Products: Consumers' Perspective. *Management Science and Engineering, 4*(2), 27–39 https://doi.org/10.3968/j.mse.1913035X20100402.002

Connell, K. Y. H. (2010). Internal and External Barriers to Eco-conscious Apparel Acquisition. *International Journal of Consumer Studies, 34*(3), 279–286 https://doi.org/10.1111/j.1470-6431.2010.00865.x

Feagan, R. B., & Morris, D. (2009). Consumer Quest for Embeddedness: A Case Study of the Brantford Farmers' Market. *International Journal of Consumer Studies, 33*(3), 235–243 https://doi.org/10.1111/j.1470-6431.2009.00745.x

Fonte, M., Eboli, M., Maietta, O., Pinto, B., & Salvioni, C. (2011). Il consumo sostenibile nella visione dei Gruppi di Acquisto Solidale di Roma. *AgriRegioniEuropa, 7*(27), 1–5 Retrieved from http://reorient.it/attachments/article/75/gasroma.pdf

Goodman, D. (2003). The Quality "Turn" and Alternative Food Practices: Reflections and Agenda. *Journal of Rural Studies, 19*(1), 1–7 https://doi.org/10.1016/S0743-0167(02)00043-8

Grunert, K. G. (2011). Sustainability in the Food Sector: A Consumer Behaviour Perspective. *International Journal on Food System Dynamics, 2*(3), 207–218 https://doi.org/10.18461/ijfsd.v2i3.232

Grunert, K. G., Hieke, S., & Wills, J. (2014). Sustainability Labels on Food Products: Consumer Motivation, Understanding and Use. *Food Policy, 44,* 177–189 https://doi.org/10.1016/j.foodpol.2013.12.001

Hassanein, N. (2003). Practicing Food Democracy: A Pragmatic Politics of Transformation. *Journal of Rural Studies, 19*(1), 77–86 https://doi.org/10.1016/S0743-0167(02)00041-4

Holloway, L., & Kneafsey, M. (2000). Reading the Space of the Farmers' Market: A Preliminary Investigation from the UK. *Sociologia Ruralis, 40*(3), 285–299 https://doi.org/10.1111/1467-9523.00149

Horne, R. E. (2009). Limits to Labels: The Role of Eco-labels in the Assessment of Product Sustainability and Routes to Sustainable Consumption. *International Journal of Consumer Studies, 33*(2), 175–182 https://doi.org/10.1111/j.1470-6431.2009.00752.x

Hughner, R. S., McDonagh, P., Prothero, A., Shultz, C. J., & Stanton, J. (2007). Who Are Organic Food Consumers? A Compilation and Review of Why People Purchase Organic Food. *Journal of Consumer Behaviour, 6*(2–3), 94–110 https://doi.org/10.1002/cb.210

Lassoued, R., & Hobbs, J. E. (2015). Consumer Confidence in Credence Attributes: The Role of Brand Trust. *Food Policy, 52*, 99–107 https://doi.org/10.1016/j.foodpol.2014.12.003

Lyson, T. A. (2012). *Civic Agriculture: Reconnecting Farm, Food, and Community.* https://doi.org/10.1017/S1742170508001452

Moore, O. (2006). Understanding Postorganic Fresh Fruit and Vegetable Consumers at Participatory Farmers' Markets in Ireland: Reflexivity, Trust and Social Movements. *International Journal of Consumer Studies, 30*(5), 416–426 https://doi.org/10.1111/j.1470-6431.2006.00537.x

Moser, R., Raffaelli, R., & Thilmany-McFadden, D. (2011). Consumer Preferences for Fruit and Vegetables with Credence-Based Attributes: A Review. *International Food and Agribusiness Management Review, 14*(2), 121–142.

Murdoch, J. (1995). Actor-Networks and the Evolution of Economic Forms: Combining Description and Explanation in Theories of Regulation, Flexible

Specialization, and Networks. *Environment and Planning A, 27*(5), 731–757 https://doi.org/10.1068/a270731

Murdoch, J. (2000). Networks – A New Paradigm of Rural Development? *Journal of Rural Studies, 16*(4), 407–419 https://doi.org/10.1016/S0743-0167(00)00022-X

Murdoch, J., Marsden, T., & Banks, J. (2000). Quality, Nature, and Embeddedness: Some Theoretical Considerations in the Context of the Food Sector. *Economic Geography, 76*(2), 107–125 https://doi.org/10.1111/j.1944-8287.2000.tb00136.x

National Geographic Society, & GlobeScan. (2014, September). Greendex 2014: Consumer Choice and the Environment – A Worldwide Tracking Survey. *National Geographic*, 1–20. https://doi.org/10.1017/CBO9781107415324.004

Nielsen. (2015). *The Sustainability Imperative. New Insights on Consumers Expectations* (pp. 1–19). https://www.nielsen.com/content/dam/nielsen-global/dk/docs/global-sustainability-report-oct-2015.pdf

Padel, S., & Foster, C. (2015). Exploring the Gap Between Attitudes and Behaviour Understanding Why Consumers Buy or Do Not Buy Organic Food. *British Food Journal Food Journal British Food Journal of Communication Management, 107*(4),606 625https://doi.org/10.1108/00070700510611002

Renting, H., Marsden, T. K., & Banks, J. (2003). Understanding Alternative Food Networks: Exploring the Role of Short Food Supply Chains in Rural Development. *Environment and Planning A, 35*(3), 393–411 https://doi.org/10.1068/a3510

Renting, H., Schermer, M., & Rossi, A. (2012). Building Food Democracy: Exploring Civic Food Networks and Newly Emerging Forms of Food Citizenship. *International Journal of Sociology of Agriculture and Food, 19*(3), 289–307.

Rey, P. J., & Ritzer, G. (2012). The Sociology of Consumption. In *The Wiley-Blackwell Companion to Sociology* (pp. 444–469). Malden, MA: John Wiley https://doi.org/10.1002/9781444347388.ch24

Soper, K. (2007). Re-thinking the "Good Life": The Citizenship Dimension of Consumer Disaffection with Consumerism. *Journal of Consumer Culture, 7*(2), 205–229 https://doi.org/10.1177/1469540507077681

Svenfelt, Å., & Carlsson-Kanyama, A. (2010). Farmers' Markets –Linking Food Consumption and the Ecology of Food Production? *Local Environment, 15*(5), 453–465 https://doi.org/10.1080/13549831003735411

Thorne, L. (1996). Local Exchange Trading Systems in the United Kingdom: A Case of Re-embedding? *Environment and Planning A, 28*(8), 1361–1376 https://doi.org/10.1068/a281361

Tregear, A. (2011). Progressing Knowledge in Alternative and Local Food Networks: Critical Reflections and a Research Agenda. *Journal of Rural Studies, 27*(4), 419–430 https://doi.org/10.1016/j.jrurstud.2011.06.003

Vermeir, I., & Verbeke, W. (2006). Sustainable Food Consumption: Exploring the Consumer "Attitude – Behavioral Intention" Gap. *Journal of Agricultural and Environmental Ethics, 19*(2), 169–194 https://doi.org/10.1007/s10806-005-5485-3

Vermeir, I., & Verbeke, W. (2008). Sustainable Food Consumption Among Young Adults in Belgium: Theory of Planned Behaviour and the Role of Confidence and Values. *Ecological Economics, 64*(3), 542–553 https://doi.org/10.1016/j.ecolecon.2007.03.007

Wallace, L. T., & Schroder, W. R. (2012). *Government and the Food Industry: Economic and Political Effects of Conflict and Co-Operation.* Springer US. Retrieved from https://books.google.it/books?id=DBfpBwAAQBAJ

Whatmore, S., Stassart, P., & Renting, H. (2003). What's Alternative About Alternative Food Networks? *Environment and Planning A, 35*(3), 389–391 https://doi.org/10.1068/a3621

Wilson, N. (1996). The Supply Chains of Perishable Products in Northern Europe. *British Food Journal, 98*(6), 9–15 https://doi.org/10.1108/00070709610131320

7

Understanding Alternative Food Networks After the Crisis: Testing Four Scenarios in Italy

Giovanni Orlando

Introduction

This chapter looks at the processes through which economic and cultural values attached to food are currently being reproduced and contested in the agri-food system—both materially and symbolically—as part of the capitalist system as a whole, exploring this topic specifically in relation to the changes that have taken place in the Italian solidarity economy sector after the crisis of 2008 and during the period of ensuing austerity. The chapter proposes four scenarios to make sense of these changes: (1) the generation of new solidarity economy phenomena, (2) the strengthening of existing ones, (3) their obstruction, and (4) the irrelevance of the crisis to the phenomena in question. The chapter examines different aspects of these scenarios through the case study of an Italian alternative food network (AFN) called 'Off The Market' (OTM).

Over the course of the last thirty years, AFNs have emerged out of the contradictions that marked the end of the second food regime, the

G. Orlando (✉)
Department of Cultures, Politics and Society, University of Torino, Torino, Italy
e-mail: giovanni.orlando@unito.it

A. Corsi et al. (eds.), *Alternative Food Networks*,
https://doi.org/10.1007/978-3-319-90409-2_7

industrial one. The term 'food regime' is used here to indicate the key role that food has played in guaranteeing the stability of capitalist accumulation on a world scale since the nineteenth century, a role that has manifested historically in the form of three specific regimes (Bernstein, 2016; McMichael, 2009).

The first regime, the colonial one (circa 1870–1929), took shape as a result of the industrial revolution and the birth of the European working classes through the importation of cereals, meat, and tropical products like tea and coffee from the colonies of Western Empires (Mintz, 1986). The second regime, the industrial one (circa 1945–1979), was based on high-input, energy-intensive agriculture in the North and aimed at the export of cereals (wheat, rice, maize) at subsidized prices toward the ex-colonies of the South. This regime allowed the partial industrialization of the South by providing it with cheap food and freeing labour for manufacturing, thus guaranteeing new markets for Euro-American capital to invest in.

The current regime, the corporate one (circa 1991–present), relies on a global division of labour that forces the world's poor to feed the rich both in the advanced capitalist nations of the North and in the emerging ones of the South, through a system of commerce—supermarkets—that has revolutionized food provision (McMichael & Friedmann, 2007). In exchange for the mass-produced calories of the North that still reach the four corners of the world, rich regions now receive increasing quantities of meat, fish, fruit, and vegetables through highly specialized supply chains that guarantee supermarket shelves are stocked 24/7, seven days a week. In this regime, financial capital has acquired considerable importance, partly thanks to the role played by multinational retail corporations (Burch & Lawrence, 2009). The corporate food regime has witnessed the development of two modes of food provisioning that reflect the tendency of world society to bifurcate into transnational classes of rich and poor consumers. Perhaps the best example of this tendency is the coexistence of retailers like Walmart and Whole Foods, which copy each other's product lines and discount strategies while defining, at least in practice, two markets for opposed classes (Friedmann, 2005).

Although food regimes guarantee stable periods of capitalist accumulation, tensions are always part of the system. Periods of transitions are as important as those of stability because the rules that allow the extraction of value are intrinsically social. Economic value is a cultural value, after all. As a result, acceptance or contestation of the 'rules of the game' represents a key factor of (in)stability. Two domains are characteristic of contestation toward the corporate food regime: food sovereignty and environmental sustainability (Friedmann, 1993; McMichael, 2008). From the 1970s onwards, social movements have been greatly influential in defining these two domains, an influence that has only increased in the age of globalization and the Washington Consensus.

On the one hand, then, the current regime rests on what have been called "food empires" (van der Ploeg, 2008) built by pushing forward a more disembedded model of economy (Polanyi, 1944/2001) where the land and labour necessary to bring food from field to table are increasingly subjected to self-regulating markets. On the other, farmers, entrepreneurs, politicians and citizens have joined forces to combat this commodification, which takes the form of higher costs and lower prices for farmers (Heatherington, 2011), food insecurity and food scandals for consumers, and a polluted environment for almost everyone (Sage, 2012). As part of this struggle, they have created AFNs inspired by values other than those of the market.

The Question of Value After the Crisis

AFNs are more widespread in the affluent societies of the North, though examples can be found also in the South (Gregson & Ferdous, 2014) and in the post-socialist world (Jung, Klein, & Caldwell, 2014), something which testifies a story that rings true all over the world: growing and eating food as we have known it after the Second World War is no longer possible. These networks comprise a great variety of phenomena: from farmer's markets to solidarity purchase groups, from farm shops to fair trade, from community-supported agriculture to web-based companies that deliver local food to people's doorsteps, and much more (Goodman, DuPuis, & Goodman, 2012). The empirical and theoretical boundaries of these phenomena with the corporate regime are constantly in question, signalling the presence of considerable tension in the system.

At a general level, AFNs can be interpreted as trying to shift the creation of value toward higher levels of social and environmental protection in a rapidly disembedding economy (Graeber, 2001; Pratt & Luetchford, 2014). Three factors of value creation have historically led to the disembedding of agri-food markets: (1) the social distance between those who grow and those who eat food, (2) the durability of industrially produced foods, and (3) the cultural construction of food as a commodity (Friedmann, 1994; Goody, 1982).[1] By favouring transactions with fewer intermediaries, from face-to-face to spatially extended ones, AFNs try to re-embed food in society (Friedmann & McNair, 2008). By promoting what they consider to be less intensive production methods, like the organic one, they seek to re-embed food in nature (Kneafsey et al., 2008). Finally, by unveiling the negative consequences of the modern world's obsession with cheapness and convenience, they attempt to change the representation of food (Petrini, 2005).

Different sorts of AFNs tackle each of these three factors in different ways (Marsden, Banks, & Bristow, 2000). In practice, two tendencies have emerged over time as a result of the relative importance assigned to two elements: product type and system of provision. Some initiatives focus on circulating specific 'quality' products regardless of the system of provision, therefore including conventional ones, even discount stores (e.g. Lidl, Aldi) or Amazon (Fonte, 2006), while other initiatives attempt to set up ethical systems of provision for food more generally (Luetchford & Pratt, 2011). This empirical difference draws from, and at the same time feeds into, a semantic slippage in the notion of 'alternative food network' that hides two possible interpretations: a weak one, alternative *food* networks, and a strong one, alternative food *networks* (Watts, Ilbery, & Maye, 2005). As Wiskerke points out, though, "very often [it is] also alternative foods that are produced, processed, distributed and consumed in many of these alternative networks" (Wiskerke, 2009, p. 378), complicating the possibility of distinguishing between the two meanings. These interpretations are themselves the result of a tension that cuts across all types of AFN, and of economic activity more generally: that between market and society.

Though we have got used to considering 'the' market as a disembodied entity whose existence is increasingly virtual, actual markets remain social institutions constructed by power elites under historically specific conditions, following interests, rules, and assumptions about property and morality that are subject to change over time, making them intrinsically arbitrary (Graeber, 2011; Hann & Hart, 2011). *Capitalist* markets are notable because they set prices in a seemingly impersonal manner through supply and demand and rely on general-purpose money (Bohannan & Dalton, 1962) for the exchange of all sorts of goods, including food but also, crucially, labour. By their very nature, then, they have the potential to be applied across social realms and whole societies. The digital revolution has amplified this potential tremendously. Herein lies the tension between market and society or the tension in the growth of one at the expense of the other (Gudeman, 2008).

Looking at this tension from the perspective of how value is created, exchanged, and used under the corporate food regime, AFNs appear to try to stem the flow of natural resources, money, and cultural meaning away from specific places, workers, and citizens toward global markets, shareholders, and elites. In other words, they try to create more closed economies where a degree of autonomy can be maintained from the immensely powerful demands of the open economy (Luetchford, 2014; Pratt, 2014). The metaphor of 'closure' can raise doubts concerning the political nature (in a broad sense) of AFNs, especially in the age of Brexit and Donald Trump (Orlando, 2017). The way in which Pratt and Luetchford use this metaphor, however, is entirely different from the values that lie behind the Brexit and Trump phenomena. The two authors' aim is essentially to adapt Polanyi's (1944/2001) concept of the self-protection of society to the food economy. Closure is therefore a useful metaphor to capture certain empirical processes and their cultural underpinnings, bearing in mind that full closure can never actually be achieved. Building a more closed food economy means strengthening personal relations of a non-exploitative kind (or weakening exploitative relations), bringing agriculture and urban spaces closer together, guaranteeing a just price to farmers and lobbying to raise the wages of those who cannot afford to pay for just prices, and favouring social and environmental regulation (De Neve, Luetchford, & Pratt, 2008). In this way, AFNs seek leverage to transform the "food-from-nowhere" economy into a "food-from-somewhere" one (McMichael, 2002).

Adapting Carole Counihan's (2004) concept of food as 'voice' of modernity, AFNs may thus be seen as representing one voice of the struggle between market and society. It therefore makes sense to ask what the effect of the 2008 financial crash has been on them. This is a difficult question to answer because of the complexity of the crash and the fact that what took place in a global disembodied sphere of exchange—the market for subprime mortgages—ended up having very different material consequences around the world (Bear, 2015; Hart, 2012; Hsing, 2012; Loftsdóttir, 2014; Ottone, 2012). In Europe, the rise of neoliberal austerity as the dominant political and economic ideology has been the main consequence (Varoufakis, 2016). But even austerity has meant very different things across the continent. In some countries, mostly southern European or peripheral ones, a sovereign debt crisis followed the financial crash, bringing with it painful structural adjustment programmes (Knight & Stewart, 2016). This has not happened elsewhere. Italy, for example, limps on the path to secular stagnation (Carlini, 2015; Furini, 2012; Pipyrou, 2014; Sassatelli, Santoro, & Semi, 2015). Countries like the UK and Germany, on the contrary, have recovered much more quickly, at least in terms of GDP and unemployment. Of course, austerity is not just about GDP and employment rates but about income levels, working hours, levels of inequality, social care, health care, and much more aside. The expression 'after the crisis,' then, can be read in many ways, but mainly in two, a double interpretation made possible by the fact that the crisis is both an event and a process. From the perspective of the event, the expression presupposes that the crisis has ended. From the perspective of process, the expression allows for the possibility that the crisis is still ongoing, regardless of macroeconomic indicators, because the event has set in motion a series of long-term phenomena inside which people now find themselves operating.

Four scenarios can therefore be imagined in order to make sense of how AFNs have changed after the crisis and during austerity: generation, strengthening, obstruction, and irrelevance. These scenarios are not mutually exclusive, taking place simultaneously across the variegated world of AFNs, often within the same initiative. In this chapter I will analyse their interplay through the study of a new Italian AFN called 'Off The Market.'

The chapter is structured as follows. The next section sets out the methodology of the research on which the chapter is based. The fourth one introduces the main actors through an ethnographic vignette, while the fifth discusses how the case illustrates the generation scenario. Section six then analyses the values that the actors in question share, highlighting strengthening, while section seven discusses the differences among the people who make up the network in order to illustrate obstruction and irrelevance. The conclusions end the chapter.

Methodology

This chapter is based on fieldwork carried out primarily in 2015 and intermittently thereafter, continuing to the present day.[2] The research began with a literature review of the topic conducted using academic and commercial search engines. The review allowed focusing on the main analytical issues discussed in the scientific community. The next step was a detailed sampling of relevant initiatives in Italy, carried out primarily using the Internet. Having thus built a general picture, the research concentrated on the AFN 'Off The Market', which was developed initially in Lombardy, near the city of Milan. The study of this particular case began by collecting as much grey material as possible on it (e.g. newspaper articles, press releases, audio-visual materials, etc.). Primary data collection followed. This phase consisted in participant observation of the network's activities and in a series of semi-structured, qualitative interviews with key informants and other actors. All the interviews and a number of significant events were audio-recorded. Considering the recent birth of OTM and its continuing evolution, the chapter will focus primarily on the history of the initiative up to the present.

'Off The Market'

In 2015 the city of Milan hosted the 33rd World Expo. Since it was first held in London at the height of colonialism, in 1851, the Expo has accompanied the history of the modern world system with increasing controversy (Sachs, 2010). The Milan Expo was all about food.[3] With the slogan of *Feeding the planet, energy for life*, the event wanted to reflect "the huge challenge of finding a balance between the nutrition of man and respecting the planet" (Expo, 2015). Praised relentlessly from all quarters, the event nevertheless attracted criticism for the poor social and environmental record of many of its partners (Cospe, 2015; Peracchi, 2015).[4] The day after its inauguration, I attended a protest picnic organized by two activist networks called Genuino Clandestino ('Illegally Genuine') and Fuori Mercato ('Off The Market'). The activists spoke from a microphone in defence of peasant agriculture and quality food, accusing the event's organizers of having jumped on the food bandwagon in order to line their pockets. The elephant in the room was Eataly, outside whose flagship store in Milan the picnic took place.

Eataly is a high-end food retailer modelled on Whole Foods Market that has made a name for itself by adding gourmet restaurants and educational spaces to this model. In the vision of its founder Oscar Farinetti (2009), people who visit Eataly are able not just to buy quality food but also to eat it on the premises and to learn about food through a variety of courses and events. From the beginning, Eataly has maintained a close relationship with Slow Food, Farinetti being a friend and fellow Piedmontese native of Carlo Petrini (Bukowski, 2015). The businessman was a vocal supporter of the Milan Expo, something that, alleged his critics, allowed him to obtain lucrative contracts for the event without going through public tender (Ferrarella, 2016). Already a symbol of culinary elitism, Eataly was targeted for its barefaced willingness to get cosy with the politicians and corporations running the mega-event. But to those who knew the retailer's past, this came as little surprise. Farinetti used to own Unieuro, Italy's biggest chain of electronic goods stores (Sartorio, 2008). At the beginning of the century, he sold the chain to the group Dixons Carphone for £230 million (Stevenson, 2002), using the money to establish his new food business. Eataly will soon be listed on the stock market thanks to a strong international presence that includes stores in New York, Tokyo, and Dubai (Insalaco, 2017). This operation will allow shareholders, potentially those in the technology sector, to (re)invest in quality food.

Eataly's story represents an excellent example of the dynamics that characterize the corporate food regime, as outlined in the chapter's introduction. The protests against it and the Expo denounced the elements of this regime. To go back to the distinction in the notion of AFN (that between a weak interpretation—alternative *food* network—and a strong one—alternative food *network*), we may say that Eataly reflects the former one, as does, for example, organic food sold in supermarkets, while Illegally Genuine and OTM reflect the latter. Piero,[5] one of the organizers of the protest, described Farinetti with the following words: "He's a very clever man who is always trying to undermine you. He will tell you he's your friend and then he will neutralize you."

OTM is an association that was born in 2013 from the collaboration between three groups of people: the ex-workers of an automotive factory near Milan that closed in 2012, a group of small farmers affiliated to Illegally Genuine, and a number of consumers from Milan's solidarity purchase groups.

The workers in question are involved in a project to create a 'recovered enterprise,' a term used to refer to instances in which failed businesses have been restarted without the involvement of their previous owners (Bryer, 2012). The term originated in Argentina in 2001, when the massive economic crisis that took place there at the time led to numerous cases of recovery. The Milan workers have not actually restarted producing car parts, which would be too expensive, but they have occupied the empty plant and use it for a number of activities, one of which is OTM. The farmers come from the Illegally Genuine network and the wider post-organic movement (Moore, 2006). The network was created in 2009 around Bologna, in Emilia Romagna, by a group of people who wanted to denounce the European Union's regulatory framework that governs organic farming and processing, which they feel unjustly favours agri-business. The initiative quickly became a national campaign (Potito & Borghesi, 2015). While these farmers agree with the philosophical principles of organic agriculture, they believe that the current EU system of regulation, and the retail sector it serves to underwrite, do not embody those principles and should therefore be superseded. Because they reject official certification, their food is 'illegally genuine.' In this sense, they represent a post-organic phase in the world of AFNs. OTM also includes a number of solidarity purchase groups who buy food directly from organic farmers in order to bypass supermarkets and stop supporting their exploitative practices.

The Generative Crisis

How did the crisis generate OTM? The answer lies in the activation of mutualism among the factory workers and among those who have helped them find new sources of income since they were laid off. It is this form of self-help and help from the 'outside'—solidarity—that has given rise to OTM. The story of the initiative clearly illustrates this.

When the workers decided to occupy the plant at the beginning of 2013, they realized that they needed to do two things: first, create support for their illegal action among the local population and political classes, and second, use the warehouse to generate income that could keep them going. They therefore embarked on a great number of actions, of the most different kind, which I will not cover here for reasons of space. During this period, one of their local contacts introduced them to a couple of members of a solidarity purchase group in Milan, who suggested they could prepare some homemade food and sell it to raise funds at one of the many events they were organizing. They also suggested buying the ingredients from farms in the neighbouring Agricultural Park, a large protected rural area whose boundary lies a short distance from the plant. The workers liked the idea and produced several hundred bottles of tomato sauce (*salsa*) and lemon-flavoured liquor (*limoncello*), common homemade foods in Italy.

The purchase group members also advised them to get in touch with a community shop in a neighbouring town where locals purchase produce directly from farmers of the Agricultural Park. Piero recounted: "One of the solidarity purchase groups in the area used to come and visit us to support the cause, and they made us realize that we are located right next to the Park, literally five hundred meters away from here. In the nearby town there's a nice little shop called Buon Mercato [Good Market], which already works with the purchase groups." The shop is run on a non-profit basis by an association and is based on premises owned by the municipality. Through a website, people order what they want and then collect it in person at the shop. The people running it suggested to the workers that they could try to set up a similar scheme in their own town, using the warehouse as delivery point. They would share the shop's website and its contacts, while the workers would help them collect the produce from the farmers. Piero again: "Good Market asked us if we could help them with the distribution part, with going around and collecting the stuff. For the previous two years this job had been done by a guy with his camper-van, on a voluntary basis, and he was sick of it." Once again, the workers thought this was a good idea and proceeded.

This is when OTM was actually born, essentially as a duplicate of the community shop. The name 'Off The Market' was adapted from the shop's milder 'Good Market.' The agreement went on for several months, until it became clear that the new initiative was not attracting enough customers to be economically viable, and was shelved. Enzo, one of the solidarity purchase group members involved, recalled: "Good Market manages to stand on its own feet, they have even created three part-time jobs. But their initiative [OTM] never really took off. They never managed to go beyond ten, fifteen orders a week, partly because they didn't put enough effort into it, partly because the area they're in isn't the best."

In the meantime, however, the workers had been put in contact with another group, a farmers' association in the southern Italian region of Calabria.[6] This association was struggling to send small parcels of food to each of the purchase groups it worked with in Milan because of the cost involved in terms of time and money. Giacomo is the factory worker who first established this contact: "One evening, during one of the many events we had organized, a man and a woman showed up. While we were chatting, he said: 'I'm in contact with a group in Rosarno that might be interested in collaborating with you. They grow citrus fruits, mainly oranges.' Basically, their problem was how to better organize the distribution here in Milan." After discussing the matter, the farmers agreed with the workers to use the warehouse as a storage facility and delegated to them the managing of the orders. Instead of one group of families in Milan ordering, for example, twelve jars of honey directly from the association in Calabria, and twenty other groups doing the same, the families would send their orders to the workers, who would collect them and then make a single order to the association. The farmers would then send the whole shipment to the warehouse, where the workers would divide it up and deliver it to the families in Milan. This arrangement proved more successful than the community shop because the workers did not have to build a new customer base from scratch, and has now been in place for five years. It represents the core of the OTM project.

Seeing the potential of this form of intermediation, in 2015 the workers started trying to expand it by including local farmers who could diversify the range of food on offer, complementing what was coming from Calabria. The formula would be the same, only this time the workers could also collect the produce directly from the farmers in Lombardy, given the shorter distances involved. In a sense, this project was a revised version of the initial one that failed (the community shop), with the addition of home delivery. To generate interest for it, the workers teamed up with the Milan node of Illegally Genuine and with other local activists. Together, they started organizing small independent farmer's markets during which they presented OTM. These markets have taken place in public squares, but also in squatted social centres and inside the occupied factory, usually to accompany cultural events. Alongside home delivery, the workers offer customers the possibility of bringing their orders to these markets, thus cutting the cost of the service. One of the promoters of this enlargement, Marco, described the process with these words:

> We began by reasoning that this arrangement [with the farmers in Calabria] could be applied also to other groups, as part of a project that links a number of different initiatives, like squatted social centres, solidarity purchase groups, various kinds of cultural associations, all in an effort to put ethical consumption at the heart of things.

The attempt to expand OTM has taken place also at the national level, once again with the help of Illegally Genuine. On this front, the workers have tried to establish new collaborations with farmers affiliated to the network all along the Italian peninsula, particularly those who are already involved in projects with special ethical connotations, like helping migrant farm workers or recovering heirloom plant varieties. In 2015, the annual gathering of Illegally Genuine was held at the occupied plant near

Milan, where the links between the two groups were strengthened and the idea of a national delivery service was officially discussed.

Food and Economic Values

To understand OTM's significance, it is particularly useful to reflect on the expressions used by its members to describe the problem posed by supermarkets and the possible solutions to it. Those involved in OTM constantly stress the importance of 'linking' the 'rings' and 'closing' the 'circles' and 'cycles' that are left open, or interrupted, by the existence of supermarkets. Marco, for example, said: "You try to create an integrated system that arrives from the producer to the consumer but which in reality promotes a meeting [of interests], going beyond the classic notions of supply and demand." Enzo spoke of "a closing of the circle of the solidarity economy." Piero of "building a circle of this kind, in which you can include the ARCI [Italy's biggest non-profit association], the CRAL [Italy's system of recreational workers' clubs], a canteen, the municipality, etcetera. You can build relations for an alternative circuit." Giacomo explained the OTM project with these words:

> The ring we want to close is the logistical one. I can be the best producer and you can be the best consumer, but in the end we've always got to use the usual guys for the delivery, DHL or whatever. OTM can become a project that connects the whole [Italian] peninsula. It could reach Tuscany to collect olive oil, or Umbria to collect lentils, or what have you. The idea is precisely to create a closed network that can prefigure an alternative system, a completely autonomous system from the supermarket one.

These spatial images convey in a direct manner the notion of a closed economy that safeguards against the siphoning off of value by the capitalist (open) economy. Through the building of such a closed economy, food is taken 'off the market.' 'Market' here is a synecdoche for supermarkets, its complexity having collapsed into a specific form of retail. It is only in this narrow sense that avoiding supermarkets can mean that food is no longer being sold ('taking something off the market' means to stop selling it, after all), even though food is still being exchanged through the medium of general-purpose money for a set price—it is still being sold, in other words. The classic definition of a commodity is 'something produced to be sold,' so for the OTM people, avoiding supermarkets means turning a commodity into its opposite, a commons or a gift. This is ultimately the meaning of the project's name.

The three groups in question (ex-workers, farmers, and consumers) share a critique of the corporate food regime that underscores their collaboration. At public events, in press releases, and on the Internet, OTM has fiercely criticized intensive agriculture, supermarkets, fast food restaurants, and agrochemical companies. The concept of food sovereignty has had a strong influence on the project, mainly as a result of the involvement of Illegally Genuine, which is inspired by the Via Campesina movement. Brazil's landless peasants, the Sem Terra, have also proven a point of contact between OTM's various actors. Also part of Via Campesina, the Sem Terra provided Argentina's recovered factories with their motto *ocupar, resistir, producir* (occupy, resist, produce), a motto which the Milan workers have also made their own, partly to recall their more famous Argentinean counterparts and partly to justify their collaboration with farmers. In Piero's words: "We've become aware of the issue of food sovereignty, of issues like those of the Sem Terra, the global justice movement, etcetera, which have mixed here with local initiatives we were also unaware of, because we used to be metalworkers." Giacomo explained further: "It's all part of what we're doing with Illegally Genuine and other movements that are involved in the fight for self-determination. We've organized a series of events. The core idea is to start talking about food again, because everyone has to eat."

One particular area of criticism has been the way in which forms of food production and consumption that used to be antagonistic to corporations, like organic and fair trade, have been turned into avenues for profit by those very corporations. Some among the solidarity purchase groups have been deeply disappointed by this turn of events, seeing their efforts to change the system through short supply chains neutralized by the new (at least in Italy) wealth of for-profit schemes that deliver local food on people's doorsteps. Marco's thoughts on this matter are particularly interesting:

> Every supermarket chain has an organic [food] line. That fight is over. The [new] fight is how to break the process that has led agriculture to produce not for [human] necessity but for the market. I have to ask myself: "How can I substitute production, logistics and consumption along the entire chain?" Because if I leave even one of these elements in the hands of the supermarkets, everything becomes completely self-referential. The fight will only be a residual one. The system will subsume you. The fact that everybody has an organic line these days means that they are able to defuse the revolutionary aspect of the desire for a different market. The whole project has to be—like we've called ours—off the market.

The OTM activists believe that to stop corporations from subsuming ever more sections of the food economy it is imperative to strengthen the relationship between those who grow food in an environmentally and socially responsible manner and those who are willing to buy such food. 'Strengthening' from this point of view means primarily organizing food provision outside the supermarket sector.

Talk of solidarity toward laid-off workers and the building of a closed economy between farmers and city dwellers can give the impression of a purposeful and coherent process whose politics are unproblematic and whose reach is only limited by the will of those involved in it. Nothing could be further from the truth. In the final substantive section, I want to discuss what the actors involved in this project of rediscovering the food common(s) do not have in common.

Conflicting Values and Practices of AFNs

The factory workers and the members of the solidarity purchase groups are aware that they have met coming from very different backgrounds. What led the workers down the path to OTM was the struggle to save their jobs. This began much earlier than the collaborations I have described thus far, back in 2009, when the company that owned their factory went into controlled administration one year into the financial crisis. After the company's clients terminated their contracts, the workers were put on benefits and the administrators began looking for a new owner. This period of limbo lasted two years, during which the workers embarked on a number of protests to draw attention to their plight and force the authorities to find a solution. At the time, their aim was finding a new buyer and securing new investments in the plant. Eventually, a Polish entrepreneur bought the business, taking advantage of generous financial incentives from the Italian state. Unfortunately, he was not interested in investing in it, but in acquiring the name, the patents, and the machinery. After the mandatory two years he had to wait to honour the agreement with the state, he closed the factory, laid off all the workers, and moved everything to Poland. It was at this point that some workers occupied the plant.

Industrial workers' struggles to save jobs and consumers' efforts to save diets or help farmers have usually little in common. However, when the Milan workers began the plant occupation, they announced that they wanted to recycle electronic goods. It is unclear to what extent they committed to this task, considering its complexities in terms of capital, authorizations, and know-how. The idea was probably part of a strategy to appear to be doing something good after having taken such a high-profile illegal action. The strategy paid off when the workers met the solidarity purchase groups, who saw favourably their desire to reconvert the plant to a more sustainable form of production. The consumers I spoke to often cited this initial impression as a reason to engage in the project, showing awareness that a 'simple' struggle to find new jobs would not have attracted their attention. Enzo, for example, had this to say on the matter:

> If we look at their initial situation, they decided to restart production on the basis of an ecological reconversion [of the plant]. I'm not saying that the solidarity purchase groups should not care about saving jobs. They should, but in terms of an ecological reconversion [of the economy]. So when they [the workers] spoke about recycling electronic appliances, it was a sign that they were thinking about environmental protection, which overlaps with the aims of a solidarity purchase group.

Still, the relationship with those involved in Milan's local food scene has been difficult. As I discussed earlier, OTM's first incarnation (the clone of the community shop) failed for lack of local interest. After five years, its core business—distributing Calabrian food in Milan—reaches only twenty purchase groups out of a total of almost 200 in the area. The workers and the consumers who help them complain that the reason for this lack of participation is that many purchase groups are not interested in the social aspect of local food consumption, but only in the health one. They accuse of this especially the newer groups. According to Piero:

> They have the most diverse motivations. Some people participate in them because they believe that the way you eat reflects your politics. Others say: "I want to eat healthily," but they're not interested in learning much more than this. If the Coop offers them something from its organic line they'll take it. "I trust the Coop, it's good stuff."

Even among those solidarity purchase groups that do participate in OTM, it is usually only a small number of individuals who push for participation, rather than the group as a whole. According to Enzo: "The gamble is all about the future of the project, but I'm thinking of some inside the purchase groups and some inside the local solidarity economy district, rather than of these groups as a whole. This need [to participate in the project] is true only for some people inside these initiatives."

The problem in question appears to be a result of the composite nature of Italy's solidarity economy. The fact that an idea which originated in Latin America with strong social connotations blended with the growth in concerns for food safety in Europe. On top of this, the activists argue that since the financial crisis, ethical consumers have become more price-conscious and thus unwilling to accept even the small extra cost that using OTM entails. Giacomo commented on this obstruction thus: "Unfortunately, solidarity purchase groups are often purchase groups, without the solidarity. They want to save money like everyone else, while it should be the project that's behind a producer that determines the choice of this product instead of that, which perhaps comes from another perfectly respectable organic farmer, but costs less than the first one."

This latter issue spills over into another area of obstruction: the disagreement about whether OTM's delivery work is at all necessary, or even justified. This difficulty stems from the fact that connecting farmers and city dwellers is a form of intermediation, something that is anathema to almost everyone in the Italian solidarity economy. Enzo was clearly concerned about this: "If the project really takes off… Of course, some solidarity purchase groups will look at it in a bad way, having to say to an organic producer who usually brings you the food once a month to bring it here [at the plant] twice a year. I'm sure someone will frown on this, because it poses some problems in terms of intermediation. There is the risk that [OTM] becomes another shop."

In Italy, fair trade set the tone of the solidarity economy back in the 1990s, emphasizing direct relations in a domestic context where people could actually meet farmers (in contrast to those in the developing world). Middlemen have long been fair trade's archetypal villains. So while this set of ideas has had many positive impacts, it has also meant that consumers who participate in AFNs largely expect farmers to bring food to the city themselves. While the cost of petrol will be included in the farmer's price, the cost of delivery *as a form of work* usually is not. Furthermore, all the paperwork required to make solidarity purchase groups function—receiving each family's order, adding everything up, sending it to the farmer, and eventually paying him—is usually done on a voluntary basis by members of the group themselves. For Giacomo, however, this is problematic: "The problem is that, in almost all cases, the purchase groups are run on a voluntary basis, which clashes with what is required when dealing with orders, shipments, crates, goods that have to be checked, etcetera: precision and punctuality. Two things you can't leave to voluntarism."

The workers and the consumers in OTM are aware of these problems and have tried to address them in three ways. First, by pointing out that they cannot be considered intermediaries in the pejorative sense that applies to middlemen, wholesalers, commercial delivery companies, and so on. The comparison would be absurd, they say. Second, they argue that the service they offer would considerably simplify the life of both farmers and consumers, especially in a heavily urbanized area like Milan, thus freeing up energy to help ethical consumption initiatives spread. As Enzo explained:

> Of course, at one level the short food supply chain should remain in place, in terms of visiting producers, of getting to know each other. This [OTM]

> can free up resources for the groups to do precisely that, not having to do all the delivery work themselves. They could invest energies in the more political aspects of the solidarity economy. But the need for this isn't recognized yet.

Thirdly, the ex-workers and (some of) the consumers have been keen to argue that any kind of work should be fairly remunerated, including that of bringing food directly from field to table, with all that it entails, from dealing with the paperwork to physically driving the van. Giacomo: "On a general level we think that work should be remunerated. Behind the management of the orders, the shipments, etcetera, there is a huge amount of work." While these are all valid points, they have failed to make any noticeable dent in the local solidarity economy. The efforts to expand the network of collaborators and supporters that I described earlier are aimed precisely at trying to achieve this.

The relationship with farmers has also been problematic. By their own admission, the workers and the consumers know that the farmers give the smallest contribution to the decision-making process in the project, simply because they are scattered, sometimes a long distance away from Milan, and already swamped with work, making them little inclined to attend endless meetings. As Piero explained: "The producers are not very integrated in the project, it's mostly the consumers. Possibly by increasing the number of producers their point of view will become more central and they will help us to fine tune certain aspects, saying for example: 'Look, it doesn't work the way you thought it would, because we've got also these problems'."

But there are other issues as well, which pertain more to the material and symbolic process of turning a commodity into a commons, or taking food 'off the market.' The crux of the matter has been the attempt to avoid conventional retailers in order to build a closed economy where value stays in the hands of those who create it. While the farmers do not have a problem with OTM acting as a middleman and delivering their produce (in contrast to some consumers, as I have shown), they do have a problem when their ethical commitments are questioned because of their dealings with retailers. Many of the individuals driving OTM have strong political beliefs, a consequence of which has been an attitude than can best be described as 'boycott.' Not organized boycotting campaigns, but rather a series of decisions about who to collaborate with. One example of this attitude was the decision to stop buying the tomatoes to make the bottles of sauce for the fundraisers from a local farmer who participated in the Milan Expo. Another one was the refusal to take part in a day of events, which included a farmer's market, also sponsored by the Expo.

While this strategy might safeguard ethical principles, it creates problems with farmers who point out that taking food 'off the market' is great if you can take a farm's entire production off it, but not so great when this operation involves only a small fraction of the produce. If the latter is true, they have to find other solutions in order to survive. Marco explained this situation well: "It's at this point that you have a discussion, knowing that you don't have a solution, because at the end of the day they will say to you—and perfectly reasonably—'Ok, if I've produced 100 and you, after all your talk, can only take away 10, what am I supposed to do with the other 90?'."

Some local farmers who participate in OTM have dealings with the high-end retailer Eataly, particularly those who specialize in artisanal foods, and this has been another area of friction. According to Marco:

> Up to now we've been guided by a few core principles: organic production, but not necessarily certified, small producers, but not re-sellers [of food grown by others], and people who don't have any links with the supermarkets and especially with the Expo. Going forward we'll have to look again at these criteria, because there are critical points. We have relations with producers against whom you can't really say anything bad, but who tell you: "Eataly has offered to stock my flour, in theory I'd like to say no to them, but I'm not in a position to do so, because I have to keep my business going."

According to Marco, even the farmers' association in Calabria, which is OTM's biggest partner, sells most of its organic oranges to a local wholesaler, through which they probably end up on the supermarkets' shelves. "In my opinion you can't simply say 'you're evil because you went with the enemy.' No. You have to take responsibility and say: 'The ethical consumption movement which I belong to is unable to absorb the whole of your production'."

Concluding Thoughts

The ex-workers and the consumers who collaborate with them in OTM are aware of the tensions and contradictions discussed in the previous section. Their attitude is mostly pragmatic, not radical for its own sake. In discussing these matters, they often talk about the state of 'power relations' or 'relations of force' to admit that there is little the farmers, and themselves, can do about these contradictions. These vivid expressions bring us back to the bigger picture of a corporate regime whose centrifugal forces tear open the places where food is grown, processed, distributed, and consumed. Financialization is a key factor in this process of economic opening, which reflects the escalating role that financial services play in our world. The crash of 2008 was the biggest wake-up call of this role to date, and its consequences are still being felt.

Drawing from a long line of thought in anthropology (Graeber, 2001, 2011; Gudeman, 2008; Hann & Hart, 2011; Hart, Laville, & Cattani, 2010; Narotzky & Besnier, 2014; Polanyi, 1944/2001, 1957), I have suggested that one way of approaching austerity is to see it as a planned reconfiguration of the boundaries between market and society. These boundaries have shifted back and forth many times since the birth of capitalism in the nineteenth century, the tension inherent to this process surfacing throughout our world. Alternative food networks are one example in which the principle of social protection, including the protection of nature, is applied in concrete experiments to try to contain the market principle. In the face of renewed assaults from the latter, four scenarios seem possible: generation, strengthening, obstruction, and irrelevance. In this chapter I chose to focus on the creation of new initiatives without silencing the many obstacles that stand in the way of envisioning, but especially of practising, food as a new commons.

Notes

1. By 'commodity' I mean the process of turning something into a commodity, not this or that object as (always) a commodity. Particular objects can take on different guises, so we should think in terms of processes of commodification rather than of objects being permanently commodities.

2. In 2015 data collection was carried out by the author under the supervision of Professor Francesca Forno, as part of the Working Group on Consumption, Networks and Practices of Sustainable Economies, Department of Humanities and Social Sciences, University of Bergamo. This part of the research was financed through the *Progetto ITALY®—Azione: Giovani in Ricerca 2014*.
3. See Teughels and Scholliers (2015) for an analysis of the role of food in World Exhibitions.
4. For a complete list of the Expo's partners, see http://www.expo2015.org/partner/ (last accessed 14 February 2017).
5. All the names used in the chapter are pseudonyms.
6. For two studies of this association, see Iocco and Siegmann (2017) and Oliveri (2015).

References

Bear, L. (2015). *Navigating Austerity: Currents of Debt Along a South Asian River*. Chicago: Stanford University Press.

Bernstein, H. (2016). Agrarian Political Economy and Modern World Capitalism: The Contributions of Food Regime Analysis. *The Journal of Peasant Studies, 43*(3), 611–647.

Bohannan, P., & Dalton, G. (Eds.). (1962). *Markets in Africa*. Evanston: Northwestern University Press.

Bryer, A. (2012). The Politics of the Social Economy: A Case Study of the Argentinean Empresas Recuperadas. *Dialectical Anthropology, 36*, 21–49.

Bukowski, W. (2015). *La danza delle mozzarelle. Slow Food, Eataly, Coop e la loro narrazione*. Roma: Edizioni Alegre.

Burch, D., & Lawrence, G. (2009). Towards a Third Food Regime: Behind the Transformation. *Agriculture and Human Values, 26*, 267–279.

Cospe. (2015). L'inaccettabile kermesse dell'insostenibilità. Retrieved from http://www.cospe.org/news/cospe-ed-expo-2015-linaccettabile-kermesse-dellinsostenibilita/

Counihan, C. (2004). *Around the Tuscan Table: Food, Family and Gender in Twentieth Century Florence*. London: Routledge.

De Neve, G., Luetchford, P., & Pratt, J. (2008). Introduction: Revealing the Hidden Hands of Global Market Exchange. In G. de Neve, P. Luetchford, J. Pratt, & D. Wood (Eds.), *Hidden Hands in the Market: Ethnographies of*

Fair Trade, Ethical Consumption and Corporate Social Responsibility (pp. 1–30). Bingley: Emerald.

Expo. (2015). The Meaning of Expo. Retrieved from http://www.expo2015.org/en/learn-more/the-history-/the-meaning-of-expo

Farinetti, O. (2009). *Coccodè. Il marketing-pensiero di Oscar Farinetti*. Milano: Giunti.

Ferrarella, L. (2016). Il giudice archivia Sala su Eataly: all'Expo non ci fu abuso d'ufficio. Retrieved from http://milano.corriere.it/notizie/cronaca/16_gennaio_19/giudice-archivia-sala-eataly-all-expo-non-ci-fu-abuso-d-ufficio-c82abfec-be8d-11e5-8000-980215fcd4e6.shtml

Fonte, M. (2006). Slow Food's Presidia: What Do Small Producers Do with Big Retailers? In T. Marsden & J. Murdoch (Eds.), *Between the Local and the Global: Confronting Complexity in the Contemporary Agri-Food Sector* (pp. 203–240). Oxford: Elsevier.

Friedmann, H. (1993). After Midas's Feast: Alternative Food Regimes for the Future. In P. Allen (Ed.), *Food for the Future: Conditions and Contradictions of Sustainability* (pp. 213–233). New York: Wiley.

Friedmann, H. (1994). Distance and Durability: Shaky Foundations of the World Food Economy. In P. McMichael (Ed.), *The Global Restructuring of Agro-food Systems*. Ithaca: Cornell University Press.

Friedmann, H. (2005). From Colonialism to Green Capitalism: Social Movements and Emergence of Food Regimes. In F. H. Buttel & P. McMichael (Eds.), *New Directions in the Sociology of Global Development* (pp. 227–264). Oxford: Elsevier.

Friedmann, H., & McNair, A. (2008). Whose Rules Rule? Contested Projects to Certify 'Local Production for Distant Consumers'. *Journal of Agrarian Change, 8*(2–3), 408–434.

Furini, L. (2012). *L'Italia in bolletta. Risparmi in fumo, debiti alle stelle: come si estingue il ceto medio*. Milano: Garzanti.

Goodman, D., DuPuis, M., & Goodman, M. (2012). *Alternative Food Networks: Knowledge, Practice, and Politics*. London: Routledge.

Goody, J. (1982). *Cooking, Cuisine and Class: A Study in Comparative Sociology*. Cambridge: Cambridge University Press.

Graeber, D. (2001). *Toward an Anthropological Theory of Value: The False Coin of Our Own Dreams*. New York: Palgrave Macmillan.

Graeber, D. (2011). *Debt. The First 5000 Years*. New York: Melville House.

Gregson, N., & Ferdous, R. (2014). Making Space for Ethical Consumption in the South. *Geoforum, 67*, 244–255.

Gudeman, S. (2008). *Economy's Tension: The Dialectics of Community and Market*. Oxford: Berghahn.

Hann, C., & Hart, K. (2011). *Economic Anthropology. History, Ethnography, Critique*. Cambridge: Polity Press.

Hart, K. (2012). The Roots of the Global Economic Crisis. *Anthropology Today, 28*(*2*), 1–3.

Hart, K., Laville, J.-L., & Cattani, A. D. (2010). Building the Human Economy Together. In K. Hart, J.-L. Laville, & A. D. Cattani (Eds.), *The Human Economy: A Citizen Guide* (pp. 1–17). Cambridge: Polity.

Heatherington, T. (2011). Introduction: Remaking Rural Landscapes in Twenty-First Century Europe. *Politicking the Farm: Transitions and Transformations in European Agriculture, Anthropological Journal of European Cultures, 20*(*1*), 1–9.

Hsing, Y. (2012). No Crisis in China? The Rise of China's Social Crisis. In M. Castells, J. Caraça, & G. Cardoso (Eds.), *Aftermath: The Cultures of the Economic Crisis* (pp. 251–277). Oxford: Oxford University Press.

Insalaco, C. (2017). Eataly, il regalo per i dieci anni è la Borsa. Retrieved from http://www.lastampa.it/2017/01/27/cronaca/la-festa-da-eataly-il-regalo-per-east-diecianni-la-borsa-farinetti-adesso-puntiamo-a-cina-india-e-far-1VU7UN4zoA7aG9v5htTlHO/pagina.html

Iocco, G., & Siegmann, K. (2017). A Worker-Driven Way Out of the Crisis in Mediterranean Agriculture. *Global Labour Column, 289*, 1–2.

Jung, Y., Klein, J. A., & Caldwell, M. L. (Eds.). (2014). *Ethical Eating in the Postsocialist and Socialist World*. Berkeley: University of California Press.

Kneafsey, M., Cox, R., Holloway, L., Dowler, E., Venn, L., & Tuomainen, H. (2008). *Reconnecting Consumers, Producers and Food. Exploring Alternatives*. New York: Berg.

Knight, D., & Stewart, C. (2016). Ethnographies of Austerity: Temporality, Crisis and Affect in Southern Europe. *History and Anthropology, 27*(*1*), 1–18.

Loftsdóttir, K. (2014). Iceland, Rejected by McDonald's: Desire and Anxieties in a Global Crisis. *Social Anthropology, 22*(*3*), 340–353.

Luetchford, P. (2014). Food and Consumption. In J. Pratt & P. Luetchford (Eds.), *Food for Change: The Politics and Values of Social Movements* (pp. 47–70). London: Pluto Press.

Luetchford, P., & Pratt, J. (2011). Values and Markets: An Analysis of Organic Farming Initiatives in Andalusia. *Journal of Agrarian Change, 11*(*1*), 87–103.

Marsden, T., Banks, J., & Bristow, G. (2000). Food Supply Chain Approaches: Exploring Their Role in Rural Development. *Sociologia Ruralis, 40*(*4*), 424–438.

McMichael, P. (2002). La restructuration globale des systems agro-alimentaires. *Mondes en Developpment, 30*(*117*), 45–54.

McMichael, P. (2008). Peasants Make Their Own History, But Not Just as They Please.... *Journal of Agrarian Change, 8*(2–3), 205–228.

McMichael, P. (2009). A Food Regime Genealogy. *The Journal of Peasant Studies, 36*(*1*), 139–169.

McMichael, P., & Friedmann, H. (2007). Situating the 'Retailing Revolution'. In D. Burch & G. Lawrence (Eds.), *Supermarkets and Agrofood Supply Chains. Transformations in the Production and Consumption of Foods*. Cheltenham: Edward Elgar.

Mintz, S. (1986). *Sweetness and Power. The Place of Sugar in Modern History*. New York: Vintage.

Moore, O. (2006). Understanding Postorganic Fresh Fruit and Vegetable Consumers at Participatory Farmers' Markets in Ireland: Reflexivity, Trust and Social Movements. *International Journal of Consumer Studies, 30*(*5*), 416–426.

Narotzky, S., & Besnier, N. (Eds.). (2014). Crisis, Value, and Hope: Rethinking the Economy. *Current Anthropology, 55*(Suppl. 9), 1–154.

Oliveri, F. (2015). A Network of Resistances Against a Multiple Crisis. SOS Rosarno and the Experimentation of Socio-economic Alternative Models. *Partecipazione e conflitto, 8*(*2*), 504–529.

Orlando, G. (2017). Solidarity Economies in the Age of Brexit and Trump. *Palaver, 6*(*2*), 165–178.

Ottone, E. (2012). A Non-Global Crisis? Challenging the Crisis in Latin America. In M. Castells, J. Caraça, & G. Cardoso (Eds.), *Aftermath: The Cultures of the Economic Crisis* (pp. 278–302). Oxford: Oxford University Press.

Peracchi, E. (2015). Il Forum Diritti Lavoro denuncia: "Volontari irregolari, Expo risparmia milioni." Retrieved from http://video.repubblica.it/edizione/milano/milano-il-forum-diritti-lavoro-denuncia-volontari-irregolari-expo-risparmia-milioni/197481/196509?ref=search

Petrini, C. (2005). *Buono, pulito e giusto: principi di nuova gastronomia*. Torino: Einaudi.

Pipyrou, S. (2014). Cutting *bella figura*: Irony, Crisis, and Secondhand Clothes in South Italy. *American Ethnologist, 41*(*3*), 532–546.

van der Ploeg, J. D. (2008). *The New Peasantries: Struggles for Autonomy and Sustainability in an Era of Empire and Globalization*. London: Earthscan.

Polanyi, K. (1944/2001). *The Great Transformation: The Political and Economic Origins of Our Times*. Boston: Beacon Press.

Potito, M., & Borghesi, R. (2015). *Genuino clandestino. Viaggio tra le agri-culture resistenti ai tempi delle grandi opere*. Firenze: Terra Nuova Edizioni.

Pratt, J. (2014). Farming and Its Values. In J. Pratt & P. Luetchford (Eds.), *Food for Change: The Politics and Values of Social Movements* (pp. 24–46). New York: Pluto Press.

Pratt, J., & Luetchford, P. (Eds.). (2014). Introduction. In *Food for Change: The Politics and Values of Social Movements* (pp. 1–23). New York: Pluto Press.

Sachs, W. (Ed.). (2010). Preface to the New Edition. In *The Development Dictionary: A Guide to Knowledge as Power* (2nd ed., pp. vi–xiv). London: Zed Books.

Sage, C. (2012). *Environment and Food*. London: Routledge.

Sartorio, A. (2008). *Il mercante di utopie*. Milano: Sperling & Kupfer.

Sassatelli, R., Santoro, M., & Semi, M. (2015). *Fronteggiare la crisi. Come cambia lo stile di vita del ceto medio*. Bologna: il Mulino.

Stevenson, R. (2002). Dixons in £230m UniEuro Takeover. Retrieved from https://www.independent.co.uk/news/business/news/dixons-in-pound230m-unieuro-takeover-613617.html

Teughels, N., & Scholliers, P. (Eds.). (2015). *A Taste of Progress: Food at International and World Exhibitions in the Nineteenth and Twentieth Centuries*. London: Routledge.

Varoufakis, Y. (2016). *And the Weak Suffer What They Must? Europe, Austerity and the Threat to Global Stability*. London: Bodley Head.

Watts, D., Ilbery, B., & Maye, D. (2005). Making Reconnections in Agro-food Geography: Alternative Systems of Food Provision. *Progress in Human Geography, 29*(*1*), 22–40.

Wiskerke, J. S. C. (2009). On Places Lost and Places Regained: Reflections on the Alternative Food Geography and Sustainable Regional Development. *International Planning Studies, 14*(*4*), 369–387.

Part III

AFNs from the Producers' Viewpoint

8

Introduction to Part III: AFNs from the Producers' Viewpoint

Alessandro Corsi, Filippo Barbera, and Silvia Novelli

A large part of the literature on Alternative Food Networks (AFNs) deals with consumers. This is because the earlier literature focused mainly on the new perspectives that AFNs opened for a critique of the globalized food system. Much of the criticism, at least in the main political arena,

A. Corsi (✉)
Department of Economics and Statistics "Cognetti de Martiis", University of Torino, Torino, Italy
e-mail: alessandro.corsi@unito.it

F. Barbera
Department of Cultures, Politics and Society, University of Torino, Torino, Italy

Collegio Carlo Alberto, Torino, Italy
e-mail: filippo.barbera@unito.it

S. Novelli
Department of Agricultural, Forest and Food Sciences, University of Torino, Grugliasco (TO), Italy
e-mail: silvia.novelli@unito.it

A. Corsi et al. (eds.), *Alternative Food Networks*,
https://doi.org/10.1007/978-3-319-90409-2_8

originated from food scandals such as mad cow disease, dioxin chickens, and the like, that deeply shocked the public and called "industrial" production into question. This was soon followed by a more general concern for the environment and attention to agricultural production techniques and methods, an attention that had been raised by the organic movement since its origins. These tendencies, however, were part of a long-term trend affecting consumption habits in developed countries, with a shift from quantity to quality. Quality is something of an umbrella term covering many concepts, from taste to safety to health, to mention only those that are most often cited by consumers and without going into the intangible attributes. All this explains why academic interest was chiefly directed to consumers, especially in the geographic and sociological fields. In a way, farmers were often implicitly viewed as beneficiaries of a support offered by consumers. Not all research shared this view, though. In particular, scholars interested in the operation of Farmers' Markets (FMs) were aware of the interplay between consumers' and producers' preferences and interests (e.g., Kirwan, 2006).

It is nevertheless interesting to put these consumption trends in perspective, because of their links with production. Food availability has historically been a major concern for the public and for governments. Famines regularly hit the population in the past, and hunger was widespread even in Europe until the twentieth century, even if it was rarely as severe as it was during the Great Famine of the 1840s in Ireland. Thus, increasing production was a priority and, since land is scarce, raising yields was the way to reach it. The huge increase in land productivity was made possible by the technological progress sparked by the application of scientific knowledge to agriculture. Both land-saving (yield-increasing) and labour-saving new technologies and inputs were widely employed. Among the former, chemical fertilizers and pesticides, as well as improvements in agronomic techniques, were the most important. Among the latter, mechanization and chemical herbicides were prominent. This technical progress created economies of scale that, although much lower than in many industrial sectors, encouraged agricultural operations to expand and thus brought about a decrease in the number of farms and, especially, the decline of small and medium-sized farms. The economies of scale are particularly strong in animal husbandry, which explains why it is the most "industrialized" sector. In economic terms, there has been a major change in the input mix, with a drastic reduction in the share of labour and land, and a dramatic increase in the share of capital per unit of output, a change in its turn driven by the shift in their relative prices. In the half century between 1950 and 2000, for instance, Italy's agricultural output doubled in real terms, notwithstanding a 80 per cent decrease in labour and one third decrease in farmed land, thanks to an approximately 5000 per cent increase in mechanization and a doubling of intermediate inputs (fertilizers, pesticides, fuel). The main driver of this change is that in the same period the price of labour increased 10 times relative to the price of mechanical inputs, 4.6 times relative to the price of land and 8.6 times relative to the price of intermediate inputs (Rizzi & Pierani, 2007), so that the input mix had changed in favour of the cheapest inputs. This change in the input mix (which is common to all developed countries) was thus a strong incentive to intensify, and as long as demand centred on undifferentiated agricultural commodities, competition was price-based, which reinforced the tendency to reduce costs. Basic food consumption is income-inelastic, and Engel's law predicts (as indeed occurs) a decrease in the proportion of total household expenditure spent on food. This steps up the competitive pressure on agriculture, which is thus pushed even harder to intensify production and exploit any available economies of scale. Remembering these facts helps in understanding that there are powerful economic reasons behind the spread of the "industrial" model of agriculture and that some of the benefits it brought are undeniable. In a way, however, the backlash against "industrial" agriculture was fuelled by its own success. Once everyone in developed countries had plenty of cheap food and a higher income, consumers could also afford to spend more for food. Since some consumers, if not all, prefer variety, they began to look for better food. A shift from a vegetable-based diet to a diet rich in protein, and animal protein in particular, usually accompanies increases in per capita income. However, a shift to a more diversified diet is also common, since standardized food no longer satisfies consumers. The demand for healthier, tastier and more environmentally friendly food grows.

What is farmers' role in these trends? Farmers differ widely in what they produce, in the size of their farms, in their skills and their preferences. Arguably, they also differ in their interest, both monetary and non-monetary, in participating in AFNs. Nevertheless, farmers are more constrained in their choices by objective, monetary constraints than consumers are. After all, farmers can go bankrupt if they make choices that are not compatible with the need to recover costs through revenues. And some agricultural production is subject to technical constraints that leave little room for different orientations in farm operation. Hence, economic accounting of revenues and costs is undoubtedly part of the decision process for choosing whether or not to participate in AFNs. As analysed in Chap. 9, both revenues and costs change with this choice. AFNs usually provide higher prices, but they very often entail higher costs as well, so that profitability is not guaranteed. Two other warnings, important for their policy implications, come from the economic analysis. The first is that shortening the chain does not make distribution costs disappear, as some of the rhetoric on AFNs and on short chains would have us believe. The second is that, when labour and capital for the new distribution chain are provided by farmers, a larger share of the value added accruing to them does not necessarily translate into higher profitability: for the new chain to be more profitable, the larger share of value added must be sufficient to adequately compensate the higher contribution in labour and capital (i.e., farmers must receive a return at least equal to the market wage and interest rate).

These considerations bring us to the issue of farmers' motivations for participating in AFNs. Since farms are economic enterprises, income is undoubtedly among farmers' concerns. When directly questioned about their motivations, farmers obviously cite higher received prices and increased sales (Brunori, Rossi, & Malandrin, 2007; Griffin & Frongillo, 2003; Hunt, 2007; Kirwan, 2006; Logozar & Schmit, 2009). However, these authors have also found other motivations, such as the direct relationship with customers, pride in raising and marketing one's own products and cooperation with other vendors. Technical reasons, such as small farms' inability to meet the volume required by wholesalers, may be another motive for choosing alternative channels (Gale, 1997).

The role of technical and economic constraints is shown by the analysis of the objective, observable determinants of farmers' participation in direct sales (Chap. 9). For example, it illustrates that not all agricultural products lend themselves to direct sales, that the difficulties of agriculture in marginal mountain and hilly areas push farmers to engage more in direct sales and that geographical proximity to consumers is important not so much because of lower transport costs, but rather in terms of potential patrons. Unlike previous studies, our analysis found that farm size is not particularly relevant, which supports the argument cited above that farms are highly heterogeneous as regards the potential revenues and costs of alternative chains. That personal characteristics such as age, gender and education have only a weak influence on the choice of alternative chains is also indicative of this heterogeneity, so that idiosyncratic factors are very important in this respect. Determinants other than income thus come into play. In fact, although earning enough income for the farm to survive is a prerequisite for farmers' choices, a certain degree of freedom nevertheless exists in family farms, since family labour is unpaid but its reward stems from farm income. Therefore, farmers can trade off a lower income for a type of operation, a farm setting or a marketing chain that suits their preferences better, and both the literature and our empirical analysis show that individual preferences do in fact count. Farmers' degree of adherence to strictly monetary or non-monetary goals differs both individually and across farmers supplying different AFNs. Different AFNs have different "degrees of alternativeness", along a continuum that sees Solidarity Purchase Groups (SPGs) and Community Supported Agriculture (CSA) at one end and district markets at the other. In a small sample of farmers selling in urban district markets in Torino, for example, Siclari (2017) finds that the highest-rated motivation for attending it is profitability, while the opportunity to promote one's products comes second. The rating assigned to the pleasure of personal contact with consumers is much lower, which is consistent with the nature of district markets, which do not target committed consumers and producers and where self-interested and income-oriented behaviour thus plays a larger role.

Social factors strongly shape the operation of AFNs through the farmers' preferences that determine their participation. They may range from enjoying the sociability found in farmers' markets (Hunt, 2007; Kirwan, 2006) to professional pride in the quality of one's products and the desire to avoid technical practices imposed by the conventional chain and which are at odds with the farmers' idea of what is right (Chap. 9). But all of these factors are connected with the personal producer-consumer relationships that are the main characteristic of AFNs. The pride fruit growers show in their product's quality stems from the patrons' recognition and praise (Chap. 9), in the same way as farmers selling in the Porta Palazzo market are careful to provide the quality, such as freshness, required by consumers (Chap. 11). Indeed, it is around the concept of quality that much of the social interplay revolves. The concepts of quality differ across consumers, individually and among participants in different chains (Chap. 5), while consumers and farmers interact in adapting to each other's concepts. Sometimes consumers send signals to producers, who update their quality conventions accordingly, abandoning certain products and introducing new ones. Sometimes producers have an educational role, teaching consumers to appreciate certain qualities of their products or suggesting how to cook them. Complex social interactions also take place among farmers, as shown by the modalities of setting prices (Chap. 11). Competition and cooperation coexist, farmers selling in the market feel part of a group, but at the same time are competitors, and must take the others' behaviour into account when setting their prices. Here again, we find that monetary and non-monetary considerations both enter the equation as drivers of farmers' behaviour. For farmers participating in AFNs, the economic variables seem more a constraint, a precondition for other objectives, than an objective per se. These farmers are not profit-maximizers, they are utility-maximizers. They are aware that their work should have an appropriate reward, but often accept that it be under-remunerated, as a result of economic constraints, such as the price levels set by other competitors, in exchange for benefits other than income.

The analysis of how Solidarity Purchase Groups operate also sheds light on social ties, personal motivations and economic constraints (Chap. 10). SPGs are organizations that connect producers and consumers, actively supporting conscious food consumption and favouring small farmers and environmentally friendly agriculture (Brunori, Rossi, & Guidi, 2012; Saroldi, 2001; Schifani & Migliore, 2011). But they also have an economic role, in buying from farmers and selling to end consumers. The question of the reconciliation of economic constraints and non-monetary objectives arises here too. The SPGs' solution lies in their members' voluntary work. It is a win-win solution, since it allows SPGs to operate with a balanced budget and at the same time satisfies the members' preferences. Members are strongly committed to the SPGs (Chap. 4), and the voluntary work they provide to the group's operation can be regarded as a measure of their commitment. The analysis of several SPGs' budgets

(Chap. 10) proves that this voluntary work is indeed the key for keeping the group viable, paying fair prices to farmers without marking up the prices paid by members. Even if members' motivations can include some monetary benefit, as well as self-interested motivations about the intrinsic attributes of AFN food (freshness, seasonality, taste, etc.), non-monetary motivations are undoubtedly dominant, and socialization among members and personal relationships with farmers are among them (Chap. 4). While intrinsic food attributes can be also provided by conventional chains, socialization and producer-consumer personal relationships cannot, which makes AFNs distinctive.

Summing up, the findings of the studies presented in this chapter suggest that (1) farmers are heterogeneous as regards the profitability of their participation in AFNs and their subjective interest in other intangible benefits of participating; (2) as participation in AFNs must be economically viable, both for farmers and in SPGs, economic and technical constraints are always at work; (3) other determinants also motivate farmers and SPG members and leaders, including preferences for intangible, self-interested or altruistic benefits from participation; (4) the strength of these determinants is not uniform, but is distributed along a continuum that sees the most "militant" AFNs, like SPGs and committed farmers, at one end and farmers who are mainly interested in the income they can receive from participating at the other; (5) complex social relationships govern the interplay between farmers and consumers, as well as between farmers; and (6) all social and economic relationships in AFNs share the characteristic of being based on *personal* knowledge and *personal* relationships, which is what makes these chains alternative.

References

Brunori, G., Rossi, A., & Guidi, F. (2012). On the New Social Relations around and Beyond Food. Analysing Consumers' Role and Action in Gruppi di Acquisto Solidale (Solidarity Purchasing Groups). *Sociologia Ruralis, 52*(1), 1–30.

Brunori, G., Rossi, A., & Malandrin, V. (2007). Co-producing Transition: Innovation Processes in Farms Adhering to Solidarity-Based Purchase Groups (GAS) in Tuscany, Italy. *International Journal of Sociology of Agriculture & Food, 18*(1), 28–53.

Gale, F. (1997). Direct Farm Marketing as a Rural Development Tool. *Rural Development Perspectives, 12*, 19–25.

Griffin, M. R., & Frongillo, E. A. (2003). Experiences and Perspectives of Farmers from Upstate New York Farmers' Markets. *Agriculture and Human Values, 20*, 189–203.

Hunt, A. R. (2007). Consumer Interactions and Influences on Farmers' Market Vendors. *Renewable Agriculture and Food Systems, 22*(1), 54–66.

Kirwan, J. (2006). The Interpersonal World of Direct Marketing: Examining Conventions of Quality at UK Farmers' Markets. *Journal of Rural Studies, 22*(3), 301–312.

Logozar, B., & Schmit, T. M. (2009). *Assessing the Success of Farmers' Markets in Northern New York: A Survey of Vendors, Customers, and Market Managers*. Department of Applied Economics and Management, College of Agriculture and Life Sciences, Cornell University, EB 2009-08. Retrieved from http://ageconsearch.umn.edu/record/55941?ln=en

Rizzi, P. L., & Pierani, P. P. (2007). *Agrefit. Ricavi, costi e produttività dei fattori nell'agricoltura delle regioni italiane (1951–2002)*. Milano: Franco Angeli.

Saroldi, A. (2001). *Gruppi di acquisto solidali. Guida al consumo locale*. Bologna: Edizioni EMI.

Schifani, G., & Migliore, G. (2011). Solidarity Purchase Groups and the New Critical and Ethical Consumer Trends: First Results of a Direct Study in Sicily. *New Medit, 10*(3), 26–33.

Siclari, I. (2017). *I Farmers' Market come canale distributivo. Il caso delle aree riservate agli agricoltori nei mercati rionali di Torino*. Tesi di Laurea Magistrale (Unpublished), University of Torino.

9

Determinants of Farmers' Participation in AFNs

Alessandro Corsi, Silvia Novelli, and Giacomo Pettenati

An Economic Framework for Farmers' Choice of Participating in AFNs

Farmers are at the beginning of any food chain, but their behaviour is particularly important for Alternative Food Networks (AFNs), in which they represent the supply side.

A. Corsi
Department of Economics and Statistics "Cognetti de Martiis", University of Torino, Torino, Italy
e-mail: alessandro.corsi@unito.it

S. Novelli (✉)
Department of Agricultural, Forest and Food Sciences, University of Torino, Grugliasco (TO), Italy
e-mail: silvia.novelli@unito.it

G. Pettenati
Department of Cultures, Politics and Society, University of Torino, Torino, Italy
e-mail: giacomo.pettenati@unito.it

A. Corsi et al. (eds.), *Alternative Food Networks*,
https://doi.org/10.1007/978-3-319-90409-2_9

From the theoretical point of view, farmers' choice to participate in an AFN is rather simple if it is assumed that their goal is maximising their profits and that the production mix and production costs are not affected by the choice of marketing chain. If this is the case, then the choice consists only of deciding which marketing chain is most profitable, and boils down to assessing revenues and costs for all available chains, and then calculating which chain offers the greatest difference between revenues and costs.

Revenues depend on quantities and prices. Choosing a different, non-conventional, chain may entail some difference in quantities produced and sold. For example, Verhaegen and Huylenbroeck (2001) cite the slight reduction in production of lettuce because of the need to have it throughout the season when selling at farmers' markets (FMs). The main difference is nevertheless in prices. There is much uncertainty about whether prices for consumers are higher or lower in AFNs. The situations may vary considerably, from higher prices in some FMs to lower ones in some Solidarity Purchase Groups (SPGs). But the crucial difference is in the prices received by farmers. From this point of view, the consensus is that they are higher than in other available chains. Nevertheless, this does not automatically translate into higher profits. The price to the end consumer reflects all costs entailed in the entire chain, that is, the production costs of the agricultural products, plus all costs connected with the subsequent stages of the chain. Depending on the product, these stages can include storage, refrigeration, sorting, packaging, possibly processing and transformation, transport, selling, and so on. In each stage of the chain, inputs (capital, labour, intermediate inputs) are used, the associated costs are incurred, and value is added to the product. In a perfectly competitive market, the final price reflects the sum of all these costs. Real markets are often different from theoretical ones, and it is quite possible that some middlemen have market power, so that they collect a rent and the retail-farmgate marketing margin is not fully justified by the costs. Direct sales between producers and consumers are frequently advocated on the grounds of the large marketing margins between farmgate and retail prices. The argument goes on to say that direct sales allow farmers to retain a larger share of the chain's added value (Brunori et al., 2016; Brunori, Rossi, & Guidi, 2012; Schmitt, Keech, Maye, Barjolle, & Kirwan, 2016). Nevertheless, even if the middlemen are cut out, the distribution costs do not disappear. Costs may be different and, above all, they are borne by different operators. For instance, a farmer who decides to sell to SPGs instead of to the wholesaler will have to buy a refrigerator for his/her fruit and bear the associated cost, which otherwise would be borne by the wholesaler. Farmers selling at FMs or at urban district markets have to bear the cost of transport, the labour cost of the sale hours and the market fees they are charged. For on-farm sales, transport costs are borne by consumers, but the farmer must still devote labour time to the sales. Value added is the remuneration of the primary factors (labour, capital, land) that, in different chains and in each stage of the chain, are provided by different operators. Hence, for a farmer considering, for instance, whether to start direct sales at an FM, the question is not only whether this change will bring an increase in income, but also whether this increase provides a sufficient return on the additional production factors he/she will have to provide. In particular, the return on the additional capital needed should be comparable to the market interest rate or to the opportunity cost of alternative investments, and the return on the additional labour should be comparable to market wages. Hardesty and Leff (2010) show that the higher revenue stemming from higher prices in AFNs can be offset by the higher marketing costs that they entail. Hence, the claim often made by farmers' unions to a larger share of the chain's value added, or the larger share of value added as a benefit for farmers (Aguglia, De Santis, & Salvioni, 2011; Darby, Batte, Ernst, & Roe, 2008; Monson, Mainville, & Kuminoff, 2008) could be misleading if the larger share does not sufficiently repay the larger resources provided by farmers.

The return on labour raises a further issue when it is provided by the farmers and by their households, that is, when it is unpaid labour in family farms. Its remuneration is then its opportunity cost, that is, what farmers could gain from an alternative use of their time. Nevertheless, when there is no opportunity cost (for instance, because there are no job opportunities due to unemployment in the area, or to lack of skills, so that it would be impossible for farmers to access other gainful activities), the cost of labour becomes a subjective wage and is the minimum return that farmers are willing to accept for working. Since AFNs are typically labour-intensive, it would not be surprising if they are more attractive for small farms where there is excess labour with low or no opportunity cost and where farmers may thus be willing to undertake an additional activity at low returns. This is certainly not the case for all farmers participating in AFNs, but it is a part of the trend. In addition to the operating costs connected with the different stages of the chain, transaction costs must also be considered (Verhaegen &

Huylenbroeck, 2001). Transaction costs are the costs incurred in collecting the information needed to perform the transaction, negotiating an agreement with the partner, and checking that the agreement is respected. In case of a new chain, they can be substantial, particularly for AFNs such as SPGs, which involve a rather complicated organisation.

The family labour provided in AFN activities raises a further consideration, connected to farmers' motivations. Indeed, it cannot be taken for granted that farmers are motivated only by the search for profits. In the language of economics, farmers try to maximise their utility (their welfare), which depends on income and on other variables, subject to constraints. There can be many objectives other than income. For example, a fruit grower we interviewed said that one of his reasons for joining an SPG was his refusal to abide by the strict production rules dictated by the cooperative to which he had formerly brought his produce, which in his view did not make it possible to convey the real quality of his fruit (Novelli & Corsi, 2018). This applies to any non-monetary motivation that farmers may have, for instance, pride in their work and their products, pleasure from socialising with customers, environmental concerns, and so on. In such cases, if the alternative chain provides a lower income than the previous one, the farmer must trade off the psychic benefit with the benefit stemming from higher profits. Non-monetary rewards of participation can actually offset monetary losses. For instance, Uematsu and Mishra (2011) find a negative impact of participation in FMs on farm incomes and suggest that farmers may continue to participate for a number of reasons: not only can farmers' markets be a risk management tool and provide opportunities to advertise their products and increase their entrepreneurial skills, there may also be a non-monetary benefit like socialisation with other farmers and consumers in the community. This justifies the empirical research found in the literature on assessing farmers' motivations for attending AFNs and on identifying characteristics that farmers participating in AFNs have in common.

Regardless of farmers' motivations, if different chains are available, farmers must decide whether to use only one or a combination. The first choice is the most appropriate if the marginal benefit (the additional benefit deriving from a small increase in the product marketed on the chain, which is the additional profit for a farmer who has only monetary motivations) is constant or increasing. In these cases, it is better to deliver all the production to the chain providing the highest profit. If, by contrast, marginal profits are diminishing (for instance, because costs increase more than proportionally with the marketed quantity), then sending the production to a combination of chains is more profitable. Another rationale for the frequently observed behaviour of utilising a conventional chain in addition to the alternative one is that there may be a maximum limit to the quantities the AFN can absorb, so that the rest of the production is sent to the conventional chain. This is what happens when, for instance, farmers cannot sell their entire production at FMs, and the remainder is sold to wholesalers or at auction. In addition, products sent to the conventional chain must often meet pack and grade standards, so that a part of the produce is sorted out and is unpaid, but can still be sold through direct marketing channels (Hardesty & Leff, 2010). Profitability (profits per dollar of revenue) nevertheless depends on production costs, and because of the different weight of marketing costs on total costs, profitability can be higher in the wholesale chain for low levels of production costs and lower in the opposite case.

This theoretical discussion cannot end without mentioning a further issue, the consequences for farms of attending AFNs. Very often, starting to sell at an FM or to SPGs forces a change in the farm setting, in order to meet demand. For instance, fruit growers are pressed to grow a wider range of types and cultivars to satisfy consumers' taste for variety and to extend the selling season, while vegetable growers similarly have to grow different crops through the seasons (Novelli & Corsi, 2018). In general, the changes tend to favour polyculture and reduce specialisation. Hence, farmers can lose some economies of scale brought by specialised production. If this is the case, then considering only the distribution costs of the goods produced would not be sufficient in order to make a rational choice of the chain. The appropriate comparison would be between the benefits and costs of alternative farm settings, one designed for the AFN and the other for the conventional chain, both considering the whole process from production to the product's final destination.

Farmers' Motivations

A number of studies have investigated farmers' motivations for attending AFNs, though not as many as those concerning consumers' motivations. The few direct surveys of farmers have found, obviously, that motivations include higher received prices and increased sales (Brunori, Rossi, & Malandrin, 2011; Griffin & Frongillo, 2003; Hunt, 2007; Kirwan, 2006; Logozar & Schmit, 2009). However, non-monetary motivations are often indicated. The same authors cite the direct relationship with customers as an important reason expressed by farmers for attending AFNs. Pride in raising and marketing one's own products, working together with other farmer-vendors, and providing customers with honest information is reported by Griffin and Frongillo (2003), while Logozar and Schmit (2009) mention the satisfaction in having customers return. Brunori et al. (2011) find in general that farmers who join an SPG "are motivated by a combination of 'push' motivations (political and ethical commitments, the search for farming styles that are consistent with their own values, unsatisfactory remuneration of prices from conventional channels, the search for better quality of life) and 'pull' motivations (opportunities emerging from contacts activated by GAS [the Italian acronym for SPG] or initiatives started by other farmers)". At times, technical reasons are indicated as determining the choice of direct sales. Gale (1997) suggests that small farms may choose this channel because they are unable to meet the volume required by wholesalers.

These studies show that there is no unique motivation for joining alternative chains and that monetary and non-monetary motivations can coexist. This is consistent with the often mixed use of different chains by farmers, who frequently "'dip in and out' of different conventional nodes [...] several 'alternative' producers are either obliged, or choose, to make use of conventional channels" (Ilbery & Maye, 2005).

Characteristics of Farmers and Farms Engaged in AFNs

Another stream of literature examines the characteristics of farms and farmers participating in AFNs. On the basis of US Agricultural Census data, Martinez et al. (2010) show that most farms that sell directly to consumers are small and that direct sales are mostly practised by produce farms, often in combination with other activities. In France (Aubert, 2015) and in Italy (Aguglia et al., 2011), farms that practise direct sales are smaller in size than those that do not.

Apart from descriptive data, the characteristics of farmers and farms that are most conducive to direct selling or other AFNs are typically assessed using discrete choice statistical models (Aguglia et al., 2011; Aubert, 2015; Bonanno, Pascucci, Caracciolo, & Cembalo, 2014; Capt & Wavresky, 2014; Corsini, Randelli, Rocchi, & Giampaolo, 2018; Detre, Mark, Mishra, & Adhikari, 2011; Dimitri, 2011; Low & Vogel, 2011; Monson et al., 2008; Sage & Goldberger, 2012; Uematsu & Mishra, 2011). One common finding is that direct sales are favoured by small farm size. There are several reasons for this outcome. It can be difficult for small farmers to overcome the entry barriers to supplying supermarkets, due to minimum-volume, quality, or certification requirements, while large farms can reduce marketing costs by selling large quantities to few buyers (Gandee, Brown, & D'Souza, 2003; Monson et al., 2008). Small farms with excess family labour can advantageously employ it in an additional gainful activity (Aguglia et al., 2011), so that the number of family members is found to favour direct or short chain sales (Aubert, 2015). High-value or specific crops (vegetables, fruits, wine, and olives, depending on the country) and organic farming are also generally associated with a higher probability of direct sales (Aguglia et al., 2011; Aubert, 2015; Bonanno et al., 2014; Capt & Wavresky, 2014; Corsini et al., 2018; Detre et al., 2011; Low & Vogel, 2011; Uematsu & Mishra, 2011).[1] This is partly due to demand factors (consumers in AFNs are usually more interested in fresh fruit and vegetables and organic produce) and partly to small farms' tendency to grow higher value crops to relax the land constraint. Also in connection with both supply and demand factors, several of the papers cited above find a positive effect of vicinity to urban centres, as do county-level studies (Low & Vogel, 2011). Metro areas offer a large number of potential customers and, from the supply side, closeness to these areas reduces farmers' transport costs. With the exception of Detre et al. (2011), these papers suggest that younger operators are more likely to opt for direct sales, which could be explained by the longer time horizon for returns on the investments in physical and human capital needed to adopt a new marketing strategy. The change to alternative chains is also favoured by agricultural education (Aubert, 2015; Corsini et al., 2018).

Some authors attempt to classify different groups of farmers participating in AFNs. Brunori et al. (2011) find that farmers supplying SPGs in

Tuscany belong to two different types, viz., "neo-peasants" ("the most important players in the 'rural renaissance' in this region, as they have been the pioneers of organic farming and of the multifunctional agricultural business model") and "local farmers", people with an agricultural family background who are strongly integrated with the local community. Cicatiello and Pancino (2012) conducted a survey of 158 farmers attending 13 Italian FMs, identifying three typologies through a cluster analysis: "traditionalist producers", mainly selling non-organic fresh produce and encouraged to participate by farmers' associations; "processing producers", large size farms mainly selling processed food, 40 per cent of which is organic; and "alternative producers", mostly organic, who diversify their supply and also look for other channels. In general, however, it is difficult to infer the rationale behind producers' participation and their monetary and non-monetary motivations from typologies.

Effects of Participation on Farm Income

Few papers have investigated the effect of participating in AFNs on farm income. Verhaegen and Huylenbroeck (2001) examine a series of innovative chains (including several cooperatives and AFNs) and compare their benefits and costs to those of the conventional chain. The analysis is qualitative, since many costs, especially transaction costs, are difficult to quantify, and for all six case studies, the conclusion is that higher costs are compensated for by higher revenues resulting from higher prices, higher turnover, and reduced uncertainty. Hardesty and Leff (2010) find poor performance for FMs in three case studies of organic farms of different sizes in California. They measure all costs (labour, purchased goods and services, and capital assets) associated with different chains (wholesale, FMs, Community Supported Agriculture—CSAs) and find significant variation in marketing costs across them, with the lowest marketing cost per dollar of revenue in the wholesale chain and the highest in FMs. Uematsu and Mishra (2011) performed an econometric analysis to estimate the effect of the predicted number of direct marketing strategies (DMSs), of the individual direct strategies, and of a set of other explanatory variables on gross cash farm income. They find that while the number of DMSs is not significant, adoption of individual DMSs showed some significant impact. Roadside stores have a negative and significant effect at some quantiles, while farm stores have a positive impact except for the highest quantile, and FMs' impact is negative and significant at all quantiles. Park, Mishra, and Wozniak (2014) and Park (2015) also model the effect of direct marketing on sales and find a negative impact, which is larger for smaller farms. According to Uematsu and Mishra (2011), the negative effect of FMs on sales can be explained by the higher competition in FMs as compared to farm stores and CSA, so that farmers are forced to reduce their selling prices, and by the fact that participating in FMs involves high costs but may not generate high revenue.

Determinants of On-Farm and Off-Farm Direct Sales in Piedmont

The foregoing considerations and short review of the literature point to the need for further investigation of the factors that favour or impede farmers' participation in AFNs. Some motivations found in the literature are linked to strictly monetary objectives, namely, income goals. Given that farms are an economic enterprise, this is not surprising and reveals the force of objective constraints on operators' behaviour. On the other hand, subjective factors, based on preferences other than income, are also widely cited. Both categories of motivation can move the same individuals. Our empirical investigation sought to address these issues in greater detail using two approaches. The first approach is based on observable data and thus focusses on the objective variables that may influence farmers' decision to participate in an AFN and, more specifically, to engage in direct sales. Working with observable data, however, does not make it possible to assess subjective motivations, except for the admittedly weak portion that can be proxied by observable individual socio-economic characteristics. Moreover, since our data were cross-sectional, it was impossible to ascertain what changes participation in AFNs brought about in the farm operation. To overcome these limitations, the second approach investigated the subjective motivations of a group of farmers who chose at least one alternative channel, and the subsequent changes introduced in their farming setting.

The first study (Corsi, Novelli, & Pettenati, 2018) concerns all family farms in Piedmont recorded in the 2010 Agricultural Census. After dropping farms belonging to joint stock companies, cooperatives and public administrations as well as farms with zero gross sales (hobby farmers), the sample consisted of 58,304 farms. From the individual farm records, it was possible to determine whether the farm was engaged in direct selling activities, separately for on-farm and off-farm direct sales. This distinction is in our view important, since, as we argued, the distribution costs differ and, more importantly, are borne by different operators in the two cases. For instance, transport costs are borne by consumers in on-farm sales and by the farmers in the opposite case. The labour time required for the two forms is also different, and so are the investments they require.

Among the variables that could affect the choice to engage in either form of direct sale, we included the economic size of the farm, as measured by the Standard Output (SO),[2] to test the frequent claim that direct sales are an especially good opportunity for small farms (Cheng, Bills, & Uva, 2011; Feenstra, Lewis, Hinrichs, Gillespie Jr, & Hilchey, 2003; Morgan & Alipoe, 2001; Uva, 2002). A second important determinant was the type of farming (TF) as determined according to the EU methodology,[3] to represent the technical feasibility of selling directly, which differs according to the product concerned (e.g., some products require processing and cannot be sold directly unless this processing is carried out on the farm). We also included other product characteristics: organic farming, Protected Designation of Origin (PDO), or Protected Geographical Indication (PGI). Other farm activities (agro-tourism, on-farm recreational activities) were included because they entail relationships with customers that may favour direct sales (more so for on-farm direct sales, as is obvious when agro-tourism includes food and beverage sales). Lastly, farm location was arguably an important variable involving several different factors. One such factor (proxied by altitude, mountains, hills, and plains) relates to the job opportunities available in different areas, the lack of which may put pressure on small farms to find alternative employment for excess family labour through direct sales. A second factor concerns the transport costs associated with off-farm direct sales, which are lower the closer the location of sale. This factor was represented by the number of main commercial cities at a half-hour driving distance from the farm. Third, location can be important in terms of potential customers visiting the farm, and we therefore included the population living within a 45-minute driving distance from the farm.

Only a small proportion of farms in Piedmont engage in direct sales. Those selling on-farm accounted for 14 per cent of the total and those selling off the farm 8.1 per cent. These percentages include the cases (3.5 per cent of the total number of farms) in which both channels were used. The shares are rather different across TFs, ranging from 5 per cent for field crops to 24.4 per cent for mixed types for on-farm sales and from 2.7 per cent for specialist cattle to 16.1 per cent for specialist horticulture for off-farm sales (Table 9.1).

Table 9.1 Percentage of farms practising direct sales by type of farming

Type of farming (European Commission Regulation (EC) No 1242/2008)	Number	Direct market (%)	
		On-farm	Off-farm
Field crops (specialist cereals—rice inclusive—and general field cropping)	18,220	5.0	3.5
Specialist horticulture	1544	13.2	16.1
Specialist vineyards	11,938	24.3	13.6
Other permanent crops (specialist fruit, olives, and various permanent crops combined)	8809	15.3	8.6
Specialist dairying	2228	13.5	5.6
Specialist cattle (rearing and fattening and dairying, rearing and fattening combined)	5363	7.5	2.7
Specialist sheep, goats, and other grazing livestock	2087	14.1	4.7
Specialist granivores (pigs, poultry, and various combined)	927	8.3	4.4
Mixed types[a]	7188	24.4	14.7
Total	58,304	14.0	8.1

Source: 2010 Agricultural Census, authors' calculations

[a]Mixed cropping, mixed livestock, field crops and grazing livestock combined, various crops and livestock combined

The type of farming undoubtedly has a strong influence on the adoption of the direct sales channel, and mixed TF and horticulture are most conducive to it. Also noteworthy is the high proportion of viticultural farms that sell on-farm, a typical feature of a renowned wine-producing area such as Langhe which attracts sizable numbers of tourists.

An analysis of the geographical distribution of the farms selling directly suggested that those engaging in off-farm direct sales were mostly concentrated in specific clusters: the hilly wine-growing areas of Langhe and Monferrato (agro-tourism areas), the hilly belt surrounding Torino (the main town of the region, and thus an attractive outlet for sales), and some low Alpine valleys in the province of Torino. Farms engaged in on-farm sales were more widespread. If the percentage of farms engaged in direct sales in each municipality is considered, relatively high shares are also found in the mountain areas.

A more formal statistical analysis was performed with probit models, estimating separately the effect of the variables listed above on the probability of adopting on-farm and off-farm sales.

First, given the apparent influence of TFs on farmers' choice, we tested whether belonging to a particular TF simply increased or decreased the probability of adopting direct sales or modified the effect of the other variables. A statistical test proved that the latter was true. In other words, the effect of, say, farm size or of operator's education on the probability of direct sales differs according to the particular TF. Hence, the picture is quite diversified, since some variables are significant for some TFs but not for others, and some variables have a positive effect on the probability of direct sales in some TFs and a negative one in others.

Here, we will present only the general results for the most interesting TFs (Table 9.2; for a full analysis, see Corsi et al., 2018). Only agro-tourism had a positive, significant, and strong effect on on-farm direct sales for all TFs, though there were differences in the effects. Having an agro-tourism activity increased the probability of on-farm sales in a range from 14 per cent (for dairying) to 36 per cent (for horticulture). In any case, the link between agro-tourism and on-farm sales is quite obvious, since it is very likely that people eating or lodging on the farm will also buy farm products. It is interesting to note that agro-tourism also has a significant and positive effect on off-farm sales for some TFs (viticulture,

Table 9.2 Selected estimates of marginal effects of the determinants of on-farm and off-farm direct sales

Type of farming	Mixed crops	Field crops	Horticulture	Vineyards	Fruits	Dairying
On-farm direct sales						
Operator's age (years)	−0.001[c]	−0.001[c]	−0.001	0.000	0.000	−0.001
Operator's gender (1 = *M*)	0.009	−0.009[c]	−0.033	0.059[c]	0.014[a]	−0.022
Operator's schooling (years)	0.009[c]	0.000	−0.003	0.003[c]	0.006[c]	0.009[c]
Op.'s ag. school (1 = yes)	0.039	0.013[a]	−0.063[c]	0.181[c]	0.012	−0.041[a]
Op.'s profess. training (1 = yes)	0.108[c]	0.019[b]	0.010	0.019	0.076[c]	0.065[b]
Hills (1 = yes)	0.156[c]	0.064[c]	−0.010	0.127[c]	0.018[a]	0.046[a]
Mountains (1 = yes)	0.254[c]	0.147[c]	0.009	0.166[c]	0.046[c]	0.150[c]
Standard Output (0,000 €)	−0.001	0.000	0.000	0.003[c]	0.000	0.002[c]
Agro-tourism (1 = yes)	0.273[c]	0.160[c]	0.364[c]	0.281[c]	0.328[c]	0.140[a]
Organic farming (1 = yes)	0.109[c]	0.070[c]	0.212[c]	0.231[c]	−0.011	0.023
PDO-PGI (1 = yes)	−0.068[b]	0.022		0.019	−0.072[c]	−0.057[c]
# commercial poles within 1/2 h driving distance	−0.002	0.000	−0.005	0.011[c]	−0.013[c]	−0.011[c]
Population living within 45 min. driving distance (000)	0.019[b]	0.003	0.031[b]	0.116[c]	0.074[c]	0.007
Off-farm direct sales						
Operator's age (years)	−0.002[c]	−0.001[c]	−0.001	−0.001[c]	−0.001[b]	−0.001[a]
Operator's gender (1=M)	−0.005	−0.007[c]	−0.080[c]	0.046[c]	−0.001	−0.002
Operator's schooling (years)	0.004[b]	0.000	−0.011[c]	0.002[c]	0.000	0.005[b]
Op.'s ag. school (1 = yes)	−0.005	0.006	−0.096[c]	0.045[c]	0.011	−0.030[c]
Op.'s profess. training (1 = yes)	0.063[c]	0.011[a]	0.007	0.049[c]	0.036[b]	0.009

(continued)

Table 9.2 (continued)

Type of farming	Mixed crops	Field crops	Horticulture	Vineyards	Fruits	Dairying
Hills (1 = yes)	0.103[c]	0.048[c]	0.052[b]	0.056[c]	0.029[c]	0.038[b]
Mountains (1 = yes)	0.065[c]	0.062[c]	−0.029	0.080[a]	0.007	0.098[c]
Standard Output (0,000 €)	−0.001	0.000	−0.001	0.002[c]	0.001[c]	0.001[c]
Agro-tourism (1 = yes)	−0.033[a]	0.027	−0.009	0.085[c]	0.082[b]	0.050
Organic farming (1 = yes)	0.102[c]	0.060[c]	0.178[b]	0.168[c]	0.026[b]	0.029
PDO-PGI (1 = yes)	−0.074[c]	0.049[a]		−0.017	−0.041[c]	−0.025[c]
# commercial poles within 1/2 h driving distance	0.013[c]	0.003[c]	0.000	0.004	−0.005[b]	0.001
Population living within 45 min. driving distance (000)	0.025[c]	0.005[c]	0.068[c]	0.036[c]	0.049[c]	0.019[c]

Source: Corsi et al. (2018)

Note: Marginal effects estimated at the mean values of the variables (at the median for dummy variables)

[a]Significant at 10%

[b]Significant at 5%

[c]Significant at 1%

fruits, and mixed crops), which can be interpreted either as a sign that their operators are particularly inclined to explore alternative chains or as an "advertising effect", whereby customers of the agro-tourism discover that the farm's products can also be bought in town.

Product quality signals differ in their effects. Organic farming favours direct sales on the farm (especially for horticulture and vineyards) and, to a lesser extent, off-farm direct sales as well. By contrast, PDO or PGI labelling generally has a negative effect, possibly because these products can be put to better advantage in other marketing channels. Contrary to many studies cited before, we found no evidence that direct sales are more likely for small farms. When significant, the associated estimates were positive, indicating that the probability increased with farm size. In these cases, however, the effect was so weak that we can conclude that farm size was not relevant in practical terms (e.g., a 100,000 euro increase in Standard Output produced only a 3 per cent increase in the probability of on-farm sales for vineyards, and in the other TFs, the results were similar).

Some interesting results concerned farm location. Farm location in the hills or in the mountains favoured both on- and off-farm direct sales. The effect (significant for most TFs) was stronger for mountains. The lower profitability of farming in these areas pushes farmers to look for alternative and more profitable outlets, but since these are also tourist areas, farmers have more opportunities to sell directly. The stronger effect of these locations on on-farm rather than on off-farm direct sales suggests that the latter effect is stronger. That the number of potential customers is an important factor was confirmed by the effect of the other location variables. The estimates suggest that each additional thousand inhabitants within the 45-minute drive increased the probability of on-farm direct sales by 2 to 11.6 per cent, depending on the TF, at the mean values of the variables. More interestingly, the effect of the population variable was also significant and positive for off-farm sales. By contrast, the farm's distance from commercial poles was either non-significant or negative for on-farm direct sales (which was in line with expectations, since it should measure transport cost for farmers), but was also non-significant for some TFs, or positive and significant but with a very weak effect in others. This supports the view that farm-to-market transport costs are not a crucial determinant for the choice of selling off the farm, while the opportunities for finding customers are much more important.

Operator's personal characteristics (age, education) either were not significant, or had a very weak effect. Gender had a contradictory effect since, for example, operators' male gender was found to favour on- and off-farm sales in viticulture, and to discourage direct sales in field crops and horticulture. All this suggests that observable characteristics did not effectively represent individual idiosyncratic preferences and that there was a large variability in subjective preferences. A major limitation of this study is indeed the lack of information on subjective motivations of participants in direct sales. This is why we decided to survey farmers directly about their motivations for participating in AFNs.

Subjective Motivations for Farmers' Participation in AFNs in Piedmont

Quantitative analysis of the determinants of direct selling based on census data shed light on which farm structure characteristics and which observable socio-demographic traits of farmers, if any, were more conducive to direct sales. Still, the weak and at times difficult to interpret effects of farmers' observable characteristics (e.g., gender, age, and education) suggest that subjective motivations and non-observable traits of participants in direct sales could play a relevant role in farmers' choices. The literature also shows that subjective motivations differ among participants in different types of alternative distribution channels (e.g., Mastronardi, Marino, Cavallo, & Giannelli, 2015).

To explore the role of farmers' attitudes and preferences in explaining part of the unexplained producers' behaviour, we carried out an in-depth qualitative analysis of producers' individual motivations (Novelli & Corsi, 2018). We set up a focus group discussion involving seven farmers operating in a hilly area located about 40 kilometres southwest of Torino. The congenial climate of this area is particularly favourable to quality fruit farming, with local farmers producing apples, kiwis, peaches, pears, and berry fruits. All focus group participants chose to engage in at least one alternative distribution channel to complement conventional channels (commercial and industrial firms or cooperatives). Four participants are fruit growers. The largest of the participants' farms (28 hectares of Utilised Agricultural Area, UAA) specialises in supplying SPGs and selling on-farm, while the smaller ones (under 3.5 hectares of UAA) chose to sell directly, mainly off-farm. Two of the participants produce both fruit and vegetables and use a mix of alternative channels, and one—specialising in horticulture—sells its produce exclusively off-farm.

The main objectives of the analysis were to solicit feedback on the personal motivations that led the participants to sell directly and to ascertain whether the use of this market channel was conducive to changes in farm management and organisation.

Regarding the first topic, participants' motivations, the group discussion brought out a general need for "freedom of choice". The decision to sell in part directly stems basically from the farmers' need to make their own management and production choices, without third party influences. In discussing this issue, group members underscored three main aspects. The first concerns the agronomic practices required by middlemen in order to meet the conventional chains' marketing standards (e.g., size, general appearance or defects, state of maturity, fruit colour). Some practices, like picking produce while still green, the use of fruit ripening gases and other chemicals, or the use of reflective cloth, were commonly considered improper and at times "extreme". Above all, such practices were considered to be far from their idea of high-quality agriculture. Hence, all participants were no longer willing to be bound by conventional market requirements that are at odds with their personal idea of quality. The second aspect concerns the dissatisfaction with conventional market prices and the payment terms set by middlemen. All the participants claimed the freedom to set their prices according to the costs they bear and to the quality standard they offer. Therefore, they consider direct marketing as an opportunity to obtain higher prices, along with the chance to have more control over the other financial aspects of the trade, for example, to avoid long waits for payment by middlemen. Lastly, a need to build and maintain a relationship of trust with customers emerged. As mentioned, the participants' beliefs concerning quality are quite different from those held in conventional channels. In the farmers' opinion, being true to these values and beliefs is important in order to maintain their reputation for high-quality produce. The consequent positive feedback from customers is a source of gratification to which the participants attach a value that goes beyond the higher prices consumers are willing to pay for their produce.

To characterise the attitude behind the stated motivations, we could say that the group members are "product oriented" rather than "market oriented". This attitude seems to be the main motive behind farmers' choice to participate in AFNs and implicitly refers to their concept of quality. With reference to the three main points that emerged through the discussion, the participants' personal notion of quality seems to be their criterion for evaluating their skills and professionalism and for assigning a value to their produce and work, as well as being a source of satisfaction when it is recognised by the consumers.

Discussion on the second topic confirmed that the conversion to direct selling—even though partial—was conducive to changes in asset endowments and in farm structure and organisation. Moreover, new cost items appeared in the farm budget.

Of course, new investments were necessary (e.g., cold stores, sheds, packaging machinery and materials, etc.), but major changes were made in the entire production chain. In accordance with one of the main motivations for selling directly, that is, the pursuit of different quality standards, all the participants changed their practices to organic. In addition, they extended the range of produce they cultivate in order to guarantee continuity of supply, extend the selling season, and meet consumers' taste for variety. For the same reasons, one of the group members who had produced a single type of fruit (berries) was able to diversify production and began to process his produce and market juices and other goods (e.g., gift baskets). For all participants, direct marketing significantly affected the farm organisation as well, especially in terms of farm labour management. Group members unanimously considered direct channels more labour-intensive than wholesale channels and stated that the availability of labour is one of the major difficulties they face day by day to strike a balance between production and distribution activities. In this connection, the group stressed that strictly marketing-related activities (e.g., packing, transportation, selling, and administration) are only a fraction of the extra labour required by direct selling. The consequent changes in agricultural practices are more time-consuming than the conventional practices, for example, weeding operations in organic farming, picking the produce gradually as it ripens, growing a wider range of fruit and/or vegetables, and so on. Since—regardless of the channel—labour is the major marketing cost for farms (Hardesty & Leff, 2010; LeRoux, Schmit, Roth, & Streeter, 2010; Uva, 2002), it is arguably one of the main extra costs the group members incurred when they started to market their produce directly.

Although some differences were found between on-farm and off-farm sales, our analysis confirms that adopting these alternative market channels brings about changes in farm assets, leads to higher costs, and requires higher skills and experience in cost and labour management. In spite of these constraints, the motivations expressed by the group members were rather strong, to the point that all participants would like to increase the share of produce sold through AFNs.

Conclusions

Both the literature review and the empirical analyses in Piedmont indicate that objective, monetary factors are important for farmers' choice of AFNs as a marketing channel. This is not surprising, since farmers are economic operators and are strongly constrained by market forces to operate in a way that is sufficiently profitable to enable them to survive. From this point of view, the higher prices fetched in AFNs are doubtless attractive, but they are not sufficient to make the AFN the most profitable choice. Choosing an alternative marketing channel involves a different distribution of marketing costs among the operators in the chain, so that farmers may incur many costs they would not otherwise bear. This is why it is not always profitable for farmers to engage in AFN sales and much depends on individual situations. Moreover, technical constraints may be strong, particularly the type of production farmers are engaged in, since only some products are suitable for selling in AFNs, and changing the production mix can be difficult and costly. A rather new finding of our empirical study is that geographical proximity to consumers does not seem to be a strong impediment because of transport cost. Rather, it is important in terms of potential patrons, not only for on-farm sales (as was expected) but also for off-farm sales. Among the characteristics that may influence the choice of AFNs, we find that farm size is not particularly relevant. This departs from previous findings, but given the heterogeneity of situations among farms, the different findings may depend on the local situations. The advantages of AFNs for small farms hinge on the latter's difficulty in meeting the volume and quality standards required by other chains and on making good use of excess family labour. In other cases, however, it might be difficult or unprofitable for small farms to invest capital and labour in accessing the alternative chain. From this point of view, it is telling that fewer farms engage in the more costly off-farm direct sales than in on-farm direct sales.

While objective economic factors are important in the choice of AFN marketing channels, subjective motivations count too. This is an area that has received little attention in the literature. In our survey of producers supplying different AFNs, in addition to profitability (seen more as a pre-requisite than as a goal), the main stated motivation was farmers' freedom to make their own production choices, without having to submit to the standards required by conventional chains, which were considered to threaten product quality and interfere with good practice. AFNs thus restore meaning to farmers' work, in terms of pride in what they produce and consumer recognition of their products' quality. This is consistent with the alternative nature of AFNs, which are not simply places where anonymous commodities are exchanged for money, since personal relationships, recognition, and reciprocal knowledge are also part of the exchange.

A further element that has been somewhat neglected in the literature concerns the changes that participating in AFNs brings about in the farm setting. That making direct sales calls for a certain farm configuration can be inferred even from the mere observation of the census data showing that direct sales are more common in specific types of farming (especially mixed ones). The personal interviews with farmers confirm this hypothesis. New investments are needed, and a production mix that meets the demand for variety and year-round availability must be introduced. Managing labour requirements for this new activity is even more important, as it may be in competition with the production activities. Many of the fixed costs entailed by the alternative chain are sunk costs, either for the materials used for direct sales or the investment in human capital needed to start the activity (e.g., information about the legal requirements). Therefore, giving up the alternative chain would mean losing the investment. Economists insist that sunk costs should not affect decisions, but in real life many operators are reluctant to adopt this view, and reconverting the farm can in any case be costly. Hence, the choice of engaging in direct sales is probably a long-term one, the more so the bigger the investments made for entering the alternative chain, which is probably more the case for off-farm than for on-farm direct sales.

Notes

1. Only Monson et al. (2008) find a negative effect of growing fruit on participation in FMs and a positive effect of non-certified organic farming.
2. The Standard Output is a standard measure of the economic size of a farm calculated in the European Union Farm Accounting Data Network (FADN). It is computed as the sum of unit standard values of production, determined for the different crops and livestock within each region, times the quantities involved.
3. The type of farming as contemplated by Regulation (EC) No. 1242/2008 classifies farms on the basis of the relative contribution of the Standard Output of specific crops or livestock to the farm's total Standard Output.

References

Aguglia, L., De Santis, F., & Salvioni, C. (2011). Direct Selling: A Marketing Strategy to Shorten Distances between Production and Consumption. In G. Baourakis, K. Mattas, C. Zopounidis, & G. van Dijk (Eds.), *A Resilient European Food Industry in a Challenging World*. Hauppauge, NY: Nova Science Publishers.

Aubert, M. (2015). *The Determinants of Selling Through a Short Food Supply Chains: An Application to the French Case*, 9. Journées de recherches en sciences sociales (JRSS), Dec. 2015, Nancy, France. Actes des journées JRSS 2015, 25 p. Retrieved from https://hal.archives-ouvertes.fr/hal-01296422

Bonanno, A., Pascucci, S., Caracciolo, F., & Cembalo, L. (2014). Farmers Participation in Short Channels in Italy: An Empirical Analysis, EAAE 2014 Congress 'Agri-Food and Rural Innovations for Healthier Societies', August 26 to 29, Ljubljana, Slovenia. Retrieved from https://ageconsearch.umn.edu/bitstream/182968/2/EAAA_2014_Short_supply_chain_final.pdf

Brunori, G., Galli, F., Barjolle, D., van Broekhuizen, R., Colombo, L., Giampietro, M., Kirwan, J., Lang, T., Mathijs, E., Maye, D., de Roest, K., Rougoor, C., Schwarz, J., Schmitt, E., Smith, J., Stojanovic, Z., Tisenkopfs, T., & Touzard, J.-M. (2016). Are Local Food Chains More Sustainable Than Global Food Chains? Considerations for Assessment. *Sustainability, 8*(5), 1–27.

Brunori, G., Rossi, A., & Guidi, F. (2012). On the New Social Relations Around and Beyond Food. Analysing Consumers' Role and Action in Gruppi di Acquisto Solidale (Solidarity Purchasing Groups). *Sociologia Ruralis, 52*(1), 1–30.

Brunori, G., Rossi, A., & Malandrin, V. (2011). Co-producing Transition: Innovation Processes in Farms Adhering to Solidarity-Based Purchase Groups (GAS) in Tuscany, Italy. *International Journal of Sociology of Agriculture & Food, 18*(1), 28–53.

Capt, D., & Wavresky, P. (2014). Determinants of Direct-to-Consumer Sales on French Farms. *Revue d'Etudes en Agriculture et Environnement, 95*(3), 351–377.

Cheng, M., Bills, N., & Uva, W.-f. L. (2011). Farm-Direct Food Sales in the Northeast Region: A Country Level Analysis. *Journal of Food Distribution Research, 42*(1), 22–25.

Cicatiello, C., & Pancino, B. (2012). Tipologie di produttori e consumatori che frequentano i farmers' market. In S. Franco & D. Marino (Eds.), *Il mercato della Filiera corta. I farmers' market come luogo di incontro di produttori e consumatori*. Gruppo 2013. Working Paper No. 19. Retrieved from http://www.gruppo2013.it/working-paper/Documents/WEB%20Working%20Paper%20n.19%20-%20Gruppo%202013.pdf

Corsi, A., Novelli, S., & Pettenati, G. (2018). Producer and Farm Characteristics, Type of Product, Location: Determinants of On-farm and Off-farm Direct Sales By Farmers. *Agribusiness*, in press (published as Early View): 1–19.

Corsini, L., Randelli, F., Rocchi, B., & Giampaolo, S. (2018). *Direct Selling and Alternative Evolutionary Patterns in the Italian Agri-food Systems*. Working Paper No. 04/2018. Università degli Studi di Firenze, Dipartimento di Scienze per l'Economia e l'Impresa.

Darby, K., Batte, M. T., Ernst, S., & Roe, B. (2008). Decomposing Local: A Conjoint Analysis of Locally Produced Foods. *American Journal of Agricultural Economics, 90*(2), 476–486.

Detre, J. D., Mark, T. B., Mishra, A. K., & Adhikari, A. (2011). Linkage Between Direct Marketing and Farm Income: A Double-Hurdle Approach. *Agribusiness, 27*(1), 19–33.

Dimitri, C. (2011). Use of Local Markets by Organic Producers. *American Journal of Agricultural Economics, 94*(2), 301–306.

Feenstra, G. W., Lewis, C. C., Hinrichs, C. C., Gillespie, G. W., Jr., & Hilchey, D. (2003). Entrepreneurial Outcomes and Enterprise Size in US Retail Farmers' Markets. *American Journal of Alternative Agriculture, 18*(1), 46–55.

Gale, F. (1997). Direct Farm Marketing as a Rural Development Tool. *Rural Development Perspectives, 12*, 19–25.

Gandee, J. E., Brown, C., & D'Souza, G. (2003, July). *The Role of Spatial and Demographic Characteristics in Direct farm Marketing: An Econometric Approach.* Paper Presented at the American Agricultural Economics Association Annual Meeting, Montreal, Canada, July 27–30. Retrieved from https://ageconsearch.umn.edu/bitstream/21912/1/sp03ga03.pdf

Griffin, M. R., & Frongillo, E. A. (2003). Experiences and Perspectives of Farmers from Upstate New York Farmers' Markets. *Agriculture and Human Values, 20*, 189–203.

Hardesty, S., & Leff, P. (2010). Determining Marketing Costs and Returns in Alternative Marketing Channels. *Renewable Agriculture and Food Systems, 25*(1), 24–34.

Hunt, A. R. (2007). Consumer Interactions and Influences on Farmers' Market Vendors. *Renewable Agriculture and Food Systems, 22*(1), 54–66.

Ilbery, B., & Maye, D. (2005). Alternative (Shorter) Food Supply Chains and Specialist Livestock Products in the Scottish–English Borders. *Environment and Planning A, 37*(5), 823–844.

Kirwan, J. (2006). The Interpersonal World of Direct Marketing: Examining Conventions of Quality at UK Farmers' Markets. *Journal of Rural Studies, 22*(3), 301–312.

LeRoux, M. N., Schmit, T. M., Roth, M., & Streeter, D. H. (2010). Evaluating Marketing Channel Options for Small-Scale Fruit and Vegetable Producers. *Renewable Agriculture and Food Systems, 25*(1), 16–23.

Logozar, B., & Schmit, T.M. (2009). *Assessing the Success of Farmers' Markets in Northern New York: A Survey of Vendors, Customers, and Market Managers.* Department of Applied Economics and Management, College of Agriculture and Life Sciences, Cornell University, EB 2009-08. Retrieved from http://ageconsearch.umn.edu/record/55941?ln=en

Low, S. A., & Vogel, S. (2011, November). *Direct and Intermediated Marketing of Local Foods in the United States*, ERR-128. U.S. Department of Agriculture, Economic Research Service.

Martinez, S., Hand, M., Da Pra, M., Pollack, S., Ralston, K., Smith, T., et al. (2010, May). *Local Food Systems: Concepts, Impacts and Issues*, ERR 97. U.S. Department of Agriculture, Economic Research Service.

Mastronardi, L., Marino, D., Cavallo, A., & Giannelli, A. (2015). Exploring the Role of Farmers in Short Food Supply Chains: The Case of Italy. *International Food and Agribusiness Management Review, 18*(2), 109–130.

Monson, J., Mainville, D., & Kuminoff, N. (2008). The Decision to Direct Market: An Analysis of Small Fruit and Specialty-Product Markets in Virginia. *Journal of Food Distribution Research, 39*(2), 1–11.

Morgan, K. T., & Alipoe, D. (2001). Factors Affecting the Number and Type of Small-Farm Direct Marketing Outlets in Mississippi. *Journal of Food and Distribution Research, 32*(1), 125–132.

Novelli, S., & Corsi, A. (2018). *Direct Selling: A Qualitative Analysis of Farmers' Motivations, Opportunities and Constraints.* Paper Presented at the 7th Conference of the Italian Association of Agricultural and Applied Economics (AIEAA), June 14–15, Conegliano (TV), Italy.

Park, T. A. (2015). Direct Marketing and the Structure of Farm Sales: An Unconditional Quantile Regression Approach. *Journal of Agricultural and Resource Economics, 40*(2), 266–284.

Park, T. A., Mishra, A. K., & Wozniak, S. J. (2014). Do Farm Operators Benefit from Direct to Consumer Marketing Strategies? *Agricultural Economics, 45*, 213–224.

Sage, J. L., & Goldberger, J. R. (2012). Decisions to Direct Market: Geographic Influences on Conventions in Organic Production. *Applied Geography, 34*, 57–65.

Schmitt, E., Keech, D., Maye, D., Barjolle, D., & Kirwan, J. (2016). Comparing the Sustainability of Local and Global Food Chains: A Case Study of Cheese Products in Switzerland and the UK. *Sustainability, 8*(5), 1–20.

Uematsu, H., & Mishra, A. K. (2011). Use of Direct Marketing Strategies by Farmers and Their Impact on Farm Business Income. *Agricultural and Resource Economics Review, 40*(1), 1–19.

Uva, W.-F. L. (2002). An Analysis of Vegetable Farms' Direct Marketing Activities in New York State. *Journal of Food Distribution Research, 33*(1), 186–189.

Verhaegen, I., & Van Huylenbroeck, G. (2001). Costs and Benefits for Farmers Participating in Innovative Marketing Channels for Quality Food Products. *Journal of Rural Studies, 17*, 443–456.

10

The Economic Viability of Solidarity Purchase Groups (*Gruppi di Acquisto Solidale*)

Silvia Novelli and Alessandro Corsi

The Economic Viability of AFNs

When food and agriculture systems are viewed in a whole-systems context, sustainability should be defined comprehensively, following environmentally sound, economically viable, and socially responsible paths (Allen, Van Dusen, Lundy, & Gliessman, 1991). In its broadest accepted meaning, the economic dimension of sustainability deals with the maintenance of non-negative net economic benefits to society. In this sense, the economic issues that are commonly considered central to sustainability in food networks include the incomes and livelihoods of the producers and other subjects involved in the network, as well as employment creation and local economic

S. Novelli (✉)
Department of Agricultural, Forest and Food Sciences, University of Torino, Grugliasco (TO), Italy
e-mail: silvia.novelli@unito.it

A. Corsi
Department of Economics and Statistics "Cognetti de Martiis", University of Torino, Torino, Italy
e-mail: alessandro.corsi@unito.it

A. Corsi et al. (eds.), *Alternative Food Networks*,
https://doi.org/10.1007/978-3-319-90409-2_10

development, particularly in rural areas (Forssell & Lankoski, 2015). However, as Alternative Food Networks (AFNs) are alternative food provisioning practices operating within the general food system, the minimum condition for their existence, and consequently for maintaining the flow of social and public benefits they produce, is their ability to succeed and be competitive in the markets. From this standpoint, the strictly economic viability of AFNs cannot be taken for granted. Economic viability deals with an organization's capacity to produce revenues that are sufficient to at least balance all operating costs and to achieve positive profits in the short to medium term. Viability becomes sustainable where continuity in balanced inflows and outflows is reasonably achievable in the longer term under changing conditions. By comparison with other dimensions of sustainability, however, little research has examined the economic performance of AFNs by focussing on the costs that producers incur when they engage in direct marketing and the profitability of these channels (Hardesty & Leff, 2010; King et al., 2010).

Producers operating in AFNs can charge higher prices than when selling wholesale and thus receive higher revenues, but they may also have to bear higher distribution and marketing costs (Corsi, Novelli, & Pettenati, 2018, Chap. 9). Several authors have analysed the net benefit to producers engaged in direct selling (Hardesty & Leff, 2010; Ilbery & Maye, 2005; Jarosz, 2008; King et al., 2010; LeRoux, Schmit, Roth, & Streed, 2009; Milestad, Westberg, Geber, & Björklund, 2010; Uematsu & Mishra, 2011; Verhaegen & Huylenbroeck, 2001),[1] suggesting that profitability—though strongly depending on the type of channel used, type of product, farm size, or location—may not always live up to theory and that efficient market strategies call for flexibility in combining alternative and conventional channels. In particular, common findings suggest that direct selling activities require significant financial resources and are time-consuming for producers. Marketing-related activities (e.g., processing, travel, selling, administration, promotion of products/channel etc.) are especially labour intensive and require a reliable and continuous labour supply. Hence, labour costs seem to be a central issue for AFNs' economic viability. Concerning this issue, LeRoux et al. (2009) warn of 'hidden operator costs'. Comparing the profitability of various channels, producers sometimes fail to account for their family's unpaid labour contribution to distribution activities. Consequently, they may select channels that reduce the farm's overall economic performance, because of misconceptions regarding the economic profit of the different channels.

Although AFNs are not always sufficiently profitable to encourage producers to leave conventional channels and to justify the adoption of the alternative strategy alone, engaging in alternative channels may improve farm economic performance by leveraging other important determinants of viability. In many contexts, direct market approaches may play an important role as risk management tools rather than profit-maximizing strategies (Hardesty & Leff, 2010; Uematsu & Mishra, 2011). Diversifying market channels increases the number of marketing options available for farmers, enabling them, for example, to allocate surpluses and apply different quality standards to different market channels. Accessing different distribution channels also mitigates the impact of price volatility in the wholesale market. In addition, forms of co-operation among farmers and collective initiatives decrease transaction costs and require less investment in labour or capital (Verhaegen & Huylenbroeck, 2001). Other networking benefits with an indirect impact on farm performance have been emphasized in farmers' markets (Brown & Miller, 2008; Feenstra & Lewis, 1999; Feenstra, Lewis, Hinrichs, Gillespie, & Hilchey, 2003). Farmers' markets may be used to promote other farm activities or to enter new businesses (e.g., agro-tourism, Community Supported Agriculture, on-farm sales, etc.). Moreover, they help producers socialize with consumers and other farmers, improving their skills in customer relations, production, and pricing, as well as increasing their business self-confidence.

In general, economic viability issues are approached by focusing on primary producers, given that in many AFNs—for example, farmers' markets and on-farm sales—they make up the entire supply side of the market. Nonetheless, new forms of market governance such as Community Supported Agriculture also involve consumers in production, purchasing, or marketing. These socially innovative approaches are based on the notion of redistributing power in the food network and sharing economic risks and/or resources (Forssell & Lankoski, 2015). Such forms of governance include the Solidarity Purchase Groups (*Gruppi di Acquisto Solidale*), an all-Italian phenomenon in which consumers take part actively in the distribution process and co-produce economic value with farmers. The ability of such complex organizations to work successfully in the long-term is an issue that deserves to be addressed from an economic perspective in order to shed light on the factors affecting their efficiency and to assess the economic implications of consumers' participation.

Values and Organizational Issues of Solidarity Purchase Groups

Solidarity Purchase Groups (SPGs) are a collective practice for food provisioning that arose in Italy in relatively recent years, that is, in the mid-1990s (Schifani & Migliore, 2011). About 1000 SPGs are currently registered throughout the country but, given their often informal nature, it is estimated that there may be at least twice as many (Economia Solidale, 2018).

Such groups are set up by citizen-consumers who cooperate in order to buy food and other commonly used goods directly from producers, at a price that is fair to both parties.[2] Even though our research suggests that purely monetary motivations for participation are not to be ruled out either for consumers (Corsi & Novelli, 2018, Chap. 4) or for producers (Corsi et al., 2018, Chap. 9), SPGs' distinguishing feature is that they are not simply interested in cost savings. The major difference from buying groups, whose main objective is the economic advantage of collective buying for utilitarian purposes (e.g., lower prices or convenience), is the principle of solidarity that guides participants in the choice of products and in relations with producers. From this standpoint, SPGs are considered one of the most significant expressions of the solidarity economy (Hankins & Grasseni, 2014). In the recent literature, they are also presented as new forms of the trust economy (Sage, 2007), since trust is a condition for solidarity (Grasseni, 2014), and of political participation, as they are hybrid organizations that can go beyond conventional forms of political consumerism by adopting innovative organizational and participatory tools (Graziano & Forno, 2012).

The general aim of SPGs is to gain control over the food they consume and of the associated production practices, through active re-appropriation on the part of the consumer (Saroldi, 2001). The main principles that shape their strategy are consciousness about food consumption, socialization, solidarity within the group and between group members and producers to guarantee fair prices and working conditions, trust relationships with producers (especially local ones), social justice, environmental sustainability, and alternative quality standards (Brunori, Rossi, & Guidi, 2012; Saroldi, 2001; Schifani & Migliore, 2011). These principles are put into practice not only through a critical approach to food consumption choices, such as supporting local and/or marginal farms, buying fresh products based on seasonality, choosing organic produce, or reducing packaging. Going beyond ethical consumerism, a more innovative approach to the solidarity economy has rethought the concept of food production, introducing the notion of co-production (Grasseni, 2014; Martino, Pampanini, & Giacchè, 2013). Participating in SPGs not only calls for establishing new direct channels but also for adopting farming styles that reflect the group's principles (Brunori, Rossi, & Malandrin, 2011). Through co-production between SPGs and farmers, some of the decision rights are shifted from the farmers to the SPGs, for example, the right to decide agricultural practices, quality features, or the time products are delivered (Martino, Giacchè, & Rossetti, 2016). On the farmer's side, the rationale for co-production is grounded in the monetary and non-monetary benefits gained in meeting this emerging demand (Corsi et al., 2018, Chap. 9). The common decision process requires negotiation both within the group, to establish a consensus on the group's principles and criteria, and between the SPG and the producers, in order to agree on protocols of production, prices, logistics, delivery frequency, and so on. The negotiation process is time-consuming and the associated transaction costs borne by the SPGs, especially in dealing with the farmers, may be sizable.

As for the governance of SPGs, the groups are run as formal or, more frequently, informal non-profit organizations. The principle of solidarity also defines the organizational form of SPGs, as their operations typically rely on occasional or regular volunteers. The organizational structure and operational aspects may vary from group to group. Nevertheless, SPGs usually appoint a group of co-ordinators who deal with specific products or producers and are tasked with liaising and negotiating with producers, making periodical calls for orders, collecting and placing the orders, and supervising delivery logistics. Producers usually deliver the orders to a point of collection where the SPG members pick up their products. Occasional or regular volunteers, as well as co-ordinators, help with the distribution operations at the meetings where members collect their orders. In formal groups, the SPGs appoint a board of directors who are in charge of the participatory process, administration, and accounting activities. It appears that the time demand on SPG volunteers is considerable and that distribution activities call for continuous commitment. The SPG approach may thus be more labour intensive in terms of organization than many other direct channels, but usually requires smaller capital investments (Hankins & Grasseni, 2014).

From the economic standpoint, the use of voluntary work has two main consequences. First, distribution costs are cut, so higher prices can be paid to producers than in conventional distribution channels. Also, as voluntary labour is the core of SPGs' non-profit nature, the groups can distribute products without having to mark up the price in order to balance their budgets. Hence, the economic viability of SPGs arguably depends on labour costs that are not borne directly. In economic terms, the cost of labour for SPGs is an implicit cost, that is, it is an opportunity cost that arises as the organization allocates internal resources to an activity without any explicit compensation for their utilization.

From this perspective, SPG members' participation is not just an element of the group's social sustainability but, by providing voluntary labour, it is also the key to the group's economic viability. Moreover, the value of volunteers' labour can be considered as a measure of the value that members assign to their participation, or in other words, a measure of the strength of their motivations. Attaching a monetary value to this voluntary labour can thus be helpful in assessing these distribution channels' long-term sustainability. Furthermore, this value can be interpreted as an indicator of the groups' adherence to the solidarity principles espoused by SPGs. As mentioned above, since labour cost in SPGs is an implicit cost item, it cannot be estimated on the basis of actual expenditure at market prices, but requires the use of indirect methods. For that reason, we analyse both explicit and implicit costs in SPGs in order to estimate the value of volunteers' participation and bring new insights to the issue of SPGs' economic viability.

The Value of Voluntary Labour in Solidarity Purchase Groups

An empirical analysis was conducted through individual in-depth interviews with the representatives of four SPGs in Torino (Italy) and other neighbouring towns (Novelli & Corsi, 2016). The general focus of the interviews was on the groups' governance framework and organizational aspects. The specific aim was to analyse the structure of their distribution costs and assess how these costs impacted their final balance. Particular attention was devoted to the implicit cost of voluntary work, for two main reasons. As mentioned earlier, since labour costs account for the majority of the total costs borne by AFNs, they are one of the key factors for these distribution channels' economic viability and possibly that of SPGs as well. Moreover, for SPGs the value of voluntary labour can be interpreted as a proxy indicator of the strength of their members' motivations.[3]

In detail, the information gathered through the interviews concerned the group's governance and general organization (structure, number of members, administration, etc.), the number of producers involved, the type and quantity of products distributed in a reference year, the value of the distributed products, the division of labour within the group, the time devoted to each operation, and the explicit costs borne by the group (e.g., any rents for private or public places used to stock and distribute food products, transportation and packaging costs—when borne by the groups—web and management software costs, etc.).

For the estimation we referred to the economic theory of production cost. We estimated both explicit and implicit costs and calculated the SPGs' balance between total costs and revenues. In economic terms, we estimated the SPGs' economic profit. In the matter in question, talking about 'profits' and 'revenues' may sound strange, since SPGs are not commercial channels and they do not actually sell any goods. It is thus necessary to stress that the analysis does not intend to consider SPGs as gainful activities. As mentioned, the aim of the evaluation is to assess whether (and to what extent) the costs of both external and internal inputs can affect the SPGs' economic viability. Clearly, the accounting profit—calculated by including only the explicit costs in the balance—is equal to zero for SPGs,[4] as is normally the case for non-profit organizations.

Among implicit costs, the cost of labour was clearly the most difficult to estimate from both a theoretical and a methodological point of view, since there is no market price for volunteer labour and its economic value must be assigned. We adopted an input-focussed approach to estimate the monetary value of volunteer time. Input approaches estimate the value of labour by assigning a monetary value to the time and labour that a volunteer donates.[5] From this group of approaches, we chose the replacement wage method. This method centres on the value of the task performed[6] and assumes that the value of the volunteer's time equals the amount that it would cost the organization to pay someone to do the same task. There are thus two main assumptions: (1) that volunteers and paid labour are substitutes and (2) that the two resources are perfect one-for-one substitutes (Bowman, 2009; Orlowski & Wicker, 2015). In many non-profit organizations, volunteers and paid workers are used together, so the substitute assumption is invalidated since, from a theoretical standpoint, two resources cannot be substitutes and complements at the same time. In SPGs, the volunteers carry out all the group's activities, so the replaceability condition is validated. Perfect substitution means that a paid employee is exactly the productive equivalent of a full-time volunteer. This condition is difficult to achieve, as volunteers normally have neither the formal training nor the experience of paid workers (Handy & Srinivasan, 2005). Accordingly, the work of an untrained generalist should be valued less than the work of a professional operator (Ironmonger, 2000). This could be the case of SPGs, especially for the most complex activities, for example, finding and selecting producers that reflect the group's values, negotiating with farmers about production techniques and food quality, and performing administrative and accounting tasks. As a consequence, the replacement wage method could overstate the value of the volunteered time, even when—as in this case—volunteers and paid workers are substitutable. Therefore, the results of our estimation should be considered as an upper bound on the economic value of voluntary labour to SPGs.

To impute labour costs, we considered mean hourly wage data from the Italian National Institute of Statistics (ISTAT, 2010). We used data for the market services sector in the northwestern area of the country, assigning the gross hourly wage of executives/employees to the board of directors, if established, and regular volunteers (i.e., co-ordinators in charge of collecting and placing orders), and the gross hourly wage of manual workers to the occasional volunteers appointed on a rotating basis for distribution at the point of collection. Other implicit costs included in the balance were rents, when waived, and other possible cost items borne by individual members and not shared within the group (e.g., transportation costs). These costs were estimated at market prices.

Table 10.1 shows general information about the four SPGs, the implicit costs borne by the groups and their balance.

Three out of the four groups are rather large SPGs, both in terms of the number of households (around or higher than 100 units) and of the value of the distributed products (over 150,000 euro/year). The number of producers supplying the groups is also sizable (more than 80 for the larger group). Just one group, the smallest, is an informal group. The others are recognized associations with a more highly organized governance structure based on a board of directors, a permanent group of co-ordinators appointed for specific products or producers, and a system of internal rules for managing the contribution of the occasional volunteers.

In absolute terms, implicit costs vary between around 5000 euro/year for the smallest group to 47,000 euro/year for the largest. As expected, voluntary labour is the major implicit cost item for all SPGs, accounting for 93 per cent of the implicit costs for Group C, 96 per cent for Group D, and all implicit costs for the two groups with the largest number of suppliers (A and B). In practical terms, implicit costs in the four SPGs analysed can be totally ascribed to labour costs (the other implicit costs are unpaid rents for sites provided free by members or public bodies for product distribution). Labour costs range from 9 per cent (Group C) to 22 per cent (Group A) of the total costs borne by the groups (which include the purchase of products from farmers). Considering that, apart from the costs of buying the goods from farmers, the other explicit and implicit costs borne by the SPGs are negligible, the analysis confirms that the SPGs' organizational model is labour intensive and that the cost of labour is the main implicit economic indicator of the groups' viability.

These findings also suggest that the SPGs' labour costs are mainly related to the number of suppliers rather than to the number of households. Evidently, building and maintaining the relations between a large

Table 10.1 General information on SPGs, groups' balance, and implicit costs (IC)

SPGs	Households (*n*)	Producers (*n*)	Product value (€/year)	IC (€/year)	Labour costs/IC (%)	Labour costs/total costs (%)	Balance without IC (€/year)	Balance with IC (€/year)	IC per €1000 of distributed goods (€)
A	156	82	164,862	47,226	100	22	212	−47,014	286
B	96	52	151,000	24,406	100	14	130	−24,276	162
C	120	29	171,440	17,830	93	9	896	−16,934	104
D	30	15	27,838	5044	96	15	214	−4830	181

number of co-ordinators (usually each co-ordinator deals with one particular set of products or with a particular farmer) and the farmers require a large amount of time.

With regard to the SPGs' balance, if labour costs were accounted for, costs would exceed revenue by a large margin in all groups[7] (the balance is always negative). Labour costs per 1000 euros of distributed goods vary between 104 (Group C) and 286 euros (Group A). In an efficient system, this ratio should decrease as the value (and the associated volume) of the distributed products increase, since increased output leads to cost advantages due to the scale of operation and to fixed costs. This phenomenon does not always occur in the observed SPGs. Especially in Group A, one of the largest in terms of value of the distributed products, the cost of labour per unit of distributed goods is particularly high, indicating that diseconomies of scale occur. A possible explanation is that, unlike the other groups, all members of Group A are appointed on a rotating basis for the distribution task at the point of collection. Due to the large number of households and to the considerable volume of distributed products, at least two members of the group are required to volunteer at the distribution meetings, otherwise their membership is not renewed. This sort of free-riding control system seems to be paid for in terms of the group's economic efficiency (much higher labour costs).

The membership fees currently paid in the four SPGs are rather low, 5–10 euro/year (Table 10.2), but more than enough to cover explicit costs. The balance considering only explicit costs is indeed positive for all SPGs. To balance the budget when implicit costs (labour costs) as well as explicit costs are accounted for, the annual membership fees would have

Table 10.2 Hypotheses for balancing explicit and labour costs

			Total cost coverage	
SPGs	Membership fee (€/year)	Average expenditure per household (€/year)	Through membership fee (€/year)	Through annual expenditure (%)
A	10	1056.81	311	+ 29.5
B	10	1572.92	263	+ 16.7
C	5	1428.67	146	+ 10.2
D	10	927.92	171	+ 18.4

to be from 17 (Group D) to 31 times (Group A) higher than they currently are. For Group A, the membership fee would rise from 10 to more than 300 euros. Of course, balancing the budget through membership fees assumes that the implicit costs are borne equally by all members. The amount of the annual membership fees needed to balance the budget when implicit costs (labour costs) are also taken into account can be interpreted as the monetary value of the volunteers' time supplied annually by the SPG members, if it were supplied equally by all members.

Alternatively, total costs could be covered by raising the prices paid by the groups' members. The average annual expenditure for the member families varies from 928 euros (Group D) to 1573 euros (Group B). To balance the budget by marking up prices to cover costs, the annual expenditure would have to be from 10 per cent (Group C) to 29 per cent (Group A) higher.

Conclusions

In food and agriculture systems, economic viability is a necessary prerequisite for achieving sustainable systems that can provide profits as well as public goods and positive economic externalities. For alternative food provisioning practices, profitability depends on many contingent aspects (e.g., type of distribution channel, type of product, farm size and endowments, location, etc.). Nevertheless, labour is typically the highest marketing cost item that producers have to bear when engaging in AFNs, and, arguably, the cost and availability of labour is the major item affecting the adoption of the alternative channel and the resulting economic performance.

Even in distribution channels based on more complex form of governance, this cost item plays an important role. In SPGs, the cost of labour refers to the implicit cost of volunteers' time and was estimated to be sizable. Large groups, such as those we surveyed, are difficult to manage, and the participatory process becomes complicated: in cases where the groups become too large, they split into independent spin-offs to keep management easy (Brunori et al., 2012; Hankins & Grasseni, 2014). In our experience, however, the implicit cost of labour seems to depend on the number of producers, rather than on group size, suggesting that the typical SPG's process of relating with farmers may result in organizational inefficiencies. Such inefficiencies are emphasized in larger groups, who implement strategies to limit free-rider behaviour. The heavy demands put on regular volunteers raises some concerns about these groups' long-term sustainability. The representatives of the larger groups complain about the difficult turnover of volunteers with formal and administrative roles and of co-ordinators and the difficulties in motivating the occasional volunteers. Usually, when there are insufficient volunteers and no one is willing to act as co-ordinator, these groups disband. Evidently, only groups showing strong motivations and internal relationships succeed despite organizational inefficiencies and the disadvantages of remaining intact.

For the SPGs, the monetary value of labour is an explicit cost savings that enables the groups to pay higher prices to producers without marking up the prices charged to members. From the group members' subjective perspective, the value of volunteers' time is a measure of the value they attach to their participation in SPGs, an indicator of the strength of their motivations and thus of the groups' resilience. This value is considerable, and assuming a high opportunity cost of the volunteers' time, it suggests that the individual ethical and ideological motivations are strong. However, participants could also derive some economic benefit from the participation. Possibly, participants who pay lower prices in SPGs than in conventional channels could trade off some of the costs they save with the value of the work they supply. On the other hand, for participants paying higher prices in SPGs, the value of participation estimated on the basis of what it would cost to hire a worker to perform the tasks would be underestimated, because in addition to their work contribution, they are willing to pay higher prices. This last consideration would appear to confirm the force of individual motivations and provide stronger grounds for concluding that non-monetary reasons for participating predominate. To gain more insight into the value of volunteers' participation, alternative estimation methods should be tested in order to quantify the subjective benefits that the volunteers receive in exchange for their work.

In conclusion, members' willingness to provide unpaid work to enable SPGs to operate constitutes the groups' strength, insofar as the monetary and non-monetary benefits members receive (lower prices, satisfaction from ethical and relational outputs) are linked precisely to personal participation. At the same time, this may be a long-term threat to SPGs' viability, since the enthusiasm of the initial phase of SPGs can fade and free-riding problems (members benefitting from others' work without contributing) can arise, which might lead to the failure of the group. SPGs' leaders should be aware of this risk, and plan measures to avoid it.

Notes

1. The estimates found in the literature usually include the costs of marketing-related activities, omitting possible changes in the structure of the production costs related to the adoption of alternative channels. In other words, production costs are considered to be independent of the choice of the marketing channel. The results of our qualitative survey conducted with a group of farmers engaged in direct selling (Corsi et al., 2018, Chap. 9) seem to confute this assumption and indicate that production costs may also arise when a direct market channel is adopted. Thus, omitting production costs when comparing profits in conventional and alternative channels may cause the latter to be overestimated.
2. The approach is similar to that of Community Supported Agriculture (CSA) in the direct contact established with farmers. However, SPGs differ from CSA in three major respects: they (1) do not share the production risks with farmers, since no payment is made at the beginning of the crop year; (2) do not apply systematic budgeting to the production process; and (3) emphasize the opportunity to practise citizenship, rather than the benefits for accessing the land or directly contributing to the establishment of a local food system (Martino et al., 2016).
3. An alternative approach to estimating the value of members' participation is based on their own statements, using stated preferences methods (Corsi & Novelli, 2018, Chap. 4).
4. As an example, the major explicit cost item in SPGs is the cost of the goods to be distributed. This cost equals the revenue, since the goods are distributed without any mark-up.
5. Output approaches, on the other hand, focus on how the outputs of voluntary work (e.g., social benefits) are valued by the beneficiaries or on the

value of volunteering, that is, the value of the benefit that the volunteers receive in exchange for their time and effort (see Orlowski & Wicker, 2015; Salamon, Sokolowski, & Haddock, 2011 for a framework of voluntary labour monetization approaches).
6. Other input approaches, such as the opportunity cost method, are individual-centred (i.e., they assess the value of an individual's time) (Orlowski & Wicker, 2015).
7. The revenue item includes membership fees, possible donations, and the revenue from 'sale' (the value) of the distributed goods (equal to the cost of buying them from farmers).

References

Allen, P., Van Dusen, D., Lundy, J., & Gliessman, S. (1991). Integrating Social, Environmental, and Economic Issues in Sustainable Agriculture. *American Journal of Alternative Agriculture, 6*(1), 34–39.

Bowman, W. (2009). The Economic Value of Volunteers to Nonprofit Organizations. *Nonprofit Management and Leadership, 19*(4), 491–506.

Brown, C., & Miller, S. (2008). The Impact of Local Markets: A Review of Research on Farmers' Markets and Community Supported Agriculture (CSA). *American Journal of Agricultural Economics, 90*(5), 1296–1302.

Brunori, G., Rossi, A., & Guidi, F. (2012). On the New Social Relations Around and Beyond Food. Analysing Consumers' Role and Action in Gruppi di Acquisto Solidale (Solidarity Purchasing Groups). *Sociologia Ruralis, 52*(1), 1–30.

Brunori, G., Rossi, A., & Malandrin, V. (2011). Co-producing Transition: Innovation Processes in Farms Adhering to Solidarity-Based Purchase Groups (GAS) in Tuscany, Italy. *International Journal of Sociology of Agriculture & Food, 18*(1), 28–53.

Corsi, A., & Novelli, S. (2018). *Determinants of Participation in AFNs and Its Value for Consumers*. Chapter 4 of This Book.

Corsi, A., Novelli, S., & Pettenati, G. (2018). *Determinants of Farmers' Participation in AFNs*. Chapter 9 of This Book.

Economia Solidale. (2018). What Is a GAS? Retrieved January 11, 2018, from http://www.economiasolidale.net/content/cose-un-gas

Feenstra, G. W., & Lewis, C. C. (1999). Farmers' Markets Offer New Business Opportunities for Farmers. *California Agriculture, 53*(6), 25–29.

Feenstra, G. W., Lewis, C. C., Hinrichs, C., Gillespie, G. W., & Hilchey, D. (2003). Entrepreneurial Outcomes and Enterprise Sizes in U.S. Retail Farmers' Markets. *American Journal of Alternative Agriculture, 18*(1), 46–55.

Forssell, S., & Lankoski, L. (2015). The Sustainability Promise of Alternative Food Networks: An Examination Through "Alternative" Characteristics. *Agriculture and Human Values, 32*(1), 63–75.

Grasseni, C. (2014). Seeds of Trust. Italy's gruppi di acquisto solidale (Solidarity Purchase Groups). *Journal of Political Ecology, 21*(1), 178–192.

Graziano, P. R., & Forno, F. (2012). Political Consumerism and New Forms of Political Participation: The Gruppi di Acquisto Solidale in Italy. *The ANNALS of the American Academy of Political and Social Science, 644*(1), 121–133.

Handy, F., & Srinivasan, N. (2005). The Demand for Volunteer Labor: A Study of Hospital Volunteers. *Nonprofit and Voluntary Sector Quarterly, 34*(1), 491–509.

Hankins, J., & Grasseni, C. (2014). Collective Food Purchasing Networks in Italy as a Case Study of Responsible Innovation. *Glocalism: Journal of Culture, Politics and Innovation, 2*, 1–14.

Hardesty, S. D., & Leff, P. (2010). Determining Marketing Costs and Returns in Alternative Marketing Channels. *Renewable Agriculture and Food Systems, 25*(1), 24–34.

Ilbery, B., & Maye, D. (2005). Food Supply Chains and Sustainability: Evidence from Specialist Food Producers in the Scottish/English Borders. *Land Use Policy, 22*(4), 331–344.

Ironmonger, D. (2000). Measuring Volunteering in Economic Terms: 2,200 Million Hours Worth $42 Billion a Year. In M. Oppenheimer & J. Warburton (Eds.), *Volunteers and Volunteering* (pp. 56–72). Leichardt: Federation Press.

ISTAT. (2010). Wage Structure Survey. www.istat.it/it/archivio/83362

Jarosz, L. (2008). The City in the Country: Growing Alternative Food Networks in Metropolitan Areas. *Journal of Rural Studies, 24*(3), 231–244.

King, R. P., Hand, M. S., DiGiacomo, G., Clancy, K., Gomez, M. I., Hardesty, S. D., et al. (2010). *Comparing the Structure, Size, and Performance of Local and Mainstream Food Supply Chains*. Economic Research Service, USDA, Economic Research Report n. 99, pp. 81.

LeRoux, M. N., Schmit, T. M., Roth, M., & Streed, D. H. (2009). *Evaluating Marketing Channel Options for Small-Scale Fruit and Vegetable Producers: Case Study Evidence from Central New York*, EB 2009-03. Department of Applied Economics and Management. Ithaca, NY: Cornell University.

Martino, G., Giacchè, G., & Rossetti, E. (2016). Organizing the Co-production of Health and Environmental Values in Food Production: The Constitutional Processes in the Relationships Between Italian Solidarity Purchasing Groups and Farmers. *Sustainability, 8*(4), 316.

Martino, G., Pampanini, R., & Giacchè, G. (2013). Exploring the Role of Consumers as Drivers of Agri-food Networks: Contexts, Beliefs, and Governance. *Brazilian Geographical Journal: Geosciences and Humanities Research Medium, 4*(1), 12.

Milestad, R., Westberg, L., Geber, U., & Björklund, J. (2010). Enhancing Adaptive Capacity in Food Systems: Learning at Farmers' Markets in Sweden. *Ecology and Society, 15*(3), 29.

Novelli, S., & Corsi, A. (2016). Economic Sustainability of Short Food Chains: The Case of the Solidarity Purchasing Groups in Italy. In *Challenges for the New Rurality in a Changing World.* Proceedings from the 7th International Conference on Localized Agri-Food Systems, 8–10 May 2016, Södertörn University, Huddinge, Sweden.

Orlowski, J., & Wicker, P. (2015). The Monetary Value of Voluntary Work: Conceptual and Empirical Comparisons. *Voluntas, 26*(6), 2671–2693.

Sage, C. (2007). Trust in Markets: Economies of Regard and Spaces of Contestation in Alternative Food Networks. In J. Cross & A. Morales (Eds.), *Street Entrepreneurs: People, Place and Politics in Local and Global Perspective* (pp. 147–163). London: Routledge.

Salamon, L. M., Sokolowski, S. W., & Haddock, M. A. (2011). Measuring the Economic Value of Volunteer Work Globally: Concepts, Estimates, and a Roadmap to the Future. *Annals of Public and Cooperative Economics, 82*(3), 217–252.

Saroldi, A. (2001). *Gruppi di acquisto solidali. Guida al consumo locale*. Bologna: Edizioni EMI.

Schifani, G., & Migliore, G. (2011). Solidarity Purchase Groups and the New Critical and Ethical Consumer Trends: First Results of a Direct Study in Sicily. *New Medit, 10*(3), 26–33.

Uematsu, H., & Mishra, A. K. (2011). Use of Direct Marketing Strategies by Farmers and Their Impact on Farm Business Income. *Agricultural and Resource Economics Review, 40*(1), 1–19.

Verhaegen, I., & Van Huylenbroeck, G. (2001). Costs and Benefits for Farmers Participating in Innovative Marketing Channels for Quality Food Products. *Journal of Rural Studies, 17*(4), 443–456.

11

Quality and Price Setting by Producers in AFNs

Filippo Barbera, Joselle Dagnes, and Roberto Di Monaco

Introduction

Prices are a key dimension of economic exchange in market-based economies. Economics and sociology offer both alternative (Chiffoleau & Laporte, 2004) and complementary (Fillieule, 2010) perspectives on price-formation mechanisms. Sociologists (see Baker, 1984; Podolny, 1993; Uzzi & Lancaster, 2004) are eager to show that the economic approach is unfit to explain why prices emerge, stabilize, and change. Economists reply that sociological variables may doubtless count in the explanation of prices, but the mechanisms that enlighten them are still economic. In this chapter, we will first illustrate three key attempts of sociologists to build an alternative

F. Barbera (✉)
Department of Cultures, Politics and Society, University of Torino, Torino, Italy

Collegio Carlo Alberto, Torino, Italy
e-mail: filippo.barbera@unito.it

J. Dagnes • R. Di Monaco
Department of Cultures, Politics and Society, University of Torino, Torino, Italy
e-mail: joselle.dagnes@unito.it; roberto.dimonaco@unito.it

A. Corsi et al. (eds.), *Alternative Food Networks*,
https://doi.org/10.1007/978-3-319-90409-2_11

view of prices and the reply that economics offers to these attempts. Second, we will argue that the explanations of prices depend on the different idea of markets the two disciplines support and more specifically on the interplay between economic and non-economic motives. We will then apply this view to the analysis of price-formation mechanisms in Alternative Food Networks (AFNs), showing why and how prices are set by producers at the intersection of different quality conventions.

Prices and the Embeddedness of Economic Exchange

Economics argues that if the competitive market holds, equilibrium prices emerge from the law of demand and supply and the law of production costs. In competitive markets agents are atomized price-takers: namely, they operate in isolation from one another and they cannot influence aggregate market outcomes. The law of production costs says that the price of a good is determined by the sum of the cost of the resources that went into making it. The cost can comprise any of the factors of production (including labor, capital, or land) and taxation. Sociology is interested in showing how social forces influence prices as deviations from competitive equilibrium and production costs. Conceptually, these "social forces" fall under the heading of "embeddedness":

> In market economies, prices are the result of supply and demand. But are they really? (…) I (…) argue instead that prices result from the embeddedness of market transactions in institutions, social networks, and culturally anchored frames of meaning. This does not deny that supply and demand play a role in price changes, but proposes that supply and demand are shaped by the social and political forces operating in market fields as well as the social and cultural contexts forming the preferences of actors. Price changes can only be explained independently from the embeddedness of economic transactions if the underlying shifts in supply and demand occur while this embeddedness remains constant. (Beckert, 2011, p. 1)

Economic action, exchange, and prices are always embedded in ongoing social relations and "thick" institutional contexts. Agents, in this perspective, are never isolated from one another and their "web of ties" influences the key dimensions of economic exchange. This point is in striking contrast with the economic assumption that—to be really competitive—markets require social atomization (Granovetter, 2017, p. 13). Economists are quite ready to accept the relevance of non-economic factors and dimensions in shaping prices, but they are more skeptical of the claim that the fundamental laws of economics (i.e., demand and supply, production costs) do not play a key role even in "embedded markets" (Fillieule, 2010).

To illustrate the point, let us first consider the research of Wayne Baker (1984) on how social structure influences equilibrium prices in two stock option markets. The key research question is simple and straightforward: how does social structure influence the volatility of prices? Is this influence in line with the assumption that the higher the number of agents, the less volatile the prices? Economics postulates that, all other things being equal, equilibrium prices are very likely to be highest with a large number of traders. Baker's answer is negative, and he reaches this conclusion by claiming that markets are kinds of social structures and identifying two different types of social structure, each with a different influence on the volatility of equilibrium prices. The first type is a small, dense social structure, while the second is made up of a greater number of actors separated into distinct subgroups. Baker shows that, contrary to the predictions of economic theory, prices do not reach the point of equilibrium as the number of agents increases, but are more stable in smaller and denser groups:

> When a market increases in size, and thus when the number of participants rises, the actors come up against the limits of their ability to process and communicate information. They no longer have time to explore all the opportunities for trading in order to discover the most advantageous one. Furthermore, the increase in market size gives problems of trust: the actors know each other less well and they have more and more reasons to be wary of possible opportunistic behaviors (…). The personal relations that each actor maintains with a fairly small number of other participants may to some extent offer protection against this opportunism. Thus when market size increases, the bounds of rationality and the risk of opportunism lead participants to reduce the number of actors with whom they trade, which

> tends to fragment the market, cause cliques to emerge and thus increase price volatility. (Fillieule, 2010, p. 673)

> Is this a rebuttal of economic reasoning? Renaud Fillieule (2010) shows this is not the case, since if the market splits, then the pricing margins will tend to move apart, the interval will widen and the price set within this interval will vary to a greater degree, which is why volatility increases: "Far from having refuted the economic argument, Baker here is offering a good illustration of it". (Fillieule, 2010, p. 681)

The second example is Uzzi and Lancaster's (2004) analysis of the prices of legal services and how they are regulated by the embeddedness of exchange within ongoing social relations (Granovetter, 1985), which may be family, friendship, or trust-based. These exchanges refer to "embedded ties" (Uzzi, 1997), namely those long-lasting social ties which reduce transaction costs. Interpersonal ties such as these are far from anonymous and allow the firm and its client to reach agreement on potentially contentious issues such as what to charge for knowledge developed for previous clients and applied to the present case (Granovetter, 2005, p. 38). Accordingly, the hourly rates of legal services are influenced by the embeddedness of exchange: the longer the actors have known each other, and have thus been able to develop shared expectations, interpersonal trust, and norms of reciprocity, the lower the price of legal services will be:

> Embedded relations between a law firm and its client companies tend to give rise to mutual trust and shared norms between the actors, which in turn facilitates the exchange of private information and limits the risks of opportunism. This results in a reduction in transaction costs, that is, a reduction in the hourly cost of producing the legal service, which tends to bring prices down. (Fillieule, 2010, p. 674)

Does this account offer an alternative perspective to economics? The effect of embeddedness would appear to be perfectly in line with the "law of costs" and the role of competition (Fillieule, 2010). As for the law of the costs, mutual ties breed key knowledge of the needs of the customer and thus reduce the hourly cost of producing the service required. Legal services deal with contentious cases and often call for applying knowledge and expertise developed in cases other than the one at hand: this "translation" is far easier if it is mediated by "embedded ties". Since we know your needs well, the reasoning goes, the costs of customizing the legal service are much lower. As for the role of competition, it has been argued that it is flawed to think that corporate actors such as law firms are making a "gift" to the customers with whom they share past social ties. Ongoing social relations also mean that the transaction will happen again in the future and hence: "They act in this way in order to avoid possible reductions in revenue due to the loss of clients. Law firms have to attract and retain their clients" (Fillieule, 2010, p. 680).

The third and last example refers to how a producer's status in the market influences its choices about product quality and the economic outcomes in terms of prices that result. Benjamin and Podolny (1999) deal with Californian wine producers and how actors occupying high-status positions obtain greater benefit from subsequent high-status affiliations than do actors occupying lower-status positions. Status is measured through "appellations of origin": the larger the number of producers from a different region who use the appellation, the higher its status. Quality is measured through the ratings awarded by wine-tasting experts in the *Connoisseur's Guide to California Wine*, where data on prices are given as well. Benjamin and Podolny's analysis shows that status is positively correlated with an increase in prices, irrespectively of quality and production costs, even after control variables are taken into account. However, in this example as well, the sociological account does not reject the economical one:

> Podolny (…) neglects to explain to us why higher demand should be reflected in a price increase. He then implicitly uses—and this is the argument we are advancing—the "law of supply and demand": the price tends to be fixed at the value that equalizes the quantities offered and those demanded ("law of supply and demand"), demand increases, the supply is assumed to remain constant, and thus the (equilibrium) price rises. (…) The sociological specificity, and the value of Podolny's study, is that account is taken of status, which is disregarded by economists but that, as he demonstrates convincingly, influences price formation. On the other hand,

his explanatory theory cannot dispense with the most standard of all economic models. (Fillieule, 2010, p. 679)

Mark Granovetter (2005) summarizes the different understanding of markets in economics and sociology by the difference between auction markets and customer markets. "Customer markets" are based on repeated purchases, while auction markets are not (Okun, 1980, p. 148). In customer markets, prices rarely equal marginal costs and customers pay premium prices to well-known sellers for their products, in return for quality. Trading only with a subset of sellers strengthens social relations and the embeddedness of economic exchange in non-economic dimensions thereof. This makes prices "sticky", since changing sellers would also mean "breaking old relations and forming new ones" (Granovetter, 2005, p. 38). Accordingly, markets tend to stabilize as niches with specific roles and ties, where economic and non-economic dimensions are strongly intertwined and generate new kinds of actions. In this line, Norkus (2000, p. 273) identified 15 possible combinations of social action, where the rational, value-driven, traditional, and affective elements combine and generate more complex empirical actions.

The Market for AFNs

With regard to price-formation mechanisms, as Mark Granovetter argues, the theoretical issue is often not one of economic and sociological arguments conflicting, but rather "of the weakness of both in understanding how actors with simultaneous economic and non-economic motives will act" (Granovetter, 2005, p. 38). Sociologists state that power, status, and social forces work as non-economic motives in shaping prices, while economists say that—even in embedded markets—the actors use their social relations for economic purposes. What both perspectives fail to acknowledge is the interplay between economic and non-economic motives. This interplay casts doubt on "the classical separability assumption that incentives and moral sentiments are simply additive in the implementation of desirable outcomes" (Bowles, 2016, p. 41). Accordingly, prices might be "sticky" or exceed the marginal cost because they are markers for the social identity of producers, or because they are means of avoiding fierce competition in given niches, or because they are signals for the "right" quality levels to competent consumers. Markets, in other words, are complex social structures where economic and non-economic motives intersect in many ways and *jointly* motivate action and shape outcomes.

The specific forms of these intersections and their effect on prices are strongly influenced by the worlds of AFN quality conventions (Boltanski & Thévenot, 2006) and the social devices that channel them (Karpik, 2010). Among the six "worlds" of legitimate common welfare (inspirational, domestic, opinion/fame, civic, market, and industrial worlds), which enable actors to reduce semantic uncertainty and facilitate coordination, AFNs are characterized by a mix of domestic, civic, and inspirational conventions. In domestic coordination, uncertainty about quality is solved through customs, traditions, and local knowledge. In civic coordination there is commitment to welfare and/or public interest. In the inspirational world, what is worthy is what cannot be controlled, what is felt in inner experience, manifested by feelings and passions, and what rejects habits and routines (Ponte, 2009). AFNs producers need first and foremost to *justify* their action within a frame grounded on these conventions. This is far from frictionless, since it requires compromises among conflicting principles: for instance, while domestic coordination emphasizes traditions and habits, the inspirational world points to novelty and the rejection of routines. Second, as we have illustrated elsewhere (see Barbera, Dagnes, & Di Monaco, 2018), the industrial world with its quest for efficiency, the market world governed by the law of costs and demand/supply, and the opinion-based world ruled by external markers of reputation pose a challenge for AFNs since large-scale distribution might "imitate" these conventions as a marketing strategy. As a consequence, for sellers as well as for consumers: "clear distinctions cannot be made between definitions of quality and (…) boundaries between categories are often blurred" (Sage, 2003, p. 7). It is fair to say that quality conventions/orders of worth combine differently in different worlds of food/worlds of production (Salais & Storper, 1992; Storper & Salais, 1997). As Stefano Ponte argued (Ponte, 2016, p. 16), analytically, the literature has developed along two distinct (but sometimes overlapping) approaches: a first approach that engages with an agro-food adaptation of the "worlds of production" framework and a second that applies the "orders of worth" approach of Boltanski and Thévenot (2006) and further elaborations of "quality conventions" (Eymard-Duvernay, 1989; Sylvander, 1995; Thévenot, 1995). Orders of worth and worlds of production mutually influence each other: for instance, the industrial world requires standardized goods (e.g., apples of the same size), which conflicts with the conventions of AFN markets. The influence can travel from consumers to producers as well (see Barbera et al., 2018), as when producers need to translate specific "aesthetics" (say, the consumers' predilection for freshness and flavor) into particular growing techniques in the field.

The social devices that channel quality conventions in AFN markets consist of networks of interpersonal relationships based on the personal and multiple interpretations of reality that are generated in the interaction. In AFNs, the seller matters and the expectation of quality is focused on the personal relationship with the seller, on the trust in her expertise and reliability. The characteristics of the sales environment, that is, the ease of access and the physical and social appeal of the shop or of the market stall, play a minor role. Trust is "an important lubricant of a social system. It is extremely efficient; it saves a lot of trouble to have a fair degree of reliance on other people's word" (Arrow, 1974, p. 23). The literature on trust converges on defining it as the belief that another person with whom you might interact will not cause you harm even though he or she is in a position to do so (Gambetta, 1988; Granovetter, 2017). The intersection between economic and non-economic motives casts doubt on the role of "interests-driven" trust, as when the decision not to cause harm is governed by something to be gained. Sellers/producers in AFNs seem to act in trustworthy ways because of their conceptions of who they are, the "logic of appropriateness" they rely on (March & Olsen, 1995, pp. 30–31). The appropriateness of rules of action includes both cognitive and normative components. Actors seek to fulfill the obligations encapsulated in a role, an identity, a membership in a group (Pizzorno, 2006): "one undertakes to see the world as others do—not because the benefit of doing so outweighs the cost, but because that is the way of being in the world with these people" (Loury, 2002, p. 44). As we will illustrate below, trust, reputation, identities, and instrumental rationality jointly motivate and shape price-setting decisions. Neither instrumental rationality nor expressive motivations act on their own and in isolation from one another.

Research Design

To explore the mechanisms underlying price formation in AFNs, we carried out a study of the farmers engaged in direct sales in Porta Palazzo, the biggest open-air urban district market in Turin and one of the largest in Europe.

The Porta Palazzo farmers' market is held in a specific area of the district market (see Fig. 11.1) protected by a historical iron shed. It hosts

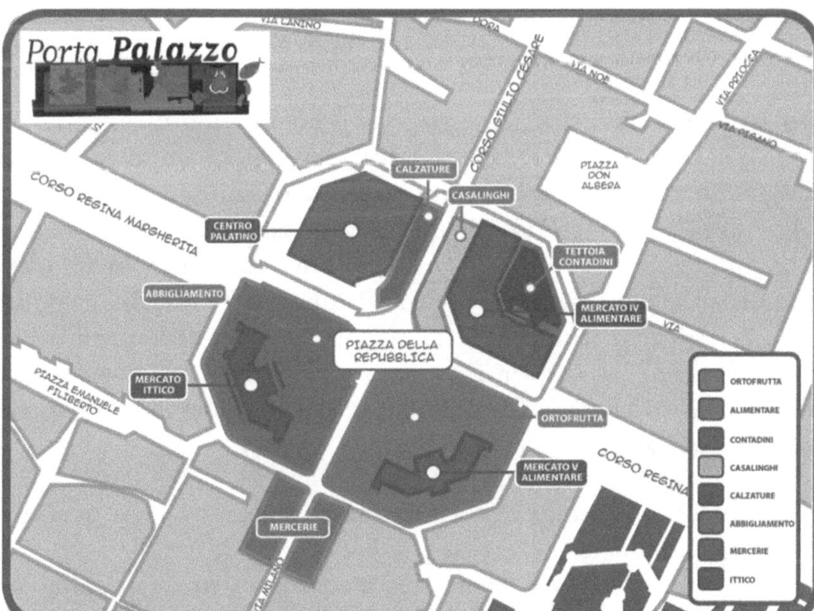

Fig. 11.1 Map of Porta Palazzo market in Turin (farmers' market area circled in black). Source: https://scopriportapalazzo.com

almost 100 small-scale farmers from neighboring rural areas, in almost all cases within 150 km from Turin, directly selling fresh fruit and vegetables, dairy goods, and cold cuts (Black, 2005, 2012). Starting from the list of producers provided by the municipal offices and verified during market days (from Monday to Saturday), we randomly selected a sample of 27 farmers, almost one third of the total, to whom we administered a semi-structured interview. Data collection took place from March to July 2015 by trained interviewers supervised by the research group. The interview addressed specific aspects of the farmer's profile and activity through an informal dialogue between the interviewer and the interviewee, starting from a list of open questions. Topics covered included the characteristics of the farm (farm name, location, foundation year, products, method of cultivation and/or breeding, area under cultivation, number of workers, annual turnover, and trend in the last three years), the sales methods (on-farm and off-farm), and the characteristics of the farmer (age, place of birth, educational qualifications). Respondents were also asked about the path they took to become a farmer, what kind of customers they have, whether they sell through middlemen, and their personal conception of quality.

To explore how small-scale agro-food producers set prices and quality conventions, we focused on the different logics behind the market strategies that farmers employ to establish prices and represent the quality of their products. Our hypothesis, in fact, is that the farmers do not act in the market following an exclusively "economic" logic, where the price is the only indicator of product quality. To test this hypothesis, we investigated the farmers' representations, attitudes, and behavior in the light of conventions theory and the judgment devices embedded in social ties. These findings will be elaborated along two specific dimensions:

1. The degree of control exercised by the producers over the quality of their own products;
2. The degree of recourse to market mechanisms in establishing and adjusting the sales price.

Quality Conventions and Price Setting in AFNs

The AFNs producers we interviewed run small-scale family businesses that have been active for generations. Some have always been located in the same place, while others moved from Southern Italy to Piedmont. Close family members such as children and spouses play a key role in business organization, either permanently or only for a limited period of time. Their help is often contingent on having "free time" during the weekends or on school holidays. More recently established businesses are mainly run by immigrants who have transformed know-how gained in their country of origin into a job here or young people who after being laid off from a job started to work on family land that had been abandoned for years.

> We've been farmers since the 16th century. Even if we went to school, our love for the land makes us come back to our origins. My daughter is studying at the moment, but my son works the land with me. He did a thousand jobs and then said "Mom, I'm coming with you to work in the fields again". (Interview number 3)

> It's only me and my mother who work but I have two little brothers who will soon come to help us. I am 29 years old, I was an electrician until 5 years ago then I left home and I decided to work with my mother. (Interview number 5)

Family bonds, local identity, personal passion, and the pride in being part of a "tradition" are the key social resources that overlap with the economic organization of the business. These resources are crucial in dealing with economic problems and market hardships: labor thus costs less and informal ties among family members provide the required flexibility. Many farmers complain that their turnover has dropped in recent years or, at most, has remained stagnant. Things are a bit better for those producers who take part in ad hoc farmers' markets, where a superior quality level and a "loyal" demand guarantee better margins even in hard times.

> Customers who go to a farmers' market are particular customers, let's say they are looking for a human touch. (Interview number 5)

> When the product is truly excellent, you attract customers; when you have the chance to produce an excellent product, then there are people who call you all the time to book the strawberries. When you have an ordinary product, people forget that you exist and go wherever is most convenient. It is truly a pursuit of quality in our case. (Interview number 8)

> In the beginning most of our customers are just regular customers. Then a friendship is established. The only thing is that you have to be honest. Don't see the customer as somebody to gouge money from. You have to give them something that you know they will appreciate that'll bring them back the next day. (Interview number 2)

As in the early analysis of "industrial districts", the economic performance of producers is closely linked to "communitarian" characteristics such as trust, reciprocity, and a shared collective identity. At the same time, the "invisible handshake" between supply and demand (Okun, 1980) builds an implicit agreement not to take advantage of market conditions by raising prices even when demand increases. Long-term stability and constant flux are thus preferred over short-term benefits. This view of price rigidity is in line with the idea that "prices should be more rigid in markets in which customers and firms interact repeatedly. There is a direct experimental evidence to this effect" (Nakamura & Steinsson, 2011, p. 222).

Sales channels are thus governed by different logics, and mixing them—as some producers do—requires a well-defined *market competence*. In addition to selling their products in the farmers' area in Porta Palazzo, the majority of the interviewees also sell in daily district markets, monthly ad hoc farmers' markets, on-farm, and/or at the wholesale market. In addition, some of them directly manage grocery stores, while a minority rely on e-commerce and Solidarity Purchase Groups. Producers who "travel" across different sale channels enact different selling strategies accordingly. This would appear to be a specific skill that is not equally distributed among AFN producers. For instance, some growers had gone wholesale, but the tiny margins and the excessive demand for product standardization made them return to the market stalls. Some decided to sell certain products wholesale and to keep others for district markets and farmers' markets. The wholesale market's industrial quality convention requires standardized parameters that are at odds with those of small-scale producers.

> Now we are back here [at the market] because in wholesale in the last few years we didn't have a margin any more [...]. To sell to the general markets, the fruit had to have a standard shape and size, so we were forced to throw the rest away. (Interview number 7)

> Switching from the wholesale market to district markets isn't easy. You are used to another type of work and find yourself reduced to a smaller company. At first, I felt that being here with this little stall was a come-down, you know, I was used to clearing pallets and pallets of stuff with 4 or 5 workers helping me every day. And now I find myself with a box of this and a box of that ... I can understand that some people maybe don't even want to take this step. (Interview number 5)

Quality in the Eyes of Producers

As we have just outlined, the direct trust relationship between demand and supply is a constitutive rule of the economic exchange in AFN markets. Along with trust, quality is also a key dimension of these markets. For AFN producers, quality is first and foremost linked to notions of "freshness", "seasonality", "genuineness", and "farm-to-table".

> People know that they pay a little more but it's good stuff. Here you find the earliest ripe fruit and seasonal products. In a supermarket you can find everything all year long, just 50 meters from here. (Interview number 8)

> People who come to the farmers come because they want a fresh product and because they want to look at the person who produces it. [...] the human relationship is very important because trust is created. (Interview number 1)

AFN producers also show a specific aesthetic conception of the product they sell: in a nutshell, vegetables and fruits have to be beautiful without being perfect. Irregularities, imperfections, and "asymmetries" are key features of a "beautiful product", while uniformity, smoothness, and symmetry are regarded as "industrial" parameters of beauty.

> For me quality means giving a fresh product, harvested the very day before. A quality product must be a good, genuine product and picked fresh the day before. Because this is the issue: from the producer to the consumer. (Interview number 7)

The role of the domestic convention by no means excludes innovation and careful application of agronomic knowledge. AFN producers are constantly striving for a balanced mix between tradition and innovation, both for the quality of the product and—above all—for the producer's quality of life and to contain production costs. Innovation is primarily aimed at optimizing the production process: this target is pursued both by "backward innovation"—namely by improving and updating a traditional solution in a new context—as well as by the use of once-innovative techniques that have now become "part of the tradition" (e.g., greenhouses).

> Traditional techniques need to be integrated with new technologies because the past is gone ... Avoiding extremes on one side or the other is the best solution, because if we go to use all the possible technologies we go right down the middle. We need to take advantage of technologies to work in the tradition, or better, to improve the working system and quality of life, because if you spend the whole day tearing out weeds ... I think you have to find the right way, in between tradition and innovation. (Interview number 10)

> Innovation helps the grower to achieve greater productivity; [...] labour costs a lot, so where you can modernize and use new techniques it turns out to be helpful ... pay a person for a week to plant twenty thousand cabbages and cauliflowers, when you can pay a person for a day and a half with mechanized planting. [...] You can't keep up with the times if you don't mechanize. (Interview number 3)

What about organic production methods? On this subject, there is no agreement among the farmers. In fact, some think that being "organic" simply means following tradition, "doing things the way they were done in the past", while others see organic methods as truly innovative:

> Many people understand organic as a traditional method, but it isn't. Organic production is highly technological, it just uses special technologies that are not used if you use chemicals. (Interview number 7)

The complex relationship between tradition and innovation is also reflected in a pragmatic and nuanced judgment of the role of standards and efficiency, as in the case of the "industrial convention":

> For quality, standardization is certainly not the best thing, not at all. At the same time, let's say that in my opinion there's a need for a good balance … a minimum of standardization is needed, because otherwise the production process takes too long. There must be a good combination and in any case standardization should not be carried so far that it's at the expense of quality. (Interview number 2)

The environmental convention displays a very close pattern: the environment is certainly a key consideration for AFNs farmers, but their grasp on it is highly "pragmatic". In terms of selling strategies, environmental safety is a central dimension for customers, but the knowledge and representation they have of environmental safety may be quite "naïve". In this regard, producers often report that their customers want to be reassured about their use of eco-friendly products, not realizing that the production process may in some cases require some chemical treatments.

> We must make people understand that in any case it is a matter of treatment, but there's a whole heap of products that are "zero-residue". It means that you do your own treatment and then leave it. There is a whole data sheet that tells you how many days when you can still find residues on the fruit. It means that if you allow 7 days, from the eighth day you can eat the fruit safely and it will always be clean. (Interview number 9)

The link with the local area also has a pragmatic slant. First of all, the local area is where embedded ties and reciprocal exchanges take place, where informal support and mutual recognition grow in support of the economic activity. We could say that the "social capital" embedded in the local web of ties and social norms reduces transaction costs and enables market behavior to be to some extent communitarian instead of "individualistic" (Bagnasco, 1988; Trigilia, 1986).

> We have a fiscal system that allows us to integrate our products with the products of other producers, the new tax systems for agriculture allow you to keep up to 50% of products that are not yours. These peppers, for instance, are from a farm that produces a lot of them, and since we produce so many peaches we barter them. We go back in order to go forward. (Interview number 11)

> We come from a small place where we all know each other, if you need something you can ask your neighbor. And at the agricultural level you can ask the neighbor quietly: there is cooperation and the community dimension is positively perceived. (Interview number 15)

> We all help each other, we were born there. If someone's tractor breaks down, somebody else lends one to him, things like that … (Interview number 13)

At the same time, these community bonds are far from deterministic, and they leave room for producers to behave opportunistically, especially when they face off on the urban market. Consumers can very rarely tell the difference between real and fake farmers and this uncertainty is exploited by some sellers. Moral suasion and informal sanctioning mechanisms are not enough as a means of controlling opportunism.

> I think everyone here looks after himself. When someone needs a hand, I give it to him, but then there are few who reciprocate. This is an anarchist place. Everyone does what he wants but looks only to his own interests. For example, we can integrate up to 50% but you must declare it and have a cash register. But they don't keep records of anything, so they can afford to buy and sell whatever they want. (Interview number 4)

> This one behind gives away a lot of things, but because he is not working properly. At 11 o'clock he has already finished everything because he sells at lower prices than ours and ruins our market. It isn't honest. (Interview number 13)

Though the price of fruit and vegetables certainly matters (cf. next section for price-setting mechanisms), it is not the only factor in consumers' purchasing choices. As stated above, the relationship of trust that can be established between the farmer and his customers is at least as important, because it is seen as a guarantee of product quality.

> People need to trust, they need to know that you are an honest person and then they trust you. Yes, because you might say that the product is organic when it isn't … (Interview number 20)

> In my experience I see that [the brand] has very little effect, because it's the person and therefore the relationship of trust that matters. (Interview number 14)

In fact, the reputation conveyed by trademarks and quality schemes for foodstuffs—such as the Protected Designation of Origin (PDO), the Protected Geographical Indication (PGI), and the Traditional Specialty Guaranteed (TSG) labels—do not seem to be very effective among the market stalls, even if producers express diverging opinions on this point. As can reasonably be expected, in fact, those who directly benefit from labelling—for example, those who have organic certification for their agricultural products—tend to emphasize the importance of the brands and their relationship with the product quality, while the others tend to downplay their relevance.

> People are a little like that, they don't know, they only look at trademarks and certifications. But in my opinion that is another thing, a joke, because many still say that if it doesn't have that label the product isn't any good … It isn't true, the product is good too. (Interview number 14)

By contrast, there is unanimous agreement among the interviewees about the importance of their intrinsic motivation, both for obtaining a quality product and for job satisfaction. In fact, the farmers' effort—and hence their labor—is not seen merely as a factor of production, but rather as being meaningful for their self-identity.

> Passion affects our effort, because as in all activities, if there's no passion you struggle and you don't succeed! (Interview number 5)

> Passion is key. The more passion you put into what you do, the more the stuff you produce is good. (Interview number 6)

The Price-Setting Mechanisms

Quality conventions influence price-formation mechanisms quite clearly. Prices and producers' market-like behavior are deeply intertwined with the rules and norms illustrated above.

In order to determinate the market value of foodstuffs, namely the price, producers must first of all take their production costs into consideration, including the costs for raw materials, work equipment, farm maintenance, transport, energy, and so on. Labor seems to be another issue, since family-based farmers usually consider only the external workforce as a cost item, but do not count their own work or that of family members.

> I calculate the costs of production and then I add something … because if I had to count my own hours … it's like I'd pay myself for one or two hours of work a day, no more. (Interview number 14)

Additional factors to be taken into consideration refer to both the supply-side and the demand-side. On the supply-side, the total amount of production, by the single farmer as well as by an entire area, obviously affects the end price of agricultural products. This dynamic is exacerbated by the seasonal nature of agro-food and the fact that agro-food processing—making preserves, jams, and marmalades, for example—is not particularly common on farms.

> When you have overproduction you can afford to lower the price (…). If you are a direct farmer, the moment arrives when you can find yourself with 30 or 40 crates of spinach to sell every day because then the season ends. If you first sold it at 3, now you can sell it at 1. (Interview number 8)

On the demand-side, the price adjustment depending on the purchase preferences shown by consumers can be almost immediate, even leading to several price changes on the same day. Expanding the observed time period, several fluctuations emerge during the week, according to the specific type of clientele and the demand they express. On Saturdays, for instance, the market attracts a larger number of shoppers, in some cases looking for foodstuffs with qualitative and quantitative characteristics that differ from those sought by daily visitors. As a result, prices are higher on Saturday than on weekdays.

> Prices along the week vary. More zucchini are sold on Fridays and Saturdays, so the price changes depending on the day. (Interview number 21)

> I obviously regulate myself based on sales … if I see that in a day I don't sell a product, the following day I cut the price. (Interview number 12)

> I evaluate on a case-by-case basis, if it is hard to sell a product then I lower the price a bit … prices change sometimes in the same day. Saturdays are a bit higher, but personally I try to keep them unchanged because then people remember, I have regular customers. (Interview number 3)

In determining the price, a major role is also played by comparison with other market actors. In this regard, there are two important aspects that should be highlighted. The first is that this comparison takes place not only with other farmers but also with district markets and large retailers. On the one hand, the farmers know that their production methods, their cost structure, and their final products are very different from those that can be found in other channels. But on the other hand, they are also aware that, unless they can carve out a quality niche market, they must compete for consumer preference in a wide arena populated by many possible suppliers. Second, the comparison does not only serve to set the end points of the price scale that the farmers use to optimize their sales strategies to be as competitive as possible on the market. In fact, it is part of a more articulated system of relations that refers to embedded ties defining—and in turn defined by—community social norms. This is of course particularly true in the farmers' market, where everyone knows each other and free riders are stigmatized (see previous section). Thus, farmers try to avoid competition on price, relying instead on customer loyalty built through personal relationship and trust.

> We look at each other, you can't sell at much more expensive prices than the others. You stay at the same level as everybody in the square, so as to not kill each other too. (Interview number 12)

> I come from (*the name of a specific area*) and we all have more or less the same prices, we know what we're doing … (Interview number 14)

> In a market with so much competition, you look at the others' prices. Nevertheless, I have higher prices because in my opinion my stuff is higher quality, is better treated and is cleaner. I work differently from many of the others who work here, look at how my table is arranged, how neat it is. I offer few products but they're special, I pick the zucchini when they are still small so I sell them at higher prices for example. So I have more expensive products but in a market niche. (Interview number 25)

Also for these reasons, producers do not always conceive of the price they set as a direct expression of product quality. Paradoxically, in some cases the downward rigidity in prices is affected by the idea of quality held by the consumer, who ignores the supply-demand mechanism and introduces expectations about the link between price and quality. This is the case, for example, of organic products. Lacking other signals known to be reliable—because organic labelling is absent, for instance, or because there is little trust in these quality certifications—price must reflect the consumer's idea of quality.

> For the organic stuff, the price is very marginal, indeed sometimes if the price is too low it isn't credible and consumers don't buy the product. (Interview number 16)

Conclusions

In this chapter we have explored the conception of quality according to producers and how the specific ideas of quality expressed both by producers and consumers affect the price set in AFNs, specifically in farmers' markets. In this last section, we will first present our main findings, focusing on the non-linear construction processes of a fuzzy and sometimes contested market, where producers and consumers continually influence each other. Then, after summarizing the major price-setting mechanisms we have identified, we will elaborate on the nexus between price and quality as a marketing strategy.

Articulating the concept of quality from the farmers' point of view, we have observed that some conflicts emerge in the definition of quality dimensions. For example, this is the case of the domestic convention, relating to the role of tradition in cultivation practices. The search for a balance between traditional ways of producing and the introduction of innovations might be complex and subject to continuous reshaping, with some farmers who are more oriented towards working the land in the old peasant way and others who are more interested in experimenting with novelty.

> Tradition is important, but it must also be innovative … If you produce nowadays doing what my grandfather did in the past, you don't get the quality you need. (Interview number 6)

A similar conflict—and a similar search for balance—stems from the dichotomy between by artisanal and standardized production, referring to the industrial convention and compliance with technical standards and reliability. In fact, there is no agreement among farmers about whether standardization is necessary to ensure a constant level of quality, or whether an artisanal approach makes it possible to better interpret and transform agricultural products.

> Standardization is important in order to guarantee the quality of the end product. Once you have found the right recipe or the right way to cultivate something, changing it can be risky. (Interview number 16)

> Too much standardization can lead to a product that's too uniform. What matters most is the producer's touch. The product must be recognized, taste can change … The highest quality, of course, but with personality. (Interview number 5)

While the attitude towards traditional/innovative and artisanal/standardized production touches directly on the issue of quality, the ecological convention seems to serve a more pragmatic and in some cases instrumental function. Since environmental concerns are central for consumers, they also become key for farmers wishing to satisfy the concept of quality expressed by the customer. And even when the producers share these ecological values, the link with the quality of the agricultural products appears much more nuanced than in the mind of the consumers.

> I don't think that the focus on the environment itself has a significant impact on my product. My company is organic because of my personal sensitivity to the environment, which has nothing to do with the quality of my product. (Interview number 26)

> We do organic products for a marketing reason. The customer wants organic products, they think they are safer, better. I personally do not really believe in organic methods. (Interview number 1)

The importance assigned to trademarks and brands as an indication of quality varies among farmers for a different reason. In general terms, those who do not directly benefit from them tend to express skepticism about the certification process and, even more, about the ways expert opinion influences consumers' opinions.

> Official schemes—such as PDO, PGI and so on—are serious, they are a guarantee. I can't say the same about experts and critics. They often promote one thing or reject another out of personal choice, a liking, acquaintance, money … (Interview number 9)

The intersections and conflicts between different quality concepts—and quality signals—found in the farmers' market highlight the mutual influence between producers and consumers. From the general analytical perspective we have assumed for this entire book, AFNs enact a specific kind of exchange between producers and consumers. Consumers thus send signals to producers on a daily basis, and producers update their quality conventions accordingly. This happens both in a negative way—as when producers abandon certain products that are no longer required—and in a positive one—as when they introduce new products and/or change their supply. These changes also affect the production and conservation methods.

> We are the first to ask the customer to enlighten us on anything, on how to improve what we do. (Interview number 17)

> Crops changed according to the people who arrived in Turin, the immigrants for example. We were among the first to introduce turnip greens and hot peppers. (Interview number 4)

> It's a continuous adjustment, you always have to give what customers ask for. For example, small onions, small potatoes, special kinds of strawberries … (Interview number 8)

The same interplay appears in price setting, which is affected by both economic and non-economic dimensions. In a nutshell, price setting depends on:

1. Production costs (without labor cost)
2. Total production
3. Average prices for retail outlets and other farmers
4. Product sales (price changes even during the same day)
5. Specific day (prices in the market are the highest on Saturday)
6. The attempt to avoid competition with neighbors by adopting similar prices
7. The quality idea expressed by the consumer (e.g., about organic products)

But what can we highlight about the nexus between price and quality? Drawing conclusions from the evidences collected among the farmers, we propose a two-dimensions scheme based on the degree of control over quality and the degree of recourse to market mechanisms in setting and adjusting sales prices. Summarizing (see Fig. 11.2), we can identify four typical situations, which may help to capture different sales conditions and mechanisms for establishing quality and price, showing the complex influences of social relations on these dimensions.

The two axes of the scheme show some implications in the experiences of the producers. The horizontal axis distinguishes the relations promoted by the producers, characterized by the attempt to 'individualize' the price

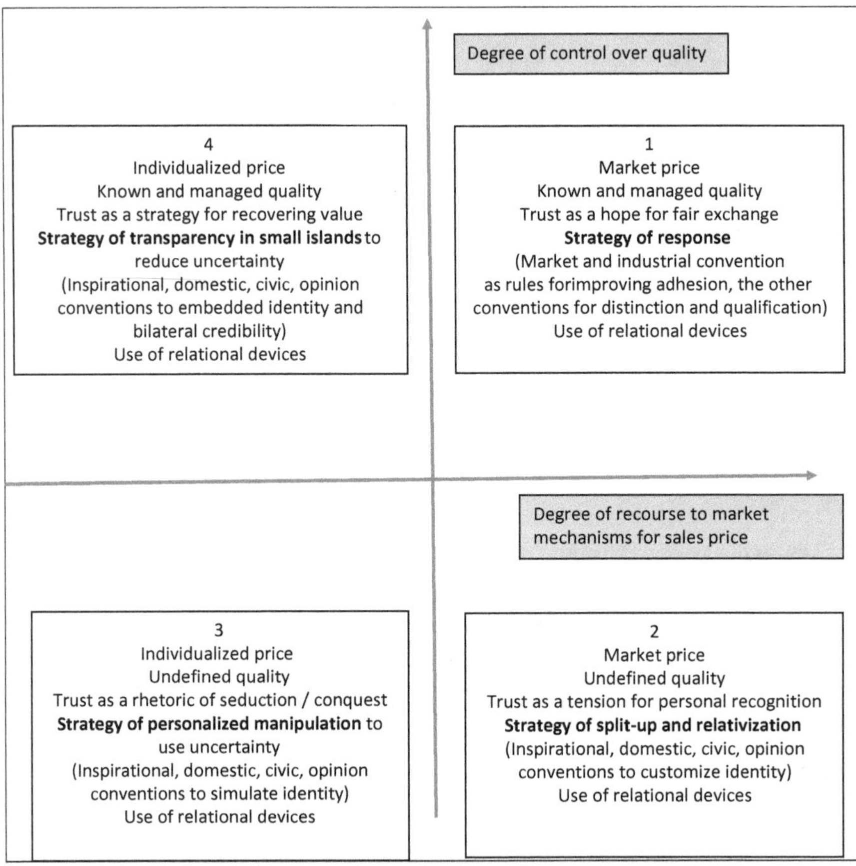

Fig. 11.2 Two-dimensions scheme for degree of control over quality and price

(establishing a special price for their customer), versus recourse to a market mechanism (current price in a similar stall). From this perspective, the producers declare that prices are in general highly opaque and variable, since they move without reference criteria. They state that these idiosyncratic factors concern all sales segments, including district markets, wholesale and large-scale retail distribution. Production costs are also considered opaque and very difficult—if not impossible—to calculate.

The vertical axis distinguishes the relationships promoted by the producers, which, in their statements, are associated with a low ability to control the intrinsic quality of their products and to limit the ability to meet their customers' quality expectations. In particular, for many producers, the technical treatments are under the control and the expertise of external specialists. Consequently, their knowledge of and control and control over their products are subject to certain limits, which are greater for products obtained from other producers, whether farmers or non-farmers.

Moreover, the producers find it difficult, if not impossible, to satisfy many of their customers' quality demands. This is true both because demand-side requirements may be "unattainable" (out-of-season products, products with non-achievable characteristics, impossible production methods, etc.) and because of prejudices and rigidity on the supply-side (e.g., producers may consider their customers' requests to be absurd or resulting from a lack of knowledge). The intersection of the two axes highlights four typical situations that emerged from our research, which have one shared trait and several differences.

The shared trait is the importance attributed, in all situations, to the relationship with customers, and in particular to gaining their trust, which is essential for qualifying the sales relationship and for influencing the representation of quality and price. However, trust, although central, appears to be quite undefined in the producers' representation. Very different ideas exist about the ways to gain trust, about its connection with the real quality of the product and with the degree of adaptation to the customer's requirements, even when they are considered inappropriate.

The difficulty in managing the relationship with the customer in a trust framework thus emerges, fluctuating between transparency and opacity, between narratives and rhetoric both about the product and the production practices. In particular, dilemmas exist with respect to the more or less strategic use of the information given to the customer, which may respond to a principle of transparency or of opportunistic construction of consistency between the product and the customer's quality expectations. This orientation is sometimes justified by disparaging the customers' beliefs and assuming a somewhat "didactic" attitude towards them. In these cases trust is essential, because it is only through trust that the customer's beliefs about quality, price, and the product can be influenced.

The differences between the four areas are thus of a strategic nature, as they describe situations in which the producers may use the relationship with the customer to achieve different objectives. In the first quadrant, where the price is more exposed to competition and the capacity for effective quality control is greater, trust relationships are interpreted as the means of achieving a fair exchange. The prevailing strategy is oriented towards bringing the qualitative and quantitative characteristics of the supply into line with demand, bringing the producer as close as possible to a tense flow, namely to an adequate response to the customer's demand. The customer, in this sense, has the task of driving the exchange. The relational devices and the conventional meanings are used to smooth this response and to orient the uncertainty on quality.

In the second quadrant, there is less capacity for effective quality control, both because there is less attention to production processes and because products from other farmers are also being sold. In this relational situation, trust is assigned to the producer and is oriented towards achieving maximum personal recognition. It is thus a strategy that aims to separate the attribution of quality from the actual characteristics of the process and of the product, relativizing the importance and significance of any discrepancies. In this operation, the judgmental devices based on the relationship and the conventional meanings of quality are fundamental.

Even in the situations represented in the third quadrant, quality control is reduced, but the producer's effort to increase the separation between price setting and market mechanisms is greater. Trust in the relationship with the customer is fundamental for this purpose, as it conveys a rhetoric of seduction that aims to endow the product with unique meaning.

We can define this operation as a strategy of personalized manipulation, as it builds shared meanings that go beyond uncertainty within the social relationship. Here again, the full range of conventional meanings is used to construct adequate representations towards the customer.

Lastly, the situations described in the fourth quadrant show an effort to individualize the price by relying on the perception that the market is inadequate in recognizing the product's actual specificity. In particular, the trust relationship strives to recover value, on the basis of production practices and product characteristics. This strategy focuses on transparency and communication, drawing on conventional meanings, conveyed in the personal relationship with the individual customer or with small groups.

The different situations that we have illustrated acknowledge that consumers are driven by very different and nuanced quality beliefs, partly conditioned from outside. However, they show different response strategies, where trust and personal relationship are a common vehicle. These strategies are not necessarily related to real changes in production processes, but in some situations (quadrants 2 and 3) they tend to support it more with words than with deeds. In these cases the producer needs to take as much control as possible in the process of conventional definition of quality and communication flows.

Once again, the relationship between product characteristics, quality, and price turns out to be a complex game in which *both* consumers and producers play a key role.

References

Arrow, K. (1974). *The Limits of Organization*. New York: W.W. Norton.

Bagnasco, A. (1988). *La costruzione sociale del mercato: studi sullo sviluppo di piccola impresa in Italia*. Bologna: il Mulino.

Baker, W. E. (1984). The Social Structure of a National Securities Market. *American Journal of Sociology, 89*(4), 775–811.

Barbera, F., Dagnes, J., & Di Monaco, R. (2018). *Consumers' Quality Conventions in Alternative, Conventional and High-quality Food Chains*. Chapter 5 of This Book.

Beckert, J. (2011). Where Do Prices Come from? Sociological Approaches to Price Formation. *MPIfG Discussion Paper* 11/3.
Benjamin, B., & Podolny, J. (1999). Status, Quality, and Social Order in the California Wine Industry. *Administrative Science Quarterly, 44*(3), 563–589.
Black, R. E. (2005). The Porta Palazzo Farmers' Market: Local Food, Regulations and Changing Traditions. *Anthropology of Food, 4*. Retrieved August 3, 2018, from http://journals.openedition.org/aof/157
Black, R. E. (2012). *Porta Palazzo: The Anthropology of an Italian Market*. Philadelphia: University of Pennsylvania Press.
Boltanski, L., & Thévenot, L. (2006). *On Justification*. Princeton, NJ: Princeton University Press.
Bowles, S. (2016). *The Moral Economy. Why Good Incentives Are No Substitute for Good Citizens*. New Haven: Yale University Press.
Chiffoleau, Y., & Laporte, C. (2004). La Formation des Prix: Le Marché des Vins de Bourgogne. *Revue Française de Sociologie, 45*, 653–680.
Eymard-Duvernay, F. (1989). Conventions de qualité et formes de Coordination. *Revue Economique, 40*(2), 329–359.
Fillieule, R. (2010). The New Economic Sociology of Prices: An Analysis Inspired by the Austrian School of Economics. *American Journal of Economics and Sociology, 69*, 668–692.
Gambetta, D. (1988). Can We Trust? In D. Gambetta (Ed.), *Trust: Making and Breaking Cooperative Relations* (pp. 213–237). New York: Basil Blackwell.
Granovetter, M. (1985). Economic Action and Social Structure: The Problem of Embeddedness. *American Journal of Sociology, 91*, 481–510.
Granovetter, M. (2005). The Impact of Social Structure on Economic Outcomes. *Journal of Economic Perspectives, 19*, 33–50.
Granovetter, M. (2017). *Society and the Economy*. Cambridge: Harvard University Press.
Karpik, L. (2010). *Valuing the Unique: The Economics of Singularities*. Princeton: Princeton University Press.
Loury, G. (2002). *The Anatomy of Racial Inequality*. Cambridge: Harvard University Press.
March, J. G., & Olsen, J. P. (1995). The Logic of Appropriateness. *ARENA Working Papers WP* 4/9.
Nakamura, E. J., & Steinsson, J. (2011). Price Setting in Forward-Looking Customer Markets. *Journal of Monetary Economics, 58*, 220–233.
Norkus, Z. (2000). Max Weber's Interpretive Sociology and Rational Choice Approach. *Rationality and Society, 12*(3), 259–282.

Okun, A. (1980). *Prices and Quantities*. Washington, DC: Brookings Institution.

Pizzorno, A. (2006). Rational Choice. In S. Turner & M. Risjord (Eds.), *Handbook of the Philosophy of Science. Volume 15: Philosophy of Anthropology and Sociology* (pp. 373–395). Dordrecht: Elsevier.

Podolny, J. (1993). A Status-Based Model of Market Competition. *American Journal of Sociology, 98*, 829–872.

Ponte, S. (2009). Governing Through Quality: Conventions and Supply Relations in the Value Chain for South African Wine. *Sociologia Ruralis, 49*(3), 236–257.

Ponte, S. (2016). Convention Theory in the Anglophone Agro-food Literature: Past, Present and Future. *Journal of Rural Studies, 44*, 12–23.

Sage, C. (2003). *Quality in Alternative Food Networks: Conventions, Regulations and Governance*. Policies, Governance and Innovations for Rural Areas: International Seminar, Università della Calabria, Arcavacata di Rende (IT), 21–23 November 2003.

Salais, R., & Storper, M. (1992). The Four 'Worlds' of Contemporary Industry. *Cambridge Journal of Economics, 16*, 169–193.

Storper, M., & Salais, R. (1997). *Worlds of Production: The Action Frameworks of the Economy*. Cambridge: Harvard University Press.

Sylvander, B. (1995). Conventions de qualité, marchés et institutions: le cas des produits de qualité spécifique. In F. Nicolas & E. Valceschini (Eds.), *Agro-alimentaire: une économie de la qualité* (pp. 167–183). INRA Editions, Economic.

Thévenot, L. (1995). Des marchés aux normes. In *La Grande Transformation de l'agriculture: lectures conventionnalistes et régulationnistes* (pp. 33–51). Paris: INRA/Economica.

Trigilia, C. (1986). *Grandi partiti e piccole imprese: comunisti e democristiani nelle regioni a economia diffusa*. Bologna: il Mulino.

Uzzi, B. (1997). Social Structure and Competition in Interfirm Networks: The Paradox of Embeddedness. *Administrative Science Quarterly, 42*(1), 35–67.

Uzzi, B., & Lancaster, L. (2004). Embeddedness and Price Formation in the Corporate Law Market. *American Sociological Review, 69*, 319–344.

Part IV

Environment, Territory, and AFNs

12

Introduction to Part IV: Environment, Territory, and AFNs

Alessandro Corsi, Egidio Dansero, and Cristiana Peano

AFNs have several implications for the environment and the territory. Environmental concerns have been a major driver behind the intensification of agricultural production and the use of chemical fertilizers and creation of AFNs. Among the criticisms of the conventional food system that were at the origin of several AFNs was the idea that it had provided cheap food at the expense of the environment, encouraging the pesticides,

---

A. Corsi
Department of Economics and Statistics "Cognetti de Martiis", University of Torino, Torino, Italy
e-mail: alessandro.corsi@unito.it

E. Dansero (✉)
Department of Cultures, Politics and Society, University of Torino, Torino, Italy
e-mail: egidio.dansero@unito.it

C. Peano
Department of Agricultural, Forest and Food Sciences, University of Torino, Grugliasco (TO), Italy
e-mail: cristiana.peano@unito.it

A. Corsi et al. (eds.), *Alternative Food Networks*,
https://doi.org/10.1007/978-3-319-90409-2_12

as well as causing a significant environmental impact by transporting food over long distances. Local food and environmental-friendly production techniques such as organic cultivation were thus proposed in order to reduce this impact. The emphasis on local food, and especially its advantages in terms of transport, was popularized by the "food miles" argument (Paxton, 1994) and attracted the interest of certain sectors of consumers, which also fuelled the debate on "locavores" (e.g., Desrochers & Shimizu, 2012; Scharber & Dancs, 2016).

However, the tenet of AFNs' environmental superiority over conventional chains has come under scrutiny. The issue is complicated because the generic term "environmental impact" covers several different aspects and calls for a number of caveats. First, an activity can impact the environment in different ways, for example, by producing greenhouse gases or consuming energy. Second, the boundaries of the analysis obviously influence the results. Some analyses focus mainly on the farm level ("cradle-to-gate"), others also involve the distribution and marketing stage ("cradle-to-market"), while rarer studies assess impacts up to the consumer stage ("cradle-to-use"). Third, the chains' settings and hence their environmental impact differ according to the individual product, as they involve different types of storage (with or without refrigeration), storage periods, shelf lives, and consumption habits. Most of these studies have cast doubt on the food miles argument, suggesting that environmental superiority should be assessed on a case-by-case basis and that evaluations are only valid for the specific indicator of the environmental impact (e.g., Coley, Howard, & Winter, 2009). Based on these premises, in Chap. 13 Peano, Tecco, and Girgenti reflect critically on AFNs' potential and limits in reducing environmental impact and present a comparative assessment of the environmental impact of alternative and conventional chains. The assessment is based on a "cradle-to-use" Life Cycle Assessment comparing a conventional chain (supermarket) to three different AFNs, namely, farmers' stands at urban district markets, farmers' markets, and Solidarity Purchase Groups. The assessment concerns different types of fruit and vegetables and considers different packaging formats, since the latter can have major effects on the impact assessment. In line with previous literature, the study concludes that AFNs are not necessarily superior to conventional chains in terms of lower environmental impact and, more importantly, that the modalities of operation are more relevant than transportation in this regard.

That AFNs have implications on the food system located in the territory is self-evident. The issue of "local food" itself is strictly related to how food is delivered from the producer to the consumer. The (physical) distance between production and consumption is one dimension of the problem and as we have seen is mostly related to the environmental concerns. But it is not only a question of physical distance between producers and consumers. Much more is at stake. Among the criticisms of the conventional and globalized food system, deterritorialization, that is, the loss of the link between food consumption and food production and the territory, is an important concern. It is on this link that a meaning of food consumption and also a specific configuration of the territory and of the networks in it are based.

On the theoretical side, this gave rise to support for different spatial configurations: relocalization (based on spatial extension, see Kremer & DeLiberty, 2011; Sonnino & Marsden, 2006); re-regionalization (Kneafsey, 2010), based on the concept of foodsheds; re-embeddedness of food in places (Sonnino & Marsden, 2006), local ecologies (Murdoch, Marsden, & Banks, 2000); and social networks (Sage, 2003).

In Chap. 14, Dansero and Pettenati analyze AFNs from three perspectives, namely, spatial distribution, reterritorialization (Dansero & Puttilli, 2013), and proximity (Dansero & Pettenati, 2015). In the first perspective, they analyze Piedmont, and the Turin metropolitan area in particular, to shed light on the connections between the spatial distribution of the different types of alternative food network and the characteristics of the places where they take place and which they connect. In the second perspective, territorialization is understood as opposed to the deterritorialization which characterizes practices associated with the conventional system (Morgan, Marsden, & Murdoch, 2006). They consider AFNs starting from three complementary dimensions, namely, spaces, resources, and relationships, and locate the chains, in particular those in Piedmont, on the axes of relationships and of spaces. In the third perspective, they break down the spatial dimension into the three categories of physical, network, and cognitive proximity that characterize the AFNs in Piedmont to varying extents. The conclusion is that proximity in its different meanings plays an important role, but that AFNs are not homogeneous in this regard, since the different types attach importance to different meanings of proximity.

References

Coley, D., Howard, M., & Winter, M. (2009). Local Food, Food Miles and Carbon Emissions: A Comparison of Farm Shop and Mass Distribution Approaches. *Food Policy, 34*(2), 150–155.

Dansero E., & Pettenati G. (2015). Alternative Food Networks as Spaces for the Re-territorialisation of Food. The Case of Turin. In G. Cinà & E. Dansero (Eds.), *Localizing Urban Food Strategies. Farming Cities, Performing Rurality* (pp. 552–565). Proceedings of the 7th AESOP Sustainable Food Planning Conference. Turin: Polytechnic of Turin.

Dansero, E., & Puttilli, M. (2013). Multiple Territorialities of Alternative Food Networks: Six Cases from Piedmont, Italy. *Local Environment, 19*(6), 626–643.

Desrochers, P., & Shimizu, H. (2012). *The Locavore's Dilemma: In Praise of the 10,000-mile Diet*. New York: PublicAffairs.

Kneafsey, M. (2010). The Region in Food – Important or Irrelevant? *Cambridge Journal of Regions, Economy and Society, 3*, 177–190.

Kremer, P., & DeLiberty, T. (2011). Local Food Practices and Growing Potential: Mapping the Case of Philadelphia. *Applied Geography, 31*, 1252–1261.

Morgan, K., Marsden, T., & Murdoch, J. (2006). *Worlds of Food*. Oxford: Oxford University Press.

Murdoch, J., Marsden, T., & Banks, J. (2000). Quality, Nature, and Embeddedness: Some Theoretical Considerations in the Context of the Food Sector. *Economic Geography, 76*(2), 107–125.

Paxton, A. (1994). *The Food Miles Report*. London: Sustainable Agriculture, Food & Environment (SAFE) Alliance.

Sage, C. (2003). Social Embeddedness and Relations of Regard: Alternative 'Good Food' Networks in South-West Ireland. *Journal of Rural Studies, 19*, 47–60.

Scharber, H., & Dancs, A. (2016). Do Locavores Have a Dilemma? Economic Discourse and the Local Food Critique. *Agriculture and Human Values, 33*(1), 121–133.

Sonnino, R., & Marsden, T. (2006). Alternative Food Networks in the South West of England: Towards a New Agrarian Eco-Economy? In T. Marsden & J. Murdoch (Eds.), *Between the Local and the Global (Research in Rural Sociology and Development, Volume 12)* (pp. 299–322). Bingley: Emerald Group Publishing Limited.

13

Applied Environmental Sustainability of Fruit and Vegetables in Different Distribution Channels (AFNs and Large-Scale Retail)

Cristiana Peano, Nadia Tecco, and Vincenzo Girgenti

Introduction

The globalized food system's social and environmental costs raise questions about its sustainability, and many possible alternatives (technical, social, and economic) have been explored by several authors in recent years (Feenstra, 2002; Goodman, 2004; Schönhart, Penker, & Schmid, 2008; Wezel et al., 2009). In this context, initiatives such as AFNs that aim both to reduce the number of intermediaries in the food system and geographically relocalize production and consumption have become increasingly worthy of consideration (Bruce & Som Castellano, 2017;

C. Peano (✉) • V. Girgenti
Department of Agricultural, Forest and Food Sciences, University of Torino, Grugliasco (TO), Italy
e-mail: cristiana.peano@unito.it; vincenzo.girgenti@unito.it

N. Tecco
Department of Cultures, Politics and Society, University of Torino, Torino, Italy
e-mail: nadia.tecco@unito.it

A. Corsi et al. (eds.), *Alternative Food Networks*,
https://doi.org/10.1007/978-3-319-90409-2_13

Goodman, 2004; Mariola, 2008; O'Hara & Stagl, 2001; Vávra, Daněk, & Jehlička, 2018).

AFNs share the ambition of meeting the various criteria of a sustainable food system, and it is mainly for this reason that localness seems to have a significant appeal for consumers. However, there are discrepancies between different countries and products in the propensity to buy local which may be due to diet habits, seasonality, consumers' preferences for local brands (Grunert, Hieke, & Wills, 2014) and to farmers' markets (Hinrichs, 2015; Pettinger, Holdsworth, & Gerber, 2008).

"Fruit and vegetables" is a category that includes many products with different roles in local cultural and agricultural landscapes (Clément, 1999; Mazoyer & Roudart, 1997), as well as on menus. Even if local is not the same as alternative (Corsi, Novelli, & Pettenati, 2018, Chap. 6), the decision to buy in Alternative Food Networks (AFNs) is often linked to a desire to support farmers and local economies. Local food, moreover, is fundamental to people's sense of identity, intimately linked to the notions of gender, class, and ethnicity, and is also important in symbolic as well as material terms (Probyn, 2000). Localness, in the case of fruit and vegetables as in many others, deserves attention because of the number of effects it can have on environmental sustainability and social wellbeing. Local is a concept that, at the very least, relates to the distance between the place where produce is grown and the place where it is consumed (Feldmann & Hamm, 2015). Even considering only this spatial dimension, the effects of local food consumption can thus be different. The economic perspective emphasizes the redistribution of increased value for farmers, the relocalization of economic flows, and a reduced reliance on non-renewable resources. From a social perspective, local food chains seem more equitable and fair, as they give renewed meaning to farm work and the social links between city and country (Hinrichs, 2000). From an environmental perspective, a number of authors have explored local food chains' ability to preserve natural resources (Hiroki, Garnevska, & McLaren, 2016) and to balance the links in the rural and urban ecosystem (Ghisellini, Cialani, & Ulgiati, 2016; Rothwell, Ridoutt, Page, & Bellotti, 2016).

While local food supply can have significant impacts on the sustainability of production processes, an increase in alternative distribution networks can also be important in helping to realize unexpressed local potential.

From a policy perspective in particular, having a clear idea of the main characteristics, strengths, weaknesses, and enabling factors of local fruit and vegetables and of what their main (positive and negative) impacts could be will help decision makers design effective measures to address the challenges involved in shortening the food supply chain. From the consumers' perspective, clearly communicated information about the impacts of local fruit and vegetables can improve the understanding of the issues connected with food consumption and the use of natural resources (Coley, Howard, & Winter, 2009; Syrovátková, Hrabák, & Spilková, 2015).

Why Life Cycle Assessment?

The term "ecology of food" refers to the study of the complex links between food and the environment (Djekic et al., 2018). In the last 16 years, several environmental assessment methods have been developed and applied to various food products (meat, dairy products, fish, fruit and vegetables, wine, beverages), mainly in order to furnish producers and industry with tools for improving food production from the environmental standpoint and identifying 'hotspots' in greenhouse gas emissions (O'Rourke, 2014). These methods have also been applied to food supply chains (Goucher-Lambert, Moss, & Cagan, 2017). For food companies, using Life Cycle Assessment (LCA) and, more generally, modeling the environmental impacts of their products and processing methods has become increasingly attractive as a means of obtaining environmental labels for the foods they produce. Grunert et al. (2014) found that although sustainability labels still do not play a major role in consumers' food choices, but whether these labels' use will be effective in the future will depend on consumers' general concerns about sustainability issues.

Many methods and models (Djekic et al., 2018) have been specifically developed and adapted to farm-to-retail-to-table planning, processing, and control, but only a few adopt a consumption-oriented approach to assess the impact of the food supply chain.

Life Cycle Assessment is the main scientific method used to measure products' environmental impact and has been applied to an increasing number of products in the agro-food sector (Arzoumanidis, Salomone, Petti, Mondello, & Raggi, 2017; Jacquemin, Pontalier, & Sablayrolles,

2012). As outlined in ISO 14040, the method consists of the following steps: mapping the process, setting the scope and boundaries, collecting data, and calculating, evaluating, and interpreting the results with a view to recommending environmental improvements.

Mapping the process and setting the scope and the boundaries are important in order to clarify parts of the food chain analyzed from the "farm to fork" perspective. In fact, most LCAs for food products apply 'cradle-to-gate' system boundaries, that is, they focus mainly on the farm level. However, other system boundaries are applied in the literature, such as 'cradle-to-market' in which the distribution and marketing stage is also involved or the more rarely cited 'cradle-to-use' LCAs, which assess impacts from the consumer stage.

A generic model of the food product's life cycle system boundaries is presented in Fig. 13.1. In this chapter, we have focused on fruit and vegetables because high-value or specific crops cultivated using organic farming methods in peri-urban areas are generally associated with a higher probability of direct sales (Corsi et al., 2018, Chap. 9).

In this case, the analyzed system is divided into four subsystems:

Subsystem 1—'Farm' includes the nursery phase and all activities which take place in the orchard (for perennial crops such as fruit trees, the impacts of the entire field cycle were calculated by taking the early field phase into consideration and then adding the subsequent adult productive phase).

Subsystem 2—'Warehouse' consists of further processing (storage, refrigeration, packaging).

Subsystem 3—'Retail' consists of activities that take place where food products are sold. These sales outlets may be supermarkets and grocery stores, or may be specialized shops and possibly AFNs.

Subsystem 4—'Household use' includes refrigeration, food preparation, and cooking.

In recent years, the literature has presented several LCA studies on the production of fruit such as apples, strawberries, raspberries, blueberries, and oranges (Cerutti et al., 2014; Girgenti, Peano, Bounous, & Baudino, 2013). In addition, an increasing number of studies have focused on vegetable crops such as beans (Abeliotis, Detsis, & Pappia, 2013), cauliflower (Martínez-Blanco, Anton, Rieradevall, Castellari, & Munoz,

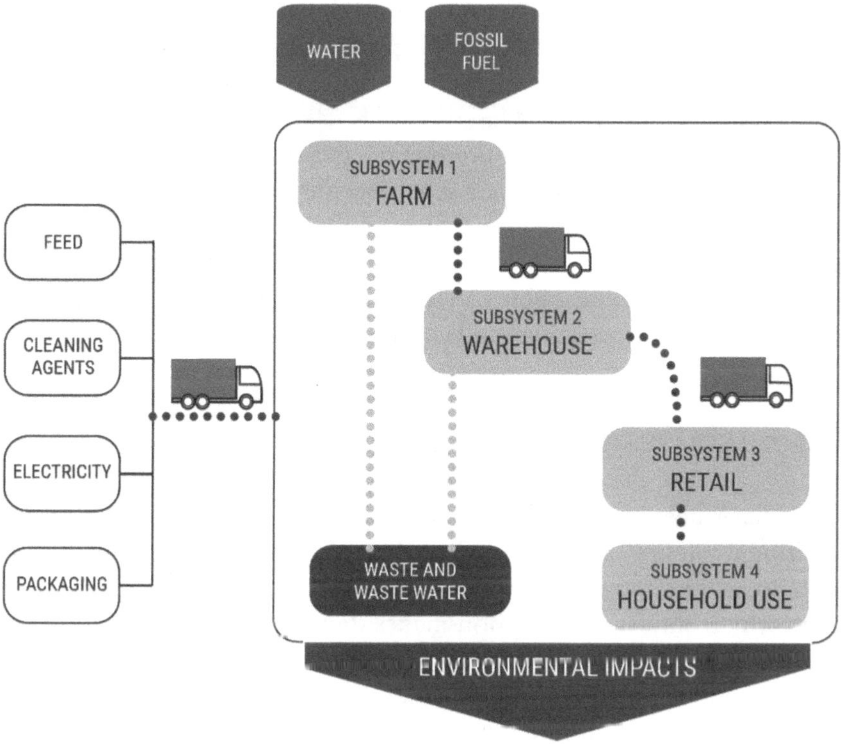

Fig. 13.1 Generic system boundaries of fruit and vegetable life cycle with four subsystems (modified from Djekic et al., 2018)

2011), potatoes (Mattsson & Wallen, 2003), tomatoes (Cellura, Longo, & Mistretta, 2012), and lettuce (Romero-Gamez, Audsley, & Suarez-Rey, 2014).

In addition to agricultural production, the subsequent stages of supply chains have also been investigated in LCAs of vegetable crops (Cellura et al., 2012). As part of the debate on local food and food miles, several studies have compared the environmental performance of the supply chains for local and imported vegetable products (Rothwell et al., 2016). AFNs and other alternative approaches to fruit and vegetable sales and delivery to the end consumer have also been investigated. The latter studies mainly address the approaches' energy and climate change performance (Coley et al., 2009). To date, very few LCA studies have focused on alternative forms of vegetable distribution and/or packaging while accounting for the entire supply chain from producers to consumers and for a variety of impact categories. For instance, Markussen, Kulak, Smith, Nemecek, and Østergård (2014) compare the production and small-scale supply of mixed organic vegetables through a box scheme with their supply via supermarkets in the UK. Some studies have questioned the assumption that the local dimension of the production and distribution system is necessarily better from an environmental point of view, demonstrating that there is a gap between theoretical assertions and empirical findings (Coley et al., 2009).

Research Design

AFNs have been proposed by food activists as a feasible alternative to traditional sales channels because of their ability to ensure a higher level of environmental sustainability as a result of their different organizational form, which almost by definition makes them "natural allies to local sustainability policies" (Geissler, 2015). AFNs are very much part of the ongoing debate on the local food system and whether it is better than a mass retail system at minimizing the farm to fork environmental impacts of fruit and vegetables, especially in terms of sink function. This debate has often claimed that there is a direct link between local food and environmental sustainability, though no specific correlation with environmental accounting studies of production and distribution chains using methods such as LCA has been made.

We thus chose to combine a theoretical approach with a group of case studies in order to critically evaluate the impacts of distribution models starting from the basis on which these relationships are established and the effects of these choices, where the scale becomes the system's boundary rather than its intrinsic purpose.

Starting from the need for co-production of knowledge by the stakeholders operating in local food systems that has been noted by several authors (Marsden, 2013), the study's objective, as regards the environmental aspect, was to propose an interpretative approach to analyzing how meanings and goals are shared among the actors in AFNs and to evaluating the environmental impact of fresh fruit and vegetables purchased at AFNs (local markets, farmers' markets) and large-scale retailers. In the past, considerations based solely on the scale as such have contributed to a rhetoric of the local as more environmentally friendly by definition. We could almost say that, paradoxically, the reflection on AFNs has long been caught in the local trap (Born & Purcell, 2006). This is why this section of our study regards the local scale as the boundary of the analyzed food systems, rather than their intrinsic purpose.

Specifically, the case investigated in this chapter covered two different systems (supply chains):

1. Large-scale retailers: as mentioned by Barbera et al. (2018, Chap. 5), large-scale retailers are more concentrated in Northern Italy than in the southern areas of the country. Several of them have endorsed the 'buy local' movement through pledges and commitments to source local produce. The Coop and Conad supermarket chains, for example, have increased the supply of produce from Italian producers in recent years, and in particular have stated that they hope to be able to source all of their fruit and vegetables locally. This situation is similar to what is happening in the UK with many British retailers such as Marks & Spencer and Tesco. In addition, a variety of environmental labels and local brands appear on products in Italian supermarkets as a consequence of the environmental impact issue. Through these initiatives, Italian retailers seek to respond to consumers' preferences for local foods.
2. Direct sales (AFNs): in addition to on-farm sales, this category includes open-air urban district markets. More than 40 daily district markets take place in the city of Turin, where farmers' markets are also held on a weekly or monthly basis, and are mainly promoted by the farmers' unions. The category also includes Solidarity Purchase Groups (SPGs), that is, self-organized networks of individuals and families who buy food—as well as other goods—directly from producers. There are no fewer than 170 SPGs in Piedmont, over 130 of which are located in the province of Turin (Pettenati & Dansero, 2018, Chap. 14).

We used the life cycle thinking approach, selecting LCA as a methodological tool for breaking down the different supply chains at different stages to determine how the internal organization of technical and distribution functions affects the products' environmental impact and thus understand the weight of individual factors in each supply chain. Though a cradle-to-grave LCA was conducted for the supply chains of a number of different types of fruit and vegetables (Fig. 13.2), this chapter will present our findings for apples, strawberries, and tomatoes, three locally produced products that have a prominent place in the eating

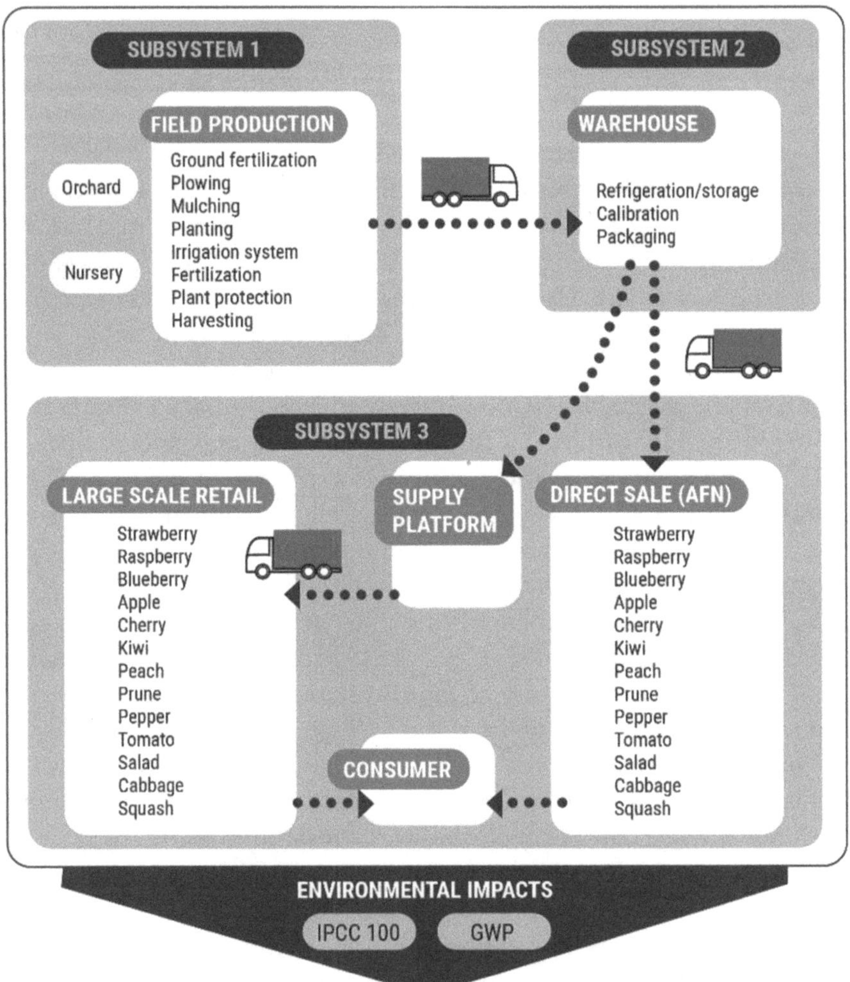

Fig. 13.2 Theoretical framework for assessing environmental impacts applied to different products in our study. The framework is limited to the first three subsystems shown in Fig. 13.1

habits of consumers in Piedmont and are on the market for several months each year.

Apples have a long product life (even in consumers' homes), while strawberries and tomatoes have a short shelf life and thus higher purchase frequencies (Tecco & Peano, 2018, Chap. 6).

Each product supply chain for the different sales channels was reconstructed by examining and collecting data from actual operating systems in Piedmont, from production to consumption and post-consumption practices (three for each product supply chain). For the production phase, two different production protocols were considered: the integrated system that follows the regional regulations for integrated farming (Piedmont Region Integrated Pest Management program) and the protocol for organic farming. In the case of organic farming, we considered only products that are in fact certified and not those from producers who claim to adopt 'natural', 'sustainable', or 'biological' methods of cultivation but do not follow EU organic farming regulations and are not certified.

LCA was conducted according the four-phase approach contemplated by ISO 14040 and 14044.

We identified different functional units according to the sales channel and the most common packaging system used in it. For apples, for example, different functional units were defined in each distribution channel, as different sales formats are used (4-cell plastic tray, 2 kg plastic bag, unpackaged apples with the CPR reusable box system).

The different functional units were used as a reference to compile the inventory of environmental burdens and then to calculate the respective impacts. The Ecoinvent 2.2 and LCA Food databases were used for the inventory. Assessment was carried out with SimaPro 7.3 software produced by PRé Consultants. For each production chain, data were standardized using mass balance methods and were subsequently organized in two impact categories: GWP (global warming potential) IPCC 100 (kg CO_2 eq.) and consumption of non-renewable energy resources, calculated from the energy content of the required resources (non-renewable primary energy in MJ eq.). As noted by Goossens et al. (2017), the product environmental footprint and International Life Cycle Data (ILCD) assessment method involves 16 impact categories. In our case, we based our selection of impact categories on the literature, focusing our analysis on two impact categories chosen in order to provide an evaluation of the examined production's impact on climate change that can be readily communicated to and understood by stakeholders. The non-renewable energy source category was selected to provide a view of the impacts on emissions and consumption, as the latter is considered to be one of the most critical issues in the primary sector.

We compared the carbon emissions resulting from a large-scale vegetable supply chain with those from a supply system where the customer buys from an AFN channel.

Data was interpreted for each fruit and vegetable product across the distribution channels taken into account.

Findings

The LCA analyses performed on different types of fruit and vegetables (data not shown) indicate that for berry fruits (including strawberries) and lettuce, the irrigation system and the operations carried out in the nursery have the highest environmental impact. It should also be noted that field operations have a decidedly greater impact than the warehouse and distribution phases (including transport). This finding, which is confirmed by the literature, is undoubtedly related to the products' short shelf life (a few days) (Peano, Girgenti, Baudino, & Giuggioli, 2017). For fruits like peaches, plums, and cherries, the greatest impacts in the field phase are due to fertilization and disease control treatments (integrated production), while in the warehouse phase, even though medium-term cold storage (1–2 weeks) involves higher energy consumption, the greatest impact is from packaging. For vegetables, however, fertigation of red cabbage and zucchini and the plastic used for mulching (even if consisting of bio-based material) peppers and lettuce have a significant effect on the environment. For all these products, the limited duration of storage (1 week) and the type of packaging mean that impacts in the warehouse phase are not high. In general, no difference was found between the overall impact of conventional and organic cultivation techniques for any given product. Though organic cultivation reduces the use of synthetic fertilizers and pesticides, significant quantities of other products such as copper are employed, while both techniques often rely on the same approaches to mulching, irrigation, and so on.

If we look at the LCA results for the three products selected for this chapter (apples, strawberries, and tomatoes), considering, for example, the lowest and the highest environmental impact score (both in terms of kg CO_2 eq. and non-renewable primary energy in MJ eq.), we see that there are no trends common to all three products or to the two sales channels and the two production methods (Tables 13.1, 13.2, and 13.3).

However, the magnitude of the differences varies, and is greater in the case of strawberries in plastic baskets sold in the direct sales system and supermarkets ($\Delta = 0.602$ kg CO_2 eq.), more modest in the case of apples sold at supermarkets in plastic bags/trays or unpackaged ($\Delta = 0.15$ kg CO_2 eq.), or for organic tomatoes sold unpackaged at the supermarkets compared to tomatoes in wooden boxes at AFNs ($\Delta = 0.117$ kg CO_2 eq.). To determine whether or not the factors intrinsic to the various organizational and logistical functions of alternative vs conventional socio-technical systems can reduce their environmental impact, it seems more interesting to break down the impact score by the individual phases rather than analyzing the final score. Breaking down the impacts into phases shows that the impact of the individual phases can vary significantly, depending on how the distribution system is organized (the production system, the logistics, the packaging system). The findings thus indicate that each channel has its own peculiarities, and neither channel can be considered more environmental friendly than the other.

The extent to which a supply chain is alternative and has the potential to reduce environmental impact is thus strictly related to the trade-offs among phases and attributes of the analyzed system (e.g., between production and centralized transport components, including logistics system km and efficiency, type of primary and secondary packaging, etc.).

If, for example, we take the case of apples sold at supermarkets, it is clear that the different packaging formats—the 4-cell plastic tray, the 20 kg plastic bag, and unpackaged apples with reusable CPR box—are crucial to impacts in the distribution phase, which in this case are the impacts that make a difference to the end result. Depending on packaging format, this phase's contribution ranges from 65% to 55% and drops to 8% for unpackaged apples.

Table 13.1 Total environmental impact (subsystems 1-2-3) for 1 kg of apples sold in different packaging formats and different markets. Production methods include integrated (PMI) and certified organic

Apples		Alternative food networks						Supermarkets	
		Farmers' stands at urban district market		Farmers' markets		SPGs			
		NRE MJ eq.	IPCC GWP 100a (kg of CO_2 eq.)	NRE MJ eq.	IPCC GWP 100a (kg of CO_2 eq.)	NRE MJ eq.	IPCC GWP 100a (kg of CO_2 eq.)	NRE MJ eq.	IPCC GWP 100a (kg of CO_2 eq.)
Integrated farming	Wood box (20 kg)	0.180	0.170	0.180	0.170	–	–	–	–
	Plastic tray	–	–	–	–	–	–	0.197	0.185
	Plastic bag	–	–	–	–	–	–	0.052	0.046
	Unpacked + CPR	–	–	–	–	–	–	0.040	0.035
Organic farming	Wood box (20 kg)	0.112	0.109	0.112	0.109	0.074	0.0717	–	–
	Plastic tray	–	–	–	–	–	–	0.115	0.099

Table 13.2 Total environmental impact (subsystems 1-2-3) for 250 g of strawberries sold in different packaging formats and different markets. Cultivation methods include integrated (PMI) and certified organic

Strawberries		Alternative food networks						Supermarkets	
		Farmers' stands at urban district market		Farmers' markets		SPGs			
		NRE MJ eq.	IPCC GWP 100a (kg of CO_2 eq.)	NRE MJ eq.	IPCC GWP 100a (kg of CO_2 eq.)	NRE MJ eq.	IPCC GWP 100a (kg of CO_2 eq.)	NRE MJ eq.	IPCC GWP 100a (kg of CO_2 eq.)
Integrated farming	Wood box (2 kg)	0.732	0.693	–	–	–	–	–	–
	Plastic basket (250 g.)	0.157	0.151	0.157	0.151	–	–	0.713	0.753
Organic farming	Wood box (2 kg)	0.683	0.583	–	–	0.574	0.583	–	–
	Plastic basket (250 g.)	0.665	0.459	0.665	0.459	–	–	0.665	0.459

Table 13.3 Total environmental impact (subsystems 1-2-3) for 1 kg of tomatoes sold in different packaging formats and different markets. Cultivation methods include integrated (PMI) and certified organic

Tomatoes		Alternative food networks						Supermarkets	
		Farmers' stands at urban district market		Farmers' markets		SPGs			
		NRE MJ eq.	IPCC GWP 100a (kg of CO_2 eq.)	NRE MJ eq.	IPCC GWP 100a (kg of CO_2 eq.)	NRE MJ eq.	IPCC GWP 100a (kg of CO_2 eq.)	NRE MJ eq.	IPCC GWP 100a (kg of CO_2 eq.)
Integrated farming	Wood box (5 kg)	0.029	0.212	0.029	0.212	–	–	–	–
	Unpacked + CPR	–	–	–	–	–	–	–	0.220
Organic farming	Wood box (5 kg)	0.029	0.212	0.029	0.212	0.166	0.244	–	–
	Unpacked + CPR	–	–	–	–	–	–	–	0.128

If we take the same 250 g plastic basket of strawberries sold directly and at supermarkets, here the difference in impacts occurs in the field. However, if we change packaging format and use a wooden box, the AFN channel's environmental impact increases and exceeds that of strawberries sold at supermarkets (Table 13.2).

In fact, the wooden boxes and plastic baskets are not reusable, as they are required to comply with EU Regulations 1935/04 and 2023/06 governing health and hygiene issues and thus must be disposed of after a single use.

In other cases, several factors concur in determining differences in impact. For unpackaged tomatoes sold through SPGs compared to unpackaged tomatoes sold at supermarkets, the loss of efficiency in the transport phase in conjunction with the type of packaging used in transport and sale resulted in a higher final score. In any case, the findings show that food packaging technologies are the most significant polluter in the food chain, as emphasized by Manfredi and Vignali (2015).

Probably the solution does not lie in zero packaging, which often reduces the shelf life of fruit and vegetables and exposes them to the risk of damage, but will depend on innovations in food packaging and in particular on combining behavioral sciences (related to retailer and consumer behavior) with LCA to improve packaging and provide valuable insights into eco-design (Williams & Wikstrom, 2011).

Evaluating the environmental burdens of these chains is thus a complex task. Consumers cannot be expected to make this type of assessment, and even after a more accurate analysis such as that carried out in this study, it is not possible to say that one marketing channel is more environmentally friendly than another. But what we can say is that different practices involved in production, transport, and distribution models across the supply chains selected as case studies can reduce their environmental impact.

Obviously, "it's the sum that makes the total", as one of Italy's best-known comic actors was wont to say, but apart from the fact that what counts in the end is the total environmental impact, using this type of LCA provided us with insights concerning the weight of single factors in the supply chain and enabled us to understand where there is room for improvement and how and where the 'local' can be environmental friendly.

Conclusions

In this chapter, we analyzed the environmental impact of three products in different agro-food supply chains, both conventional (integrated production and large-scale retail) and alternative (organic production and AFN). The supposed advantages of 'eating locally' for energy consumption (and greenhouse gas emissions) have already been studied by many researchers (Edwards-Jones et al., 2008; Mariola, 2008; Milà i Canals, Cowell, Sim, & Basson, 2007; Rizet et al., 2008; Saunders, Barber, & Taylor, 2006; Schlich & Fleissner, 2005).

One of the first conclusions that can be drawn from our study's observations along the entire farm to fork supply chain is that local food chains have significant potential for logistical optimization. These chains are accumulating logistics experience, and they have levers for improvement which could significantly improve their performance (Blanquart et al., 2010; Van Hauwermeiren, Coene, Engelen, & Mathijs, 2007; Wallgren, 2006). Indeed, the findings show that gains in efficiency are still possible, since in most cases the logistics are rather simple and affected by the location of distribution sites and the distance between farms and consumers. This indicates that agricultural spaces in urban peripheries could play a decisive role in the energy performance of local food chains. It is also important to emphasize that simply measuring energy efficiency (or greenhouse gas emissions) does not enable us to gauge the true extent of the set of economic and social benefits provided by consuming local products in local sales chains, and—as has been noted by Mariola (2008) and Kruse, Flysjö, Kasperczyk, and Scholz (2009)—their sustainability cannot be measured by means of a single indicator.

In view of the plurality of benefits that may accrue from relocalizing food consumption, we have attempted to go beyond considering energy efficiency as the sole criterion for sustainability which takes all local sales chain actors and modes of food distribution into account. Observing producers' and consumers' actual practices shows that building a network can improve the food system, for example, through careful choice of place of distribution, mutualizing transportation, and ensuring that there is a plurality of reasons for making a trip. It is in any case important to emphasize, as Sonnino and Marsden (2006) have done, that it is a mistake to see 'alternative' and 'conventional' food networks as separate spheres. Rather, there is a range of competing agro-food geographies built upon "different sets of quality and commercial conventions and different degrees of horizontal and vertical embeddedness".

The food consumer is not faced simply with a choice between 'local' and 'global'. As our data show, purchasing the most geographically local produce does not necessarily mean the lowest carbon impact.

In addition to greenhouses emissions, many other factors are involved in evaluating the impact of purchasing decisions. We must also factor in the implications for biodiversity and landscape, for local employment, for fair trade, and for social justice. Lastly, Coley et al. (2009) remind us that we cannot expect consumers to take the life cycle analysis of every product they buy into account, and it is thus important to base public debate on food systems on strategic case studies of specific retail systems, including AFNs. In conclusion, the interpretative approach developed here could also include the other social and economic dimensions of sustainability in a hierarchical structure where each of the three dimensions corresponds to specific measurement variables in the framework of Life Cycle Sustainability Analysis combining LCA, s-LCA, and LCC (Tecco, Baudino, Girgenti, & Peano, 2016).

References

Abeliotis, K., Detsis, V., & Pappia, C. (2013). Life Cycle Assessment of Bean Production in the Prespa National Park, Greece. *Journal of Cleaner Production, 41*, 89–96.

Arzoumanidis, I., Salomone, R., Petti, L., Mondello, G., & Raggi, A. (2017). Is There a Simplified LCA Tool Suitable for the Agri-food Industry? An assessment of selected tools. *Journal of Cleaner Production, 149*, 406–425.

Barbera, F., Dgnes, J., & Di Monaco, R. (2018). *Consumers' Quality Conventions in Alternative, Conventional and High-end Food Chains*. Chapter 5 of This Book.

Blanquart, C., Gonçalves, A., Kebir, L., Petit, C., Traversac, J.-B., & Vandenbossche, L. (2010). *The Logistic Leverages of Short Food Supply Chains*

Performance in Terms of Sustainability. 12th WCTR, July 11–15, 2010, Lisbon, Portugal.

Born, B., & Purcell, M. (2006). Avoiding the Local Trap: Scale and Food Systems in Planning. *Research Journal of Planning Education and Research, 26*, 195–207.

Bruce, A. B., & Som Castellano, R. L. (2017). Labor and Alternative Food Networks: Challenges for Farmers and Consumers. *Renewable Agriculture and Food Systems, 32*(5), 403–416.

Cellura, M., Longo, S., & Mistretta, M. (2012). Life Cycle Assessment (LCA) of Protected Crops: An Italian Case Study. *Journal of Cleaner Production, 28*, 56–62.

Cerutti, A. K., Beccaro, G. L., Bruun, S., Bosco, S., Donno, D., Notarnicola, B., & Bounous, G. (2014). Life Cycle Assessment Application in the Fruit Sector: State of the Art and Recommendations for Environmental Declarations of Fruit Products. *Journal of Cleaner Production, 73*, 125–135.

Clément, A. (1999). *Nourrir le people, entre état et marché, contribution à l'histoire intellectuelle de l'approvisionnement alimentaire*. Paris: L'Harmattan.

Coley, D., Howard, M., & Winter, M. (2009). Local Food, Food Miles and Carbon Emissions: A Comparison of Farm Shop and Mass Distribution Approaches. *Food Policy, 34*(2), 150–155.

Corsi, A., Novelli, S., & Pettenati, G. (2018). *Determinants of Farmers' Participation in AFNs*. Chapter 9 of This Book.

Djekic, I., Sanjuán, N., Clemente, G., Režek, J. A., Djukić-Vuković, A., Brodnjak, U. V., et al. (2018). Review on Environmental Models in the Food Chain – Current Status and Future Perspectives. *Journal of Cleaner Production, 176*, 1012–1025.

Edwards-Jones, G., Mila`i Canals, L., Hounsome, N., Gruninger, M. T., Koerber, G., & Hounsome, B. (2008). Testing the Assertion That "Local Food Is Best": The Challenges of an Evidence-Based Approach. *Trends in Food Science & Technology, 19*, 265–274.

Feenstra, G. W. (2002). Creating Space for Sustainable Food Systems: Lessons from the Field. *Agriculture and Human Values, 19*(2), 99–106.

Feldmann, C., & Hamm, U. (2015). Consumers' Perceptions and Preferences for Local Food: A Review. *Food Quality and Preference, 40*, 152–164.

Geissler, J. B. (2015). Short Food Supply Chain and Environmental "Foodprint": Why Consumption Pattern Changes Could Matter More Than Production and Distribution and Why It Is Relevant for Planning, 7th International Aesop Sustainable Food Planning Conference Proceedings, Torino, 7–9 October 2015.

Ghisellini, P., Cialani, C., & Ulgiati, S. (2016). A Review on Circular Economy: The Expected Transition to a Balanced Interplay of Environmental and Economic Systems. *Journal of Cleaner Production, 114*, 11–32.

Girgenti, V., Peano, C., Bounous, M., & Baudino, C. (2013). A Life Cycle Assessment of Non-renewable Energy Use and Greenhouse Gas Emissions Associated with Blueberry and Raspberry Production in Northern Italy. *Science of the Total Environment, 458–460*, 414–418.

Goodman, D. (2004). Rural Europe Redux? Reflections on Alternative Agro-food Networks and Paradigm Change. *Sociologia Ruralis, 44*(1), 3–14.

Goossens, Y., Annaert, B., De Tavernier, J., Mathijs, E., Keulemans, W., & Geeraerd, A. (2017). Life Cycle Assessment (LCA) for Apple Orchard Production Systems Including Low and High Productive Years in Conventional, Integrated and Organic Farms. *Agricultural Systems, 153*, 81–93.

Goucher-Lambert, K., Moss, J., & Cagan, J. (2017). A Meta-analytic Approach for Uncovering Neural Activation Patterns of Sustainable Product Preference Decisions. In J. Gero (Ed.), *Design Computing and Cognition '16*. Cham: Springer.

Grunert, K. G., Hieke, S., & Wills, J. (2014). Sustainability Labels on Food Products: Consumer Motivation, Understanding and Use. *Food Policy, 44*, 177–189.

Hinrichs, C. (2015). Farmers' Markets. Setting for Food Politics and Sites for Consumption. In D. T. Cook & J. M. Ryan (Eds.), *The Wiley-Blackwell Encyclopedia of Consumption and Consumer Studies*. Malden, MA: Wiley-Blackwell.

Hinrichs, C. C. (2000). Embeddedness and Local Food Systems: Notes on Two Types of Direct Agricultural Market. *Journal of Rural Studies, 16*, 295 and 303.

Hiroki, S., Garnevska, E., & McLaren, S. (2016). Consumer Perceptions About Local Food in New Zealand, and the Role of Life Cycle-Based Environmental Sustainability. *Journal of Agricultural and Environmental Ethics, 29*(3), 479–505.

Jacquemin, L., Pontalier, P. Y., & Sablayrolles, C. (2012). Life Cycle Assessment (LCA) Applied to the Process Industry: A Review. *The International Journal of Life Cycle Assessment, 17*, 1028–1041.

Kruse, S., Flysjö, A., Kasperczyk, N., & Scholz, A. J. (2009). Socioeconomic Indicators as a Complement to Life Cycle Assessment – An Application to Salmon Production Systems. *The International Journal of Life Cycle Assessment, 14*(1), 8–18.

Manfredi, M., & Vignali, G. (2015). Comparative Life Cycle Assessment of Hot Filling and Aseptic Packaging Systems Used for Beverages. *Journal of Food Engineering, 147*, 39–48.
Mariola, M. J. (2008). The Local Industrial Complex? Questioning the Link Between Local Foods and Energy Use. *Agriculture and Human Values, 25*(2), 193–196.
Markussen, M. V., Kulak, M., Smith, L. G., Nemecek, T., & Østergård, H. (2014). Evaluating the Sustainability of a Small-Scale Low-Input Organic Vegetable Supply System in the United Kingdom. *Sustainability, 6*, 1913–1945.
Marsden, T. K. (2013). Sustainable Place-Making for Sustainable Science: The Contested Case of Agri-food and Urban-rural Relations. *Sustainability Science, 8*(2), 213–226.
Martínez-Blanco, J., Anton, A., Rieradevall, J., Castellari, M., & Munoz, P. (2011). Comparing Nutritional Value and Yield as Functional Units in the Environmental Assessment of Horticultural Production with Organic or Mineral Fertilization: The Case of Mediterranean Cauliflower Production. *International Journal of Life Cycle Assessment, 16*(1), 12–26.
Mattsson, B., & Wallen, E. (2003). Environmental Life Cycle Assessment (LCA) of Organic Potatoes. *Acta Horticolturae, 619*, 427–435.
Mazoyer, M., & Roudart, L. (1997). Histoire des agricultures du monde, du Néolithique à la crise contemporaine. *Économie rurale, 245–246*, 119–121.
Milà i Canals, L., Cowell, S. J., Sim, S., & Basson, L. (2007). Comparing Domestic Versus Imported Apples: A Focus on Energy Use. *Environmental Science and Pollution Research, 14*(5), 338–344.
O'Hara, S., & Stagl, S. (2001). Global Food Markets and Their Local Alternatives: A Socio-ecological Economic Perspective. *Population and Environment, 22*(6), 533–554.
O'Rourke, D. (2014). The Science of Sustainable Supply Chains. *Science, 344*, 1124–1127.
Peano, C., Girgenti, V., Baudino, C., & Giuggioli, N. (2017). Blueberry Supply Chain in Italy: Management, Innovation and Sustainability. *Sustainability, 9*, 261.
Pettenati, G., & Dansero, E. (2018). *Reterritorialization, Proximity and Urban Food Planning: Research Perspectives on AFN*. Chapter 14 of This Book.
Pettinger, C., Holdsworth, M., & Gerber, M. (2008). All Under One Roof? Differences in Food Availability and Shopping Patterns in Southern France and Central England. *The European Journal of Public Health, 18*, 109–114.

Probyn, E. (2000). *Carnal Appetites: Food Sex Identities*. London: Routledge.

Rizet, C., Browne, M., Léonardi, J., Allen, J., Piotrowska, M., Cornélis, E., et al. (2008). Chaînes logistiques et consommation d'énergie: Cas des meubles et des fruits & légumes. Contrat INRETS/ADEME No. 05 03 C 0170.

Romero-Gamez, M., Audsley, E., & Suarez-Rey, E. M. (2014). Life Cycle Assessment of Cultivating Lettuce and Escarole in Spain. *Journal of Cleaner Production, 73*, 193–203.

Rothwell, A., Ridoutt, B., Page, G., & Bellotti, W. (2016). Environmental Performance of Local Food: Trade-offs and Implications for Climate Resilience in a Developed City. *Journal of Cleaner Production, 114*, 420–430.

Saunders, C., Barber, A., & Taylor, G. (2006). Food Miles – Comparative Energy/Emissions Performance of New Zealand's Agriculture Industry. Lincoln University, Research Report, no. 285.

Schlich, E. H., & Fleissner, U. (2005). The Ecology of Scale: Assessment of Regional Energy Turnover and Comparison with Global Food. *International Journal of Life Cycle Assessment, 10*(3), 219–223.

Schönhart, M., Penker, M., & Schmid, E. (2008). Sustainable Local Food Production and Consumption – Challenges for Implementation and Research. 8th European IFSA, Symposium, 6–10 July 2008, Clermont-Ferrand (France).

Sonnino, R., & Marsden, T. (2006). Beyond the Divide: Rethinking Relationships Between Alternative and Conventional Food Networks in Europe. *Journal of Economic Geography, 6*, 181–199.

Syrovátková, M., Hrabák, J., & Spilková, J. (2015). Farmers' Markets' Locavore Challenge: The Potential of Local Food Production for Newly Emerged Farmers' Markets in Czechia. *Renewable Agriculture and Food Systems, 30*(4), 305–317.

Tecco, N., Baudino, C., Girgenti, V., & Peano, C. (2016). Innovation Strategies in a Fruit Growers Association Impacts Assessment by Using Combined LCA and s-LCA Methodologies. *Science of the Total Environment, 568*, 253–262.

Tecco, N., & Peano, C. (2018). *The Environmental Quality Factors Sought by Consumers in Alternative and Conventional Market*. Chapter 6 of This Book.

Van Hauwermeiren, A., Coene, H., Engelen, G., & Mathijs, E. (2007). Energy Lifecycle Inputs in Food Systems: A Comparison of Local Versus Mainstream Cases. *Journal of Environmental Policy & Planning, 9*(1), 31–51.

Vávra, J., Daněk, P., & Jehlička, P. (2018). What Is the Contribution of Food Self-Provisioning Towards Environmental Sustainability? A Case Study of Active Gardeners. *Journal of Cleaner Production, 185*, 1015–1023.

Wallgren, C. (2006). Local or Global Food Markets: A Comparison of Energy Use for Transport. *Local Environment, 11*(2), 233–251.
Wezel, A., Bellon, S., Dore, T., Francis, C., Vallod, D., & David, C. (2009). Agroecology as a Science, a Movement and a Practice: A Review. *Agronomy for Sustainable Development, 29*(4), 503–515.
Williams, H., & Wikstrom, F. (2011). Environmental Impact of Packaging and Food Losses in a Life Cycle Perspective: A Comparative Analysis of Five Food Items. *Journal of Cleaner Production, 19*, 43–48.

14

Reterritorialization, Proximity, and Urban Food Planning: Research Perspectives on AFNs

Egidio Dansero and Giacomo Pettenati

Introduction

This chapter presents some of the work carried out since 2011 by a group of geographers at the University of Turin, coordinated by Egidio Dansero. Starting from a research project on Alternative Food Networks (AFNs) in Turin and Piedmont (Dansero & Puttilli, 2013), we gradually enlarged our research focus with the "Atlante del cibo" (Atlas of Food) project, conducted together with other research groups from the University of Turin, the Polytechnic of Turin, and the University of Gastronomic Sciences. The aim of the Atlas is to provide a comprehensive view of the characteristics and dynamics of the food system in the Turin metropolitan area (Dansero, Pettenati, & Toldo, 2015).

While this chapter presents the results of a joint effort by both authors, sections "Introduction" and "Theoretical Framework" were drafted by Egidio Dansero and the remaining sections by Giacomo Pettenati.

E. Dansero • G. Pettenati (✉)
Department of Cultures, Politics and Society, University of Torino, Torino, Italy
e-mail: egidio.dansero@unito.it; giacomo.pettenati@unito.it

A. Corsi et al. (eds.), *Alternative Food Networks*,
https://doi.org/10.1007/978-3-319-90409-2_14

In addition to the aspects of AFNs discussed in this chapter, the topics explored by the research group include urban food policies in the world's North (Calori, Dansero, Pettenati, & Toldo, 2017) and South (Bini, Dansero, Magarini, & Nicolarea, 2017); the role of social actors in considering food as a field of political action (Pettenati & Dansero, 2018); food and urban poverty (Toldo, 2018); and the relationships between food supply chains and development that arise at different scales (Pettenati & Toldo, 2018).

Alternative Food Networks have been among the group's main research topics from the beginning. The first significant contribution, which was the starting point for the work, carried out as part of the project entitled Alternative Food Networks: an Interdisciplinary Approach (AFNIA), a proposed interpretation of AFNs' territoriality developed by Dansero and Puttilli (2013), which laid the foundations for part of the theoretical framework used during the project. Drawing on the huge Italian and French literature about the relationships between actors and territory that define territoriality (Raffestin, 2012), we identify three dimensions that can be used to analyze and describe AFNs' territoriality, considering both the functional and substantial aspects: *space*, *resources*, and *relations*.

Starting from this territorial perspective on AFNs, which will be expanded below, this chapter presents the main geographic findings emerging from the broad framework of the AFNIA project, where several research questions were posed.

The first question concerns the spatial distribution of AFNs in Piedmont and of the Turin metropolitan area in particular and attempted to shed light on the connections between the spatial distribution of the different types of Alternative Food Network and the characteristics of the places where they take place and which they connect.

The second research question is related to the role that these practices can play in a potential reterritorialization of the food system at different scales.

Thirdly, we tried to understand the adequacy and congruity of the concept of proximity as a lens for interpreting and integrating the three dimensions of AFNs' territoriality indicated above.

In conclusion, we reflected on the role that the practices that fall within the broad category of AFNs play and can play in the framework of urban food planning.

The information provided by this chapter comes from various sources and from the wide range of methodologies used during three years of engagement with the vibrant AFN scene in Turin and Piedmont: quantitative data analysis, participant observation, surveys, and interviews with experts and key informants. Most of all, however, we benefited from many formal and informal relationships that we were able to cultivate in these years with many actors involved in different types of AFN in the area.

The Spatial Distribution of AFNs in the Turin Metropolitan Area[1]

The mapping activities indicated that AFNs are mainly urban practices. The major types of AFN considered in the study (farmers' markets and GASs or solidarity purchase groups[2]) are concentrated in Piedmont's larger urban areas. The Turin metropolitan area hosts over three quarters of the region's AFNs, with around half of the total in the city of Turin alone. In addition, most of the AFNs are located in the main regional cities, such as Cuneo, Asti, and Novara, while some of the most interesting initiatives are in medium-sized towns such as Pinerolo and Ivrea. However, as the geographical analysis of AFNs shows, the different types of AFN correspond to different spatial distributions.

As can be seen from the distribution of farmers' markets (FMs) in the Turin metropolitan area, there is a clear difference between the two main types of farmers' market in the region (Fig. 14.1).

The first type is represented by the sections reserved for local agricultural producers in the "ordinary" city markets that take place at least once a week in the region's main municipalities. In the city of Turin alone, 42 food markets are organized every day, 38 of which host farmers' stalls where local producers sell seasonal fruit and vegetables, cheese, honey, and eggs.

At the provincial scale, 209 municipalities out of a total of 316 organize at least one farmers' market, in some cases more than once a week. The areas where this kind of FM is absent are chiefly small municipalities in mountain areas.

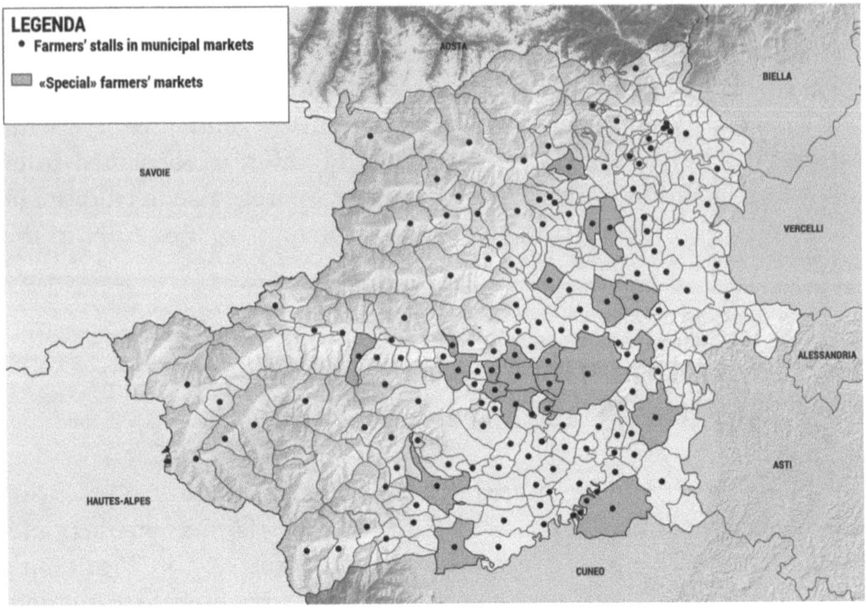

Fig. 14.1 Distribution of farmers' markets in the Turin metropolitan area municipalities (2016)

The second type consists of periodic markets organized by various groups in order to promote locally produced fresh food. The main role here is played by farmers' organizations, in particular Coldiretti, which through its Campagna Amica program organizes more than 600 markets throughout Italy. In Turin, there are about 15 farmers' markets of this type, most of them organized by Coldiretti. Other organizers of significant interest are Slow Food (with the "Mercati della Terra"), the Italian Confederation of Agriculture (CIA), and other more radically alternative networks (e.g., Associazione Solidarietà Campagna Italiana (ASCI) or Genuino Clandestino). This second type of FM is mainly concentrated in the area's chief urban centers, particularly in Turin and in its suburbs (the towns of Moncalieri, Rivoli, Venaria Reale, Chieri, etc.), while their density decreases in rural areas and around smaller cities.

The concentration in urban areas is even more marked for the GASs (solidarity purchase groups). Out of approximately 175 GASs in

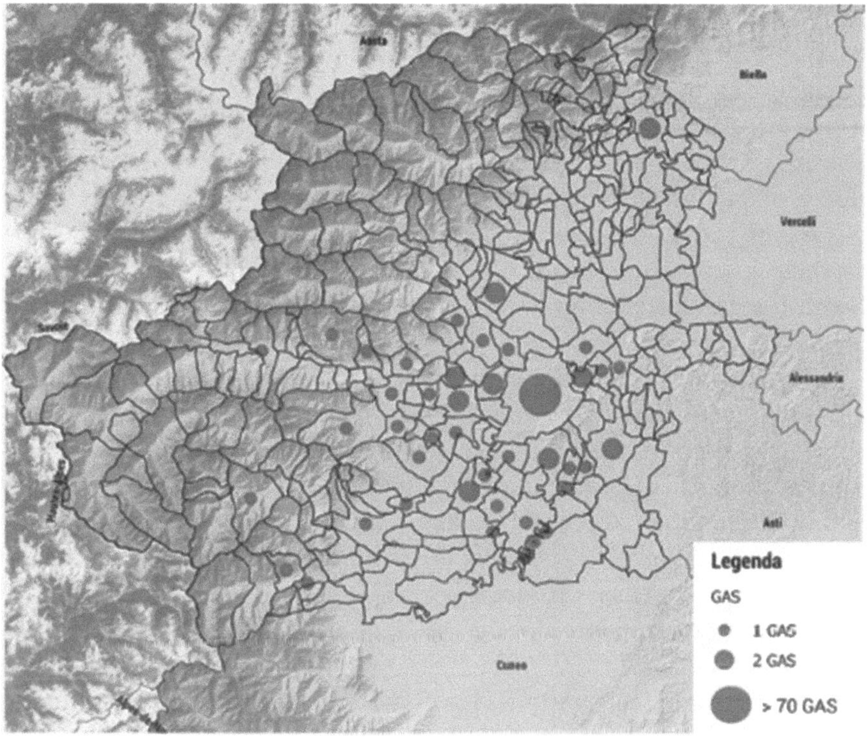

Fig. 14.2 Distribution of GASs in the Turin metropolitan area (2016)

Piedmont (the exact number is very difficult to determine, due to the high rate of “hidden” informal GASs), about 70 are located within the boundaries of the city of Turin and almost 50 are in the city’s surrounding suburbs (Fig. 14.2).

A few words are in order concerning the reasons behind AFNs’ concentration.

The main explanation is related to the connection between AFNs and the typically urban nature of many forms of political activism, such as the practices promoted by the creative and sharing economies and the quality turn in the choice of food. From the outset, the debate about alternative ways of providing food from producers to consumers recognized their prevailingly urban nature, and identified the city as “the space, place, and scale where interesting new forms of extrafirm relationships are emerging” and "where demand is also greatest for alternative food products." (Donald & Blay-Palmer, 2006, pp. 1902 and 1904). Urbanization and rural restructuring in metropolitan areas can be seen as drivers for the emergence of AFNs, creating demand and opportunities for consumers (wealthy or middle-class urban dwellers seeking quality food) and producers at small-scale farms (Jarosz, 2008).

Despite the largely urban nature of AFNs, rural areas are also involved in their spatial articulation, not only as places of production but also because many interesting initiatives are based in rural and/or mountain areas.[3]

AFNs are also promoted by a number of projects initiated by small cities in order to reconnect rural and urban areas by engaging urban consumers in supporting sustainable small-scale local agriculture and the local economy. The most interesting example analyzed during the study is that of the project Ecoredia in the urban area of Ivrea, north of Turin, which promotes relationships between GAS consumers and local producers and works together with local government in sustainable local development projects (e.g., promoting local food in school canteens) (Dansero & Puttilli, 2013).

So far, our considerations have mostly taken a consumer-based perspective.

Shifting from the consumers' point of view to the producers', another key spatial issue that was investigated in order to understand AFNs' territoriality in Piedmont is the provenance of producers participating in FMs and GASs in the city of Turin.

The importance assigned to producers' origin varies significantly according to the characteristics of individual consumers and type of AFN. It is probably at its highest for GASs, where direct knowledge of the producers is central to the buying experience (Grasseni, 2013).

The fundamental role of farm location is demonstrated by the visibility given to place of production in many AFNs, for example, through descriptive cards placed on the sales counters in many farmers' markets.

Nevertheless, there are no complete official lists of producers supplying the individual alternative agro-food networks based in Turin. This makes it difficult to carry out an exhaustive analysis of the spatial extension and organizational characteristics of these networks and shows that there is still a lack of the clear connections between food and its producers and places of origin that could enable direct sales to reach their full potential.

The extensive fieldwork carried out during the AFNIA project, however, made it possible to build a database—not exhaustive but significant—of about 650 agro-food producers who in the last five years sold their products through one or more of Turin's AFNs, farmers' markets, and GASs in particular.

As Fig. 14.3 (limited to Piedmont-based producers) shows, most of these farmers are from an area within 50 km of Turin, confirming the importance assigned to the local provenance of products sold through the AFNs, over and above their processes of production.

The highest concentrations of producers are found in three areas:

1. The hilly region surrounding Turin on the eastern and southeastern side of the metropolitan area, especially along the Po river (e.g., the municipalities of Castiglione Torinese, Gassino Torinese, San Mauro Torinese, and Moncalieri, which are particularly notable for horticulture.
2. The Roero hill region, about 40–50 km south of Turin (fruit and vegetables).
3. The areas between Turin and the Alpine valleys of Susa, Chisone, and Pellice (fruit, vegetables, and dairy products).

These three sub-regions are very different as regards their agricultural and economic structure and their relationships with the city of Turin. It is thus instructive to scrutinize why so many of the producers participating in Alternative Food Networks are located in these areas, in order to understand if this concentration is related to the development of a new relationship between urban and rural, possibly through the reterritorialization of food practices and networks.

The study found a substantial absence of projects that are territorial in scope, that is, which attempt to leverage strong connections between producers from these regions and urban consumers. So far, in fact, any such connections have mostly been due to individual entrepreneurial choices.

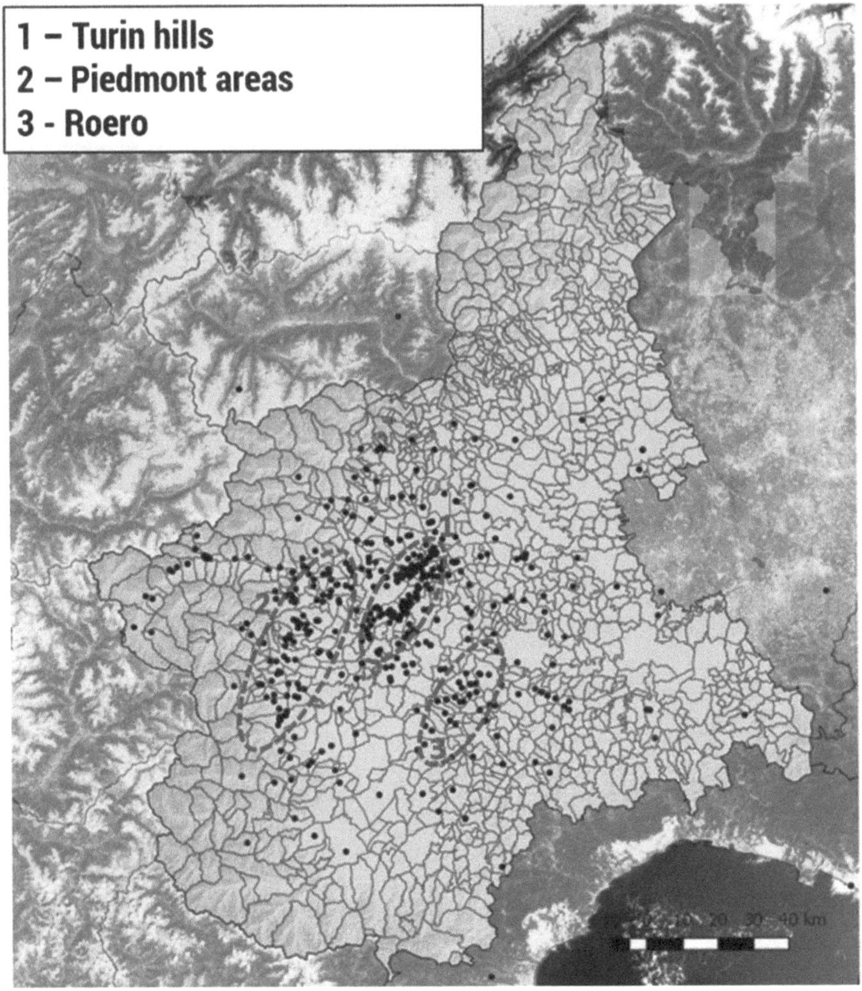

Fig. 14.3 The distribution of Piedmont-based producers participating in farmers' markets and GASs in the city of Turin (2016)

Generally speaking, the GASs' foodshed is broader than that of farmers' markets, as the "shopping basket" of consumers participating in collective purchase schemes commonly contains products coming from other regions and even other countries. In this case, the main motivation for choosing such products is not their local provenance, but the fact that they are representative of an alternative model of food production and distribution. With the exception of olive oil, which mostly comes from Liguria—the closest region to Piedmont where it is produced—products that cannot be found locally are to a large extent chosen on the basis of ethical or environmental considerations, such as sustainable fishing practices (fish from the Tyrrhenian Sea), support for the people of Emilia-Romagna after the 2012 earthquake (Parmigiano Reggiano cheese produced in the areas devastated by the event), or support for organizations (e.g., Libera) that fight the mafia in Southern Italy by cultivating land confiscated from the criminal organizations.

Alternative Food Networks and the Reterritorialization of the Food System[4]

Theoretical Framework

Today's dominant globalized food system can be seen as characterized at every scale by a productivistic, market-oriented approach, ruled by a few powerful economic actors, usually transnational corporations (Morgan, Marsden, & Murdoch, 2006). This scenario has led to what can be termed the *deterritorialization* of food, which can be broken down into the *disconnection* between production and consumption, the *disembedding* of food from its places of production, and the *disentwining* of the stages of the food chain and the dimensions of food (Wiskerke, 2009). The notion of deterritorialization harks back to the debate on territoriality, used by geographers to describe the cycles of production and reproduction of territory through the action of the networks of actors operating in it (Raffestin, 1980, 2012). The Italian planner Alberto Magnaghi (2010) considers deterritorialization as a structural factor of the present economic system, based on efficiency, resulting in a sprawled urbanization and weakened relations between societies and places, territories, landscapes, the environment—and food.

The power relations that sustain this system are highly unbalanced, as a very few powerful political and economic actors make most of the decisions affecting the system, and there is a significant loss of power on the part of both producers and consumers.

Despite the important role that rural areas still play as spaces of production, they have lost much of their cultural and economic stature: no longer considered as complex places in their own right, they are little more than neutral supports for industrial agriculture.

This system produces "placeless foodscapes" (Ilbery & Kneafsey, 2000), where the relationships between food and the place where it is produced are broken, and the food most people eat is the homogeneous and standardized product of a globalized non-place-based value chain.

A system of this kind optimizes the food chain's efficiency and production costs, but yields several negative externalities: downward pressure on farm incomes and the consequent loss of jobs, skills, expertise, and knowledge in the agricultural sector; an increase in environmental pollution in the form of waste, dependence on fossil fuels, greenhouse gas emissions, and increased consumption of water resources for production; loss of agricultural and natural biodiversity; decline in the organoleptic quality and diversity of products; increased competition for land, land grabbing, and new forms of food colonialism; and an increase of diseases related to obesity and poor eating habits, notably in the lowest-income population groups (Wiskerke, 2009).

As one of the pillars of an imagined and practiced "alternative food geography" (Wiskerke, 2009), AFNs contribute to redefining the spatial and network organization of food systems, sometimes as the specific aim of their promoters and participants, in other cases as an unintended side effect.

In summarizing the prolific debate about the food geographies produced by alternative agro-food networks, we can identify different spatial configurations.

The first is the *relocalization* of the food system (Hendrickson & Heffernan, 2002), often considered as a reduction of the *food miles* and an increase in the market share of local food. The relocalization of food can be imagined starting from an idea of "local" based purely on spatial extension (e.g., by identifying an optimal circular area within which food can be considered "local"), or with a more complex understanding of "local" as a variable scale, produced by relationships between people, places, and resources (Kremer & DeLiberty, 2011; Sonnino & Marsden, 2006).

The relationships between AFNs and the relocalization of the food system must be approached from a critical perspective to avoid falling into the so-called local trap (Born & Purcell, 2006) or unreflexive localism (DuPuis & Goodman, 2005) of judging local food as inherently "better". Even localized systems can reproduce the dynamics of socio-spatial injustice (DuPuis & Goodman, 2005), and it is necessary to define precisely which negative aspects of the conventional system can be at least partially solved by small-scale alternative models (Allen, 2010). The risk of uncritically assigning positive value at the local scale is also that of denying the political dimension of the local, failing to recognize the scale's multidimensionality and underestimating both the role of powerful supra-local actors in orienting local dynamics and practices (DuPuis & Goodman, 2005) and the possibility that some local actors may have reactionary defensive attitudes (Hinrichs, 2003). Increasing the physical proximity between producers and consumers and between stages of the supply chain does not necessarily contribute to improving the food system (Casey, 2001; Feagan, 2007).

The idea of the short food supply chain, which sometimes overlaps or complements the notion of AFN (Marsden, Banks, & Bristow, 2000; Renting, Marsden, & Banks, 2003), then, should not be limited to its spatial interpretation, but must encompass a wider understanding of proximity as discussed below.

A second spatial shift of the food system which is often mentioned in the debate is its *re-regionalization* (Kneafsey, 2010). One of the key dimensions of the spatial perspective in studying food systems is the analysis of the *foodshed* of a city or an area (Kremer & DeLiberty, 2011), that is, the set of (usually not contiguous) areas where the food consumed in a place comes from. While analyzing the foodshed can be seen as an assessment of existing dynamics, the idea of regionalization (or re-regionalization) usually has regulatory connotations, as it applies to attempts to define what areas food (and not only local food) should mostly come from, in order to achieve more sustainable or just food systems. As the difference between relocalization and regionalization is decidedly nuanced, regionalization can be considered an upper scale process that connects different "locals" in a complex and open territorial food system (Clancy & Ruhf, 2010).

A third concept, which supports and enriches relocalization and re-regionalization, is the *re-embeddedness* of food in places (Sonnino & Marsden, 2006), local ecologies (Murdoch, Marsden, & Banks, 2000) and social networks (Sage, 2003). This is potentially a very useful analytical category because it includes the spheres of the cultural, social, and political environment (horizontal dimension) and the institutional sphere (vertical dimension) of food systems (Sonnino & Marsden, 2006).

The theoretical thrust of this chapter is that the concept of *reterritorialization*, understood as opposed to the deterritorialization which characterizes practices associated with the conventional system (Morgan et al., 2006), could more effectively synthesize and describe the characteristics of alternative geographies of food and AFNs. As suggested by Dansero and Puttilli (2013), the geographical and territorial approach is particularly valuable for studying AFNs for two reasons. First, because these practices can be seen as a redefinition of the relationship between food and territory, the reaffirmation of social relationships, and a new economic and cultural relation between places, producers, and consumers. Second, the concepts of territory and territoriality can offer a new analytical perspective for food networks, with particular reference to their spatial configurations. We propose to consider AFNs starting from three complementary dimensions (Fig. 14.4):

a. *Spaces*: the organization of AFNs in space, specifically the physical and functional distance between the actors participating in the network. The focus is on both the spaces of production—whence a new urban-rural linkage can be developed—and the spaces of sale and consumption, which often become new spaces of socialization.
b. *Resources*: the type of resources used in AFNs. These resources can be quite varied: at one extreme, they can be highly locally specific, unavailable or unreproducible elsewhere, while at the other extreme, they can be standardized resources, reproducible anywhere. Is the food sold in AFNs the expression of a specific place or a specific network of

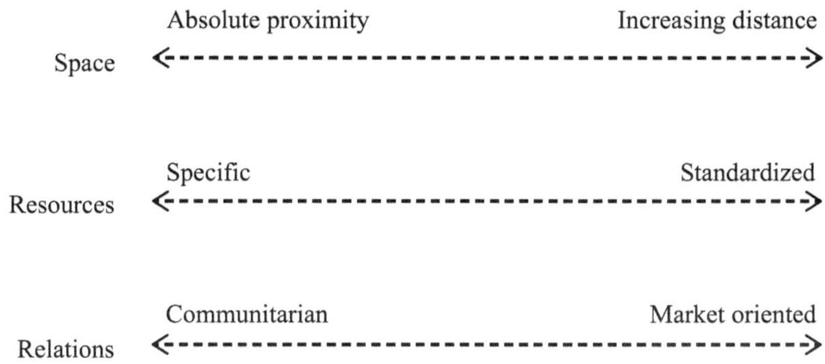

Fig. 14.4 Dimensions of AFNs' territoriality (Dansero & Puttilli, 2013). Source: Dansero and Puttilli (2013)

actors? To what extent do the relational, cultural, and material resources mobilized through the network come from the milieu of specific places?

c. *Relationships*: the type of social relations between the actors who belong to the AFN. At one side, we can find experiences with an explicit community dimension, based on face-to-face relations and trust, on the other side more structured, market-oriented, organizational models. What is the AFNs' main aim? A new market space for economic activities? A new space of social relationships? Supporting development of a weak area? How do these different aims mix together in each AFN?

The Role of Piedmont's AFNs in the Reterritorialization of the Food System

Figure 14.5 breaks down the most common types of AFN in Turin, using a theoretical framework that draws on the dimensions of AFNs' territoriality proposed by Dansero and Puttilli (2013).

Dansero and Puttilli's "relations" dimension is shown on the Cartesian x-axis, with a market-oriented approach of the food network on the right and a community-/territory-oriented approach on the left. The y-axis is

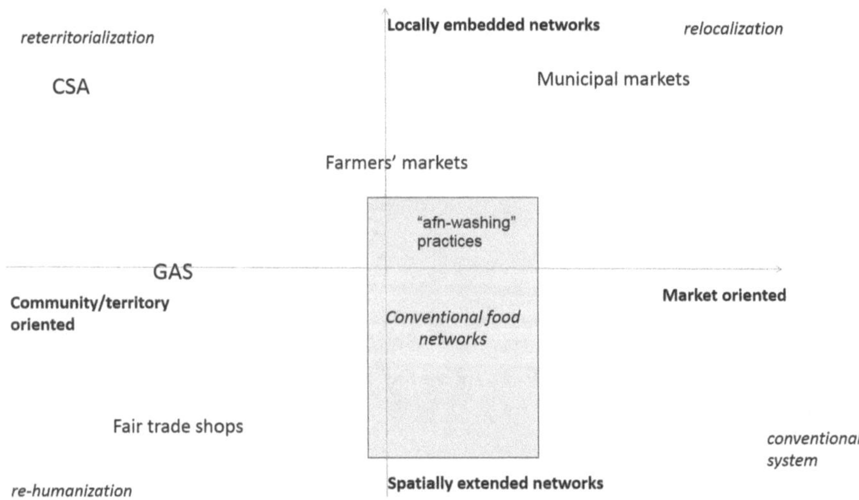

Fig. 14.5 Interpretive framework for AFNs' territoriality (Dansero & Pettenati, 2015). Source: Dansero and Pettenati (2015)

based on the "space" dimension, with spatially extended networks at the bottom of the graph and locally embedded networks at the top.

The four quadrants deriving from the intersection of the four axes represent four different fields of development and practice of (alternative) food networks:

- In the lower right quadrant, we have the *conventional food system* based on market-oriented spatially extended networks that sometimes use mimetic strategies of "AFN-washing", such as local food shelves in supermarkets or marketing strategies for providing geographical information about food.
- In the lower left quadrant, we have spatially extended networks animated by a community-oriented approach, which aim at *re-humanizing* (or re-moralizing) food systems. This is the case of fair trade networks, whose labels guarantee that food arriving on consumers' tables—often from far away—is produced and transported in accordance with ethical and environmental criteria. GASs also fall into this quadrant to

some extent, as some of the food products they carry travel along spatially extended networks, but are chosen according to criteria of ethics and sustainability.

- In the upper right quadrant, we have locally embedded market-oriented networks, whose general aim is the *relocalization* of the food system, represented by practices that sell local food, often through face-to-face interactions, but do not radically subvert economic exchange relationships between producers and consumers.
- In the upper left quadrant is the only real example of potential reterritorialization of the food system, represented by practices that radically overcome the idea of food as a market good and the traditional contraposition of producers and consumers. This is the case of Community Supported Agriculture (CSA), a term that denotes different forms of agreement between producers and consumers, where the latter commit to purchasing products for a set period of time, paying for them in advance. Producers, for their part, undertake to supply consumers with the agreed quantities of products, usually in the form of baskets whose composition varies according to season and availability, and to guarantee a sufficient variety to meet consumers' needs. Through these practices, producers and consumers are no longer bound by a competitive relationship that aims at achieving an economic advantage, but share risks and benefits of production, contributing concretely to co-producing the food system according to a shared vision (Galt, 2013) and the mutual understanding of the food system as a commons (Pettenati, Toldo, & Ferrando, 2018). The AFNIA project found that there were no CSA initiatives in Piedmont at the time of the survey. However, some of the projects and practices that were investigated aim at developing close new relationships between consumers and producers through box schemes (such as those developed by the cooperatives Agricoopecetto in Pecetto Torinese and Il frutto permesso in Bibiana) that guarantee regular support to producers from consumers, based not only on commercial exchange but also on mutual trust (Guadagno & Cavallo, 2016).

Proximity as a Conceptual Framework for Analyzing and Understanding Alternative Food Networks[5]

Theoretical Framework: For a Conceptual Definition of Proximity

Proximity—and its opposite, distance—have always been two of the main concepts guiding theoretical and applied research in geography and territorial studies. One of the main theorists of the role of the proximity/distance combination in social life is Jacques Lévy (1997), according to whom the goal of geography can be summarized by the understanding of the role of distance in the functioning and evolution of societies, starting from the idea that proximity, that is, the absence of distance, is a condition of existence of all social life.

Many studies hinge on a dual conception of geographical and organized proximities (Rallet & Torre, 2004). In our research, drawing on Boschma's (2005) theories, we used a slightly different taxonomy of proximity that in addition to spatial proximity introduces an organizational—or network—proximity between the actors participating in a process and a cognitive—or values—proximity linked to the actors' sharing of knowledge or values.

On a spatial level, this categorization reflects the division proposed by David Harvey (2006), who identifies: (a) *absolute space*, Cartesian, continuous, geometrically measurable, whose points are separated and related according to distance and linear proximity; (b) *relative space*, topological space of the networks, measurable with nonlinear metrics, which deform the continuous space by using the characteristics of the relations between the points which constitute it (network proximity); (c) *relational space*, defined by values (material and immaterial) given by the actors who inhabit and transform it, through social, cultural, and economic processes (cognitive proximity).

In summary, this chapter will consider three broad categories of proximity, closely related to each other:

1. A *spatial and physical proximity*, which characterizes the coexistence of subjects or phenomena in the same spatial context, on a variable scale.
2. A *network proximity*, linked to the mutual position of the nodes of an organization.
3. A *cognitive proximity*, linked to the sharing of values, knowledge, and perspectives between different actors.

Spatial Proximity

The spatial proximity between the actors is one of the factors that characterize the examples of AFNs analyzed during the study and can be considered from various perspectives.

First, spatial proximity between producers and consumers is one of the criteria that characterize the interactions of most AFNs. For example, 520 of the almost 600 producers who supply the AFNs in Turin (farmers' markets and GASs) come from the surrounding region, and 374 of them are based in the Turin metropolitan area. The local provenance of the producers is almost total in farmers' markets, which mostly focus on local food, whereas the origin of the products is more varied in the case of the GASs, which also buy food from producers based in other regions and even other countries.

Second, spatial proximity can be considered as a means of fostering interactions between the actors participating in AFNs. This is clear if we consider the importance vested in the physical space where AFNs take place. Farmers' markets, for example, are thought of and frequented not only as places to sell and buy food but also as meeting places and places of exchange.

Third, spatial proximity between consumers seems to be crucial for the emergence of some types of AFN, such as GASs. Many of the participants in GASs are people who live in the same neighborhood, and even their name often evokes their location (in Turin, e.g., the San Salva Gas is located in the San Salvario neighborhood, while the Vanchiglia neighborhood is home to the Gas Vanchiglia).

Fourth, spatial proximity between producers could be a factor of cooperation and an incentive for territorial projects that aim at sustaining new relationships between urban and rural areas, often based on AFNs.[6] Some sub-regional sustainable local development projects where AFNs play a crucial role seem to confirm this hypothesis. An example is Ivrea's Ecoredia project, even if it is still an exception in Piedmont.

Network Proximity

Alternative Food Networks do not only shorten the food chain in terms of the origin of products but also through the desire to establish direct face-to-face relations between producers and consumers (Marsden et al., 2000; Renting et al., 2003).

The need to consider the multiple dimensions of short food supply chains is well described by Renting et al. (2003), who explore the various "proximities" of AFNs that go beyond the reduction of food miles.

The different types of AFN examined in Piedmont have very different levels of network proximity.

For farmers' markets, the clearest example is probably that of those set up by farmers' organizations (e.g., Coldiretti), where only producers belonging to the organization can participate. Network proximity is mixed with the other dimensions in the case of FMs organized according to different criteria: for example, spatial proximity for markets that generally target local producers and cognitive proximity in the case of the more "political" markets, where producers share common visions of agro-food production.

In the case of the GASs, network proximity is present from different points of view. First, most GASs spring from existing associations or networks (e.g., neighborhood associations, sports, cultural and religious organizations, or groups of work colleagues, students, roommates, or parents), whose participants decide to cooperate in the purchase of food, often seen as a civic/political field of action. Second, the activity of a GAS contributes to increasing the complexity of local networks and to creating new network proximity among actors. Third, there is a "second-level" network proximity, made up of the relationships between different GASs that cooperate on specific issues. Despite their very horizontal structure, in fact, many GASs belong to higher-level networks that aim to increase their efficiency through coordinated actions of small-scale logistics or shared purchases.[7]

Cognitive Proximity

Together with issues like distrust in industrial food, the general demand for "quality food", and other individual or pragmatic reasons (e.g., costs, desire for specific food, time) (Tregear, 2011), the principal motivations of some consumers who participate in AFNs include the will to oppose the globalized industrial agro-food system, perceived as unsustainable and unfair, and to sustain alternative models of rural development (Goodman, Du Puis, & Goodman, 2012).

These practices would thus appear to be linked to a desire for critical consumption and civic engagement (Grasseni, 2013; Graziano & Forno, 2012) in a shared vision of the values that should characterize the food system and that are associated with food consumption (environmental sustainability, social justice, etc.). Food purchase becomes a field of political and civic action, where actors are connected by cognitive proximity, based on sharing common values and a common idea of the food system.

The analysis of producers involved in Turin-based AFNs shows that when non-local producers are selected, the choice is mainly based on criteria relating to cognitive proximity. Most of these producers belong to—or are explicitly connected with—organizations or networks engaged in political or social initiatives and actions whose values are shared by the consumers, notably in the case of GASs. This is clear in the cases mentioned above of producers in southern Italy who belong to the Libera anti-mafia network or producers of Parmigiano Reggiano cheese in the areas affected by the 2012 earthquake and supported by GASs throughout the country. The desire to associate civic engagement with food consumption is reflected in the many activities that some GASs add to the purchase of products, such as organizing meetings with producers or with experts on specific topics related to food, self-production workshops, and so on.

Value proximity between the actors participating in the AFN appears to be weaker for farmers' markets (Marino & Cicatiello, 2012), with the exception of the more radical ones that are explicitly engaged in opposition to the dominant system (in Turin, this is the case of markets organized locally by the nationwide Genuino Clandestino network).

A Fruitful Interpretative Category

Proximity appears to be a fruitful interpretative category for analyzing food systems from a geographical and territorial point of view. The capitalist and globalized agro-industrial system can be interpreted as characterized by a loss of proximity, while the movements and practices of "alternative food geography" can be seen as an attempt to reconstruct relations of proximity, variously understood.

In practices falling into the broad category of Alternative Food Networks, proximity plays a decisive role, with its three dimensions: spatial proximity (reconstruction of local food systems), cognitive proximity (transformation to food systems based on shared values), and network proximity (to move towards more inclusive food systems).

The AFNIA project's findings confirm the importance of proximity as a characterization of alternative production, distribution, and consumption practices.

Using the three dimensions of proximity as an interpretive framework for two families of AFNs (farmers' markets and GASs) shed light on the main differences between them. In the case of farmers' markets, the main role is played by spatial proximity (local producers) and network proximity (if the markets are organized by professional associations). For GASs, network proximity seems to be important (the GASs were created by existing associations or groups), as is cognitive proximity (selection of producers and participation in the GAS deriving from a common understanding of how producers and consumers should interact in the food system).

Alternative Food Networks and Urban Food Planning: Convergence Fields

Urban food policies (UFP) or urban food strategies are heterogeneous sets of objectives, forms of governance, content, and actions, initially developed in the United States and Canada as a response to negative externalities (connected in particular to public health problems and access to food) generated by the dominant food system, which have repercussions at local level and whose consequences tend to intensify in urban nodes (Morgan & Sonnino, 2010). In more general terms, they are voluntary policies which share some aspects of strategic planning, such as the presence of shared visions, integrated objectives, mixed partnerships, and stakeholder involvement (Calori et al., 2017).

Most UFPs take a systemic approach to the theme of food (Sonnino, 2016; Sonnino & Spayde, 2014), which translates into policies aimed at integrating and connecting the multiple dimensions of food (environment, production activities, logistics and transport, education and training, economic and employment development, health and social welfare aspects, culture and tourism); the different phases of the agro-food supply chain; geographical scales and related levels of territorial governance; urban and rural areas; and public sector, private sector, and civil society.

Arriving at a definition of urban food policies that brings all this complexity together is far from easy. Some authors regard UFPs as processes of change in cities' food systems (Sonnino, 2016), which influence the ways in which food is produced, purchased, consumed, and disposed of by those who live there. Concretely, UFPs capitalize on existing experiences and networks and propose complex strategies that aggregate and provide a framework for different interventions and policies (urban agriculture, alternative forms of distribution, food education, fight against waste, etc.). The general aim is to guarantee that everyone—and the weakest groups in particular—has access to healthy, nutritious, socially just, environmentally compatible, and culturally appropriate food (Sonnino, 2009). Recurring and interrelated strategies for achieving these general objectives include the relocation of production and consumption and the reconnection of urban and rural (Sonnino, 2009), the "remittance" of food systems, and education and training programs aimed at changing habits and lifestyles.

According to Matacena (2016, p. 55), "Urban food policies and alternative food networks appear as the two sides of the same coin, both products of the general recognition of the unsustainability attached to the food system, and both intended to generate mechanisms to cope with those 'failures of coordination' (Lang, Rayner, Rayner, Barling, & Millstone, 2005) that created the space for a corporate-controlled productivist model to establish as the only available development paradigm for the food system".

Actually, most of the actions that existing UFPs single out as essential in order to achieve their purposes are examples of AFNs: farmers' markets, urban gardens, community shops, CSAs, purchasing groups, and so on.

UFPs can thus be the political framework for supporting existing AFNs (in an outscale and/or upscale perspective) or promoting the emergence of new ones.

Despite local actors' engagement in initiatives to establish a Turin food policy, no such tool has yet been formally approved in Piedmont (Calori et al., 2017). If we look at the "food assembly" of actors involved in these processes, however, it is clear that many of them are involved in local AFNs as organizers or coordinators of farmers' markets, GASs, urban gardens, or other innovative, sustainable, or socially inclusive initiatives (Bottiglieri, Pettenati, & Toldo, 2016; Pettenati & Dansero, 2018).

Interesting attempts to integrate AFNs in an UFPs framework are now taking place in several rural areas surrounding small cities, but functionally connected to Turin through commuter movements and flows of economic goods. Many of these efforts have set up AFNs conveying local fresh food. The area around the small city of Chieri (with a population of about 35,000) on the eastern side of the Turin hills, for example, has begun to engage local actors in formulating food policies and establishing up a "food district" (see note 6), where AFNs play a crucial role (Pettenati & Vittone, 2018).

Concluding Remarks

This chapter summarized the different research paths explored during the AFNIA project by the geography research group, in close interaction with project members from other disciplines.

The analysis of AFNs' spatial distribution showed that they are a highly place-based phenomenon whose characteristics differ according to the territorial context. Specifically, they assume a different articulation and meaning in urban and rural contexts. In urban areas, where they are more widespread, AFNs often seem to be an expression of the desire of a part of the urban population (critical consumers) to have a different relationship with food supply, as the AFN literature cited in this volume suggests.

In rural areas, however, the contemporary agro-industrial system's separation of production and consumption is mitigated by physical proximity between producers and consumers, who are often part of the same local networks where physical proximity and cognitive proximity coincide (see above). This co-incidence, however, is threatened by the city's steady encroachment on peri-urban agricultural areas, where lifestyles are becoming increasingly similar to those of inner cities and where "urban" AFNs are more and more common.

The second research question that guided the work of geographers in the AFNIA project concerned the potential role of AFNs in reterritorializing globalized and deterritorialized food systems. Analysis of the different types of AFNs in Piedmont shows that they deal with only some of the dimensions of a real reterritorialization (relocation or rehumanization), while examples of practices such as CSA that aim to truly overcome the economic and relational logics of the dominant food system are almost unknown.

Third, the heuristic and interpretative potential of the concept of proximity, in its various dimensions—spatial, network, and cognitive—was confirmed through an analysis and interpretation of AFNs' spatial and social articulation, demonstrating that it can fruitfully explain the rationalities and the dynamics of different types of AFN.

Fourth, we highlighted the importance that AFNs have in many urban food planning and urban food policies, which aim to integrate food policies, in increasing environmental sustainability, social justice, and the economic competitiveness of food systems. From this perspective, it should be emphasized that in Turin, as in many other cities, AFNs preexist urban food policies and are important area of politics, networking, and practice that can and should constitute the foundations of processes for developing and implementing integrated local food policies at any scale.

To conclude, the spatial and geographical analyses of AFNs summarized in this chapter found major differences between the various types of Alternative Food Network. Farmers' markets, GASs, CSA, and other practices have different relationships with and effects on the territorial context where they develop. The category of Alternative Food Networks—as well as other similar umbrella definitions such as Short Food Supply Chain (Marsden et al., 2000; Renting et al., 2003) or Civic Food Networks (Renting, Schermer, & Rossi, 2012)—is useful in describing the general turns of food-related social, economic, and political behaviors, but probably encompasses practices that are too dissimilar to be treated as a whole in studies aiming at a better understanding of how such practices work and how they can affect people, places, and food systems.

Notes

1. In 2015, the Turin metropolitan area replaced the Province of Turin as the NUTS-3 level of government, following the local administration reform pursuant to national law 56/2014. It covers 6830 km^2, has a population of about 2.3 million, and is divided into 316 municipalities.
2. For a deeper understanding of the role of GASs as Alternative Food Networks in Italy, see Grasseni (2013).
3. This is the case of two networks based in the Susa valley (west of Turin). The first is "Genuino Valsusino", a network of commercial and non-commercial producers linked to the national grassroots network Genuino Clandestino and to the local movement opposing the Turin-Lyon high-speed railway line. The second is "Etinomia", a network of self-defined ethical businesses, cooperating for sustainable and fair local development.
4. Part of this section was presented at the 7th AESOP Sustainable Food Planning Conference that took place in Turin in 2015 and was published in the conference proceedings (Cinà & Dansero, 2015).
5. Part of this section was presented at the Colloque International "Construire le proximités dans un monde global"—8me Journées de la Proximité (Tours, May 20–22, 2015) and was published in the conference proceedings (Dansero, Pettenati, & Toldo, 2016).
6. Italian national law 205/2017 established the "*distretti del cibo*" (food districts), that is, groups of local authorities and businesses that cooperate to promote local development, social cohesion and inclusion, food security,

environmental sustainability, landscape protection, and so on through agro-food activities. One of the possible food district models is based on local productive systems relying heavily on direct sales of agro-food products through solidarity economy networks (e.g., GASs, etc.), thus confirming AFNs' potential for promoting and sustaining new models of territorial development that are potentially more sustainable.

7. The most important case is that of GAS Torino, which gathers together most of the Turin-based groups.

References

Allen, P. (2010). Realizing Justice in Local Food Systems. *Cambridge Journal of Regions, Economy and Society, 3*, 295–308.

Bini, V., Dansero, E., Magarini, A., & Nicolarea, Y. (2017). Urban Food Policies in the Global South: Themes, Approaches, Reference Cases. *Bollettino della Società Geografica Italiana, 10*(1–2), 47–64.

Born, B., & Purcell, M. (2006). Avoiding the Local Trap: Scale and Food Systems in Planning Research. *Journal of Planning Education and Research, 26*, 195–207.

Boschma, R. (2005). Proximity and Innovation: A Critical Assessment. *Regional Studies, 39*(1), 61–74.

Bottiglieri, M., Pettenati, G., & Toldo, A. (Eds.). (2016). *Toward the Turin Food Policy. Good Practices and Visions.* Milano: FrancoAngeli.

Calori, A., Dansero, E., Pettenati, G., & Toldo, A. (2017). Urban Food Planning in Italian Cities: A Comparative Analysis of the Cases of Milan and Turin. *Agroecology and Sustainable Food Systems, 41*(8), 1026–1046.

Casey, E. S. (2001). Between Geography and Philosophy: What Does It Mean to Be in the Place-World? *Annals of the Association of American Geographers, 91*, 683–693.

Cinà, G., & Dansero, E. (Eds.). (2015). Localizing Urban Food Strategies. Farming Cities and Performing Rurality. *Proceedings of the 7th AESOP Sustainable Food Planning Conference*, Polytechnic of Turin, Turin.

Clancy, K., & Ruhf, K. (2010). Is Local Enough? Some Arguments for Regional Food Systems. *Choices, 25*, 123–135.

Dansero, E., & Pettenati, G. (2015). Alternative Food Networks as Spaces for the Re-territorialisation of Food. The Case of Turin. In G. Cinà & E. Dansero (Eds.), *Localizing Urban Food Strategies. Farming Cities and Performing*

Rurality. Proceedings of the 7th AESOP Sustainable Food Planning Conference (pp. 552–565). Turin: Polytechnic of Turin.

Dansero, E., Pettenati, G., & Toldo, A. (2015). The Atlas of Food. Processes, Actors and Representations Toward the Food Strategy of Torino Metropolitana. *GeoProgress Journal, 2*(I), 17–33.

Dansero, E., Pettenati, G., & Toldo, A. (2016). Si proche et pourtant si loin. Etudier et construire la proximité alimentaire à Turin. In P. Mundler & J. Rouchier (Eds.), *Alimentation et proximité: jeux d'acteurs et territoires.* Educagri: Dijon.

Dansero, E., & Puttilli, M. (2013). Multiple Territorialities of Alternative Food Networks: Six Cases from Piedmont, Italy. *Local Environment, 19*(6), 626–643.

Donald, B., & Blay-Palmer, A. (2006). The Urban Creative-Food Economy: Producing Food for the Urban Elite or Social Inclusion Opportunity? *Environment and Planning A, 38*(10), 1901–1920.

DuPuis, M., & Goodman, D. (2005). Should We Go "Home" to Eat?: Toward a Reflexive Politics of Localism. *Journal of Rural Studies, 21*, 359–371.

Feagan, R. (2007). The Place of Food: Mapping Out the 'Local' in Local Food Systems. *Progress in Human Geography, 31*(1), 23–42.

Galt, R. E. (2013). The Moral Economy Is a Double-Edged Sword: Explaining Farmers' Earnings and Self-Exploitation in Community-Supported Agriculture. *Economic Geography, 89*(4), 341–365.

Goodman, D., Du Puis, M., & Goodman, M. (2012). *Alternative Food Networks.* Milton Park: Routledge.

Grasseni, C. (2013). *Beyond Alternative Food Networks: Italy's Solidarity Purchase Groups.* London: Bloomsbury.

Graziano, P. R., & Forno, F. (2012). Political Consumerism and New Forms of Political Participation: The Gruppi di Acquisto Solidale in Italy. *The ANNALS of the American Academy of Political and Social Science, 644*(1), 121–133.

Guadagno, R., & Cavallo, A. (2016). I Box Scheme. In D. Marino (Ed.), *Agricoltura urbana e filiere corte: Un quadro della realtà italiana.* Milano: FrancoAngeli.

Harvey, D. (2006). *Spaces of Global Capitalism: Towards a Theory of Uneven Geographical Development.* New York: Verso.

Hendrickson, M., & Heffernan, W. (2002). Opening Spaces Through Relocalization: Locating Potential Resistance in the Weaknesses of the Global Food System. *Sociologia Ruralis, 42*(4), 347–369.

Hinrichs, C. (2003). The Practice and Politics of Food System Localization. *Journal of Rural Studies, 19*, 33–45.

Ilbery, B., & Kneafsey, M. (2000). Registering Regional Specialty Food and Drink Products in the United Kingdom: The Case of PDOs and PGIs. *Area, 32*(3), 317–325.

Jarosz, L. (2008). The City in the Country: Growing Alternative Food Networks in Metropolitan Areas. *Journal of Rural Studies, 24*, 231–244.

Kneafsey, M. (2010). The Region in Food – Important or Irrelevant? *Cambridge Journal of Regions, Economy and Society, 3*, 177–190.

Kremer, P., & DeLiberty, T. (2011). Local Food Practices and Growing Potential: Mapping the Case of Philadelphia. *Applied Geography, 31*, 1252–1261.

Lang, T., Rayner, G., Rayner, M., Barling, D., & Millstone, E. (2005). Policy Councils on Food, Nutrition and Physical Activity: The UK as a Case Study. *Public Health Nutrition, 8*(1), 11–19.

Lévy, J. (1997). *Europe. Une géographie*. Paris: Hachette.

Magnaghi, A. (2010). *Il progetto locale*. Torino: Bollati Boringhieri.

Marino, D., & Cicatiello, C. (2012). *I Farmers' Market: la mano visibile del mercato*. Milano: FrancoAngeli.

Marsden, T., Banks, J., & Bristow, G. (2000). Food Supply Chain Approaches: Exploring Their Role in Rural Development. *Sociologia Ruralis, 40*(4), 424–438.

Matacena, R. (2016). Linking Alternative Food Networks and Urban Food Policy: A Step Forward in the Transition Towards a Sustainable and Equitable Food System? *International Review of Social Research, 6*(1), 49–58.

Morgan, K., Marsden, T., & Murdoch, J. (2006). *Worlds of Food*. Oxford: Oxford University Press.

Morgan, K., & Sonnino, R. (2010). The Urban Foodscape: World Cities and the New Food Equation. *Cambridge Journal of Regions, Economy and Society, 3*(2), 209–224.

Murdoch, J., Marsden, T., & Banks, J. (2000). Quality, Nature, and Embeddedness: Some Theoretical Considerations in the Context of the Food Sector. *Economic Geography, 76*(2), 107–125.

Pettenati, G., & Dansero, E. (2018). Alternative Food Networks and Food Citizenship in Turin Metropolitan Area. In N. Baron & J. Romero (Eds.), Cultura territorial, innovaciòn social y reorientaciòn de los modelos metropolitanos. *Proceedings of the Conference* MESCRIM – *Métropoles espagnoles crises et mutations*, Valencia, May 30th–June 1st 2018, pp. 437–448.

Pettenati, G., & Toldo, A. (2018). *Il cibo tra azione locale e sistemi globali*. Milano: FrancoAngeli.

Pettenati, G., Toldo, A., & Ferrando, T. (2018). Food System as Commons. In J. Vivero-Pol, T. Ferrando, O. de Schutter, & U. Mattei (Eds.), *Routledge Handbook of Food as a Commons*. London: Routledge.

Pettenati, G., & Vittone, I. (2018). Il sistema del cibo del Chierese, verso una politica locale del cibo. In *2° rapporto dell'Atlante del cibo di Torino Metropolitana* (pp. 119–175). Torino: Celid.

Raffestin, C. (1980). *Pour une geographie du pouvoir*. Paris: Litec.

Raffestin, C. (2012). Space, Territory, and Territoriality. *Environment and Planning D: Society and Space, 30*(1), 121–141.

Rallet, A., & Torre, A. (2004). Proximité et localisation. *Économie Rurale, 280*(1), 25–81.

Renting, H., Marsden, T. K., & Banks, J. (2003). Understanding Alternative Food Networks: Exploring the Role of Short Food Supply Chains in Rural Development. *Environment and Planning A, 35*(3), 393–411.

Renting, H., Schermer, M., & Rossi, A. (2012). Building Food Democracy: Exploring Civic Food Networks and Newly Emerging Forms of Food Citizenship. *International Journal of Sociology of Agriculture and Food, 19*(3), 289–307.

Sage, C. (2003). Social Embeddedness and Relations of Regard: Alternative 'Good Food' Networks in South-West Ireland. *Journal of Rural Studies, 19*, 47–60.

Sonnino, R. (2009). Feeding the City: Towards a New Research and Planning Agenda. *International Planning Studies, 14*(4), 425–435.

Sonnino, R. (2016). The New Geography of Food Security: Exploring the Potential of Urban Food Strategies. *The Geographical Journal, 182*(2), 190–200.

Sonnino, R., & Marsden, T. (2006). Beyond the Divide: Rethinking Relationships Between Alternative and Conventional Food Networks in Europe. *Journal of Economic Geography, 6*, 181–199.

Sonnino, R., & Spayde, J. (2014). The New Frontier? Urban Strategies for Food Security and Sustainability. In T. Marsden & A. Morley (Eds.), *Sustainable Food Systems: Building a New Paradigm* (pp. 186–205). London: Earthscan.

Toldo, A. (2018). Povertà e assistenza alimentare. Il sistema del cibo d'emergenza a Torino. *Sociologia urbana e rurale, 115*, 82–97.

Tregear, A. (2011). Progressing Knowledge in Alternative and Local Food Networks: Critical Reflections and a Research Agenda. *Journal of Rural Studies, 27*(4), 419–430.
Wiskerke, J. (2009). On Places Lost and Places Regained: Reflections on the Alternative Food Geography and Sustainable Regional Development. *International Planning Studies, 14*(4), 369–387.

Part V

Conclusions

15

Conclusions: An Interdisciplinary Assessment

Alessandro Corsi, Filippo Barbera, Egidio Dansero, and Cristiana Peano

A. Corsi (✉)
Department of Economics and Statistics "Cognetti de Martiis", University of Torino, Torino, Italy
e-mail: alessandro.corsi@unito.it

F. Barbera
Department of Cultures, Politics and Society, University of Torino, Torino, Italy

Collegio Carlo Alberto, Torino, Italy
e-mail: filippo.barbera@unito.it

E. Dansero
Department of Cultures, Politics and Society, University of Torino, Torino, Italy
e-mail: egidio.dansero@unito.it

C. Peano
Department of Agricultural, Forest and Food Sciences, University of Torino, Grugliasco (TO), Italy
e-mail: cristiana.peano@unito.it

A. Corsi et al. (eds.), *Alternative Food Networks*,
https://doi.org/10.1007/978-3-319-90409-2_15

A General Assessment

In this chapter, we will summarize the main findings of our research, discussing the contribution it has made as well as the areas in which it has confirmed the received literature or called it into question.

Both theoretically and empirically, our research has adopted a conception of the "alternativeness" of food chains that departs somewhat from those currently found in the literature. The definition of "alternative" we propose is based on the kind of exchange among operators: namely, we propose to shift the analytical emphasis from the product to the exchange relationship and its correlates (e.g., value-chain organization, multiple forms of embeddedness, environmental consequences, quality conventions, mixed motivations, etc.). In fact, several intrinsic and intangible attributes that are normally considered as constitutive of Alternative Food Network (AFN) products, such as freshness, taste, healthiness, and localness, can also be provided by conventional chains like supermarkets, as they increasingly are. Walmart starting to sell local products and supermarket chains like Carrefour creating lines of high-quality locally designated products under their private labels are examples in point. But AFNs are also dealing with large-scale distribution systems to reach a larger number of consumers.

Originally, in fact, these chains were defined as alternative largely on the basis of the characteristics of food that could be found there, in addition to the type of organization. Food in supermarkets was considered to be anonymous, fungible, tasteless, and damaging to health and the environment. Accordingly, food that had different qualities—since it came from different sources—was considered as an alternative, thus also acquiring a social and political meaning of opposition to the globalized food system. From this standpoint, the food system's local organization and its degree of globalization clearly affected the perception of the "alternative" chains when they originated and, consequently, the theorization of the academic research on the issue. For instance, farmers' markets (FMs) in the UK and in the USA were perceived—and theorized—as "alternative" exactly because they were new and drastically different from the conventional chains. In Italy and in France, by contrast, forms of direct sales by farmers to consumers in urban markets were not new at all. They had survived from time-honoured forms of urban provision, when farmers brought their produce from the countryside to town to sell. In Italy, farmers' markets as a means of fighting intermediation and of bringing producers and consumers into contact have only recently been promoted by farmers' unions, mainly as an economic initiative intended to save a larger share of value added for farmers. But direct sales by farmers in urban open-air district markets are customary and—as we have illustrated—Torino is exemplary in this respect, both in its home region of Piedmont and nationwide. Hence, in some areas, AFNs are not really "new", but they nevertheless allow a personal acquaintance and relationship to develop between consumers and producers. Of course, other chains, such as Solidarity Purchase Groups (SPGs), are often in intentional and declared opposition to the conventional chain, though not all of them take such a strong stance. But all build "embedded ties" between producers and consumers, so that the act of purchasing is not simply an exchange of money for commodities. Mindful of Sage's remarks (Sage, 2003) on the relations of "regard", we maintain that "alternativeness" hinges on the different quality of the exchange and that all these chains to some extent entail an addition to the trade itself, namely, a psychic benefit from the very modalities of the exchange.

It is not by chance that we say "to some extent". One of the findings of our work, which confirms much of the received literature, is that alternativeness is a continuum and not a dichotomy (Hinrichs, 2000; Tregear, 2011) and its borders are blurred. This also holds for the related concept of "local food", for which it is difficult to find precise definitions (Brunori et al., 2016). AFNs involve a complex interplay of motives, both consummatory and instrumental, which are intertwined with the kind of social relations that characterize AFNs. These two dimensions—the mix of motives and interpersonal relations—are the real constitutive dimensions of AFNs, and they act both as a resource and a constraint. In this continuum, consumers and producers are highly heterogeneous in their preferences. Moreover, it is crystal clear that preferences and motivations coexist in each consumer and producer.

Our empirical findings strongly support this concept of alternativeness as a continuum rather than a dichotomy. The empirical research design we favoured over conceptual elaboration per se added significantly to the state of knowledge on AFNs. First, our analysis showed that the strength of the preferences for AFNs differed according to the type of AFN. Consumers' average willingness-to-pay (WTP) for staying with their favourite farmer vendor in district markets was less than SPG members' average WTP to stay with their SPG, and the value of voluntary work provided by SPG members is high and is the key factor in these groups' economic viability. This also suggests that consumers self-select in attending the chain that best reflects their preferences. Our analyses concern chains ranging from urban district markets—traditional facilities that are not particularly committed to alternative food culture—to organizations like the "Off The Market" chains presented in Chap. 7, which are openly political in orientation and strongly opposed to the current food system. The differentiation and self-selection of consumers into different chains might also hold when comparing consumers' concept of quality (and hence preferences) between conventional and alternative chains (Chap. 5), as well as when determining the environmental attributes that consumers in different chains attach to food (Chap. 6).

One reason for the existence of different "degrees of alternativeness" is thus consumers' heterogeneous preferences for the chains, and whether they are more or less explicitly opposed to the food system and the mass food models. A second reason is the coexistence in individual consumers of different motivations for participating in AFNs and for the food characteristics they can find in each of them. In accordance with much of the literature, we find that intrinsic characteristics of food are the main drivers of the choice, as "quality" in general was the most widely cited reason for buying at farmers' stands and at SPGs. If these hedonistic and self-interested motivations are dominant and concern food as a private good, other motivations are at work as well, concerning food as a public good. Hence, concern for the environment and for local farmers is also cited, as is typically found in the literature. These intangible characteristics of AFN food are not in contrast with its intrinsic quality (freshness, seasonality, safety). They can nevertheless be at odds with monetary concerns, if food in AFNs is more expensive than elsewhere, or they operate together with these concerns if it is cheaper. One contribution of our study is in drawing attention to the trivial but frequently overlooked fact that all consumers are budget-constrained, though in differing degrees. How tight this constraint is depends mainly on consumers' income, which explains why the literature frequently finds that consumers attending AFNs are wealthier (note that this applies in situations where AFN food is more expensive than food in the conventional chain). Monetary motivations coexist to varying extents with the other motivations, but are always present. For example, consumers at district markets who are concerned with prices are less willing to continue buying from farmers at higher prices (though not to a statistically significant degree), and those members who state they enjoy lower prices in their SPG than in the supermarkets are also more reluctant to leave it if prices increase. Nevertheless, AFNs are operating in developed countries with relatively high average incomes and where the expenditure for food accounts for a small share of consumers' household outlays. It is thus unsurprising that strictly monetary concerns are secondary to the preferences for the intrinsic and intangible attributes of food.

Also consistent with the existing literature is our finding that no clear-cut division can be made between the environmental impacts of conventional and alternative chains (Chap. 9). Here, our analysis concludes that when looking at the chain in its entirety, most of the environmental impact may occur in the agricultural production phase, with neither organic nor conventional agriculture being consistently superior to the other in terms of its impact. Even if we look only at the distribution phase, much of the environmental impact depends on specific modalities of each particular chain (packaging, for instance), rather than on the nature of the chain. This reinforces the findings in the literature that there is no clear superiority of AFNs over conventional chains in this respect (Coley, Howard, & Winter, 2009; Markussen, Kulak, Smith, Nemecek, & Østergård, 2014) and that food miles are a poor indicator of environmental impact (Coley et al., 2009; DEFRA, 2005; Edwards-Jones et al., 2008; Van Passel, 2013).

The idea of different motivations coexisting across operators and in the same operators also holds among producers. The determinants of producers' participation in AFNs have been investigated rather less than those of consumers. Farmers selling directly are a minority. The objective constraints, not surprisingly, were found to be more binding for them than for consumers (Chap. 4). Constraints are both technical and economic. From the technical standpoint, the type of farming was shown to be strongly associated with the choice of selling directly to consumers, both on- and off-farm. This clearly is because many agricultural products need processing before they can be sold, and on-farm processing is definitely unprofitable when there are strong economies of scale in processing, as is true for milling, slaughtering, and pasteurization. Selling directly, in addition, requires that production be diversified, both seasonally and as regards products. Farmers selling in farmers' markets or to SPGs need to have a variety of products and to provide them year-round. This is the reason why mixed types of farming lend themselves more than others to direct sales. There are differences and exceptions, though. Fruit growers supplying SPGs are often specialized farmers, and the variety in their case means different types of fruit. Wine growers are another category that is particularly interested in on-farm direct sales, due to the widespread wine tourism in Piedmont's famous vineyard areas. Unlike much of the previous literature, we do not find evidence that small farms are more likely to practise direct sales. This might be a particular feature of the region, but there are reasons why this might occur. Direct sales require an investment (higher for off-farm sales than for on-farm sales) both in terms of capital and—more importantly—in labour. It is quite possible that the fixed costs involved are such that the investments are not profitable for very small farms, since fixed costs are distributed over small quantities. In addition, the labour required for sales activities—which can hardly be delegated to waged workers—may interfere with farm activities or be excessive for small part-time farmers. On the other hand, large farms might find it difficult to sell their entire production on the alternative chain. There is a wide heterogeneity among farmers concerning these determinants, with some finding it profitable to adopt the alternative chain, at least for part of their production, while others remain with the conventional chains. This heterogeneity might explain our finding that farm size is in practice irrelevant to the likelihood that a farm will adopt direct sales.

Farmers' subjective motivations for supplying AFNs are another field where the literature is rather scanty. Our survey of a group of producers selling to different AFNs (Chap. 4) confirmed that income motivations are, obviously, one of the main determinants, but at the same time that farmers' motivations also include personal preferences. Among these preferences, one that was unanimously indicated was linked to the defence of their personal professional skills and to their idea of product quality, in opposition to the standard practices imposed by conventional chains. Their idea of quality went hand in hand with consumers' recognition of quality. Farmers' pride in the quality of their products derived from the praise they personally received and the satisfaction it gave. This is further proof that personal knowledge and relationships are at the core of AFNs and give meaning and recognition to the producers' work, as well as to food consumption by consumers. Of course, the strength of these motivations can differ across individuals and across different food chains. Just as consumers have different motivations for purchasing at AFNs, farmers can differ in the strength of their non-monetary motivations. In some cases, simple profitability can be their reason for choosing the alternative chain, more so when the "degree of alternativeness" of the particular chain is low. Again, a continuum of motivations and of strength in the relationship between consumers and producers, and the coexistence of monetary and non-monetary determinants, also emerges for the producers.

The heterogeneity of motivations and preferences, and of their strength, along a continuum, can be rationalized with sociological and economic concepts. According to a sociological discourse (Block, 1990; Hinrichs, 2000), transactions take place along opposing levels of marketness and embeddedness. Marketness indicates the relevance of price in the transaction, with a high level meaning that price is the only or dominant driver of the transaction. At lower levels of marketness, the transaction becomes more and more embedded in a web of social relationships. Marketness is strictly related to instrumentalism, that is, the subjective motivation, and high levels of instrumentalism are equivalent to strict self-interest, while low levels are tantamount to a great interest in non-economic goals and concerns (friendship, social ties, ethics). Hinrichs rightly argues that prices have a role in every transaction and that social embeddedness does not exclude instrumentalism and marketness. Hinrichs nevertheless equates high instrumentalism with prioritization of price. However, self-interest is not necessarily limited to concern with price. It may encompass all food attributes that are personally and exclusively enjoyed. Participants in FMs or SPGs may only be interested in having fresh, seasonal, tasty produce, while all other attributes (local farmers, environmental friendliness) may be purely instrumental to the goal of getting the kind of food they want. Put in economic terms, the crucial distinction is between attributes that are private goods and those that are public or club goods, that is, attributes that are rival or non-rival (rival goods are those goods whose consumption by one person precludes consumption by anyone else, while for non-rival goods this does not apply). Intrinsic food quality is a rival good, insofar as no one else can consume the same food.

By contrast, intangible attributes such as support for local farmers or environmental protection are non-rival, since someone else can benefit from the same effect of the consumption of AFN food.

The continuum along the population of chains can thus be interpreted along two related dimensions. One is the degree of consumers' preferences for rival vs non-rival goods, equivalent to higher or lower levels of instrumentalism; the other is the relevance of personal relationships, which may add meaning to the transactions via social and/or affective relationships. To a certain extent, this differentiation is also linked to the subjective opposition to the existing food system, since some AFNs (CSAs, SPGs) display open rejection of the existing chain and of the existing eating models. At the opposite end, patronizing district markets and FMs may not entail any socio-political criticism and may simply spring from a different attitude towards food consumption.

These considerations help put in perspective our findings about the different structure of preferences in the different chains and the strategic mimicry employed by supermarkets and high-end food retailers. District markets, farmers' markets, and Solidarity Purchase Groups all assign considerable importance to the seller, showing high-quality expectations for the relationship with a specific seller. In district markets, the centrality of the personal relationship with the seller channels a generic quality expectation on the part of consumers. In farmers' markets, the seller is perceived as an intermediary and a guarantor of a specific kind of quality grounded on intangible dimensions of food. In Solidarity Purchase Groups, the personal relationship with the seller is crucial for quality expectations of consumers, who have a somewhat negative attitude towards the dimensions of quality which are key in large-scale distribution (prices and trademarks). In the case of hybrid organizations such as Eataly, quality strategies combine different worlds of quality. Eataly, in fact, combines the ability to respond to soft quality expectations and to leverage features of the retail environment. In other words, consumers at high-end retailers are not looking for a specific seller, but for a particular *sales atmosphere*. The retail environment is the organizational lever that Eataly relies on to generate the experience of soft quality. Eataly mimics the trusting relationship between consumers and sellers in AFNs through *impersonal* judgment strategies where the atmosphere *substitutes* for the personal relationships with specific sellers. What is interesting to underline is that there seems to be a "chain-effect" on quality conventions which is independent of individual level attributes. This opens onto two interpretations. One is that quality conventions are not psychological traits of consumers, but rather are enacted by the specific setting of the chain. For instance, the atmospheric dimensions of farmers' markets differ from those of supermarkets and encourage consumers to value qualities like freshness, taste, and so on. A different interpretation is that consumers self-select in different food chains, so that those interested in freshness and taste attend FMs and those who do not are more inclined to go to the supermarket. Whatever the preferred interpretation, different quality conventions have distinctive effects on the working of food chains.

For instance, they explain our findings on the mechanisms underlying the operation of SPGs. The economic sustainability of SPGs, that is, their ability to pay fair prices to producers and charge their members reasonable prices while balancing the SPG's budget, clearly depends on the unpaid labour contributed by members. This contribution is possible because of the members' strong commitment to the SPG, which is shown by their high willingness-to-pay, that is, to remain with the SPG even if it charges much higher prices. In other words, it is explained by the members' strong preferences for the SPG itself. The commitment has both selfish and altruistic determinants (different levels of instrumentalism), since the stated motivations for preferring to purchase in the SPG include food quality and distrust of food available in supermarkets, as well as non-rival attributes such as environmental protection and concern for farmers. In addition, for some members it is also important to pay lower prices than elsewhere, as shown by the statistical analysis. Therefore, SPG members thus make an implicit trade-off between their labour contribution to the SPG's operation and what they receive in return, that is, food characterized by intrinsic and intangible attributes, and for some, lower prices. For many members, contributing labour is not a cost, but a benefit, since they enjoy cooperating with the other members in running the SPG. To use sociological terminology, they are at a low level of instrumentalism and a high level of embeddedness. This is a characteristic of "committed AFNs" and similar results would be probably found for Community Supported Agriculture, though the latter is almost absent in Italy.

Interdisciplinarity and Understanding AFNs

Did the interdisciplinary approach taken by this research actually help in understanding and assessing AFNs? We are convinced that it did. The main advantage is that adopting different disciplinary lenses allowed us to look at AFNs from different vantage points and thus calibrate and balance out the emphasis on particular aspects that each discipline tends to give.

The economic approach tries to find common behavioural patterns and to model their underlying mechanisms. It is mainly deductive, assuming a behavioural model which it attempts to verify or falsify with empirical data. Specificities, both local and individual, are seen as statistical variations of the assumed behaviour. The economic approach also stresses the objective income constraint that sets limits to individual preferences and, more generally, tries to detect the incentives that influence individual behaviour. The sociological and anthropological approaches are more deductive-oriented. Though they too refer to theoretical models, they give greater emphasis to individual behaviour and stress the differences as the main objects of analysis. They focus on the symbolic and intangible attributes of food in AFNs, and the social relationships connected with economic life. The geographical approach draws from both, giving more emphasis to the territorial implications. In a way, there is a trade-off between a higher level of abstraction that illuminates the underlying mechanisms and a more detailed analysis that more accurately reflects the multiple facets of reality.

Contrasting these approaches was reciprocally fruitful. Economists became more aware of the social implications of transactions and were thus spurred to explicitly include symbolic and intangible attributes of food as determinants of consumers' preferences in their empirical models (to be sure, contrary to a widespread view, economists do not only deal with monetary variables). Second, economists also became aware of a distinctive feature of exchanges in AFNs, namely, the fact that the modalities of the transaction may yield a benefit, that is, that the transaction itself provides utility. This was included in a model of consumer behaviour that made it possible to estimate the WTP for this benefit (Corsi & Novelli, 2015), thus adding to the understanding of the mechanism underlying the chain's operation. Likewise, understanding and assessing the non-monetary motivations of SPG members shed light on the groups' economic operation and provided insights into their resilience. Sociologist and anthropologists were reminded of the sad reality of the monetary constraints that, though to a lesser extent than social determinants, influence individuals' behaviour. Both producers' and consumers' choices in AFNs take the role of monetary constraints on their behaviour into account. It would be meaningless to simply think that the "alternativeness" of AFNs does not contemplate any role for time, money, and costs. Why should that be so? The key point is to shed light on how economic constraints and social dimensions jointly shape producers' and consumers' choices. Even the most radical forms of AFN (such as SPGs) must be economically sustainable in the long term. Scaling-up dynamics, the role of new technologies and efficient logistics are inescapable challenges AFNs need to come to grips with. The crucial issue is to understand how the intrinsic motivations that support AFNs can be sustained even when face-to-face interaction and "militancy" against the conventional food system tend to decrease for whatever reason.

A final result of the interdisciplinary approach was that it helped reduce the risk of an ideological bias that is always present when dealing with a socially and politically sensitive issue like AFNs. The literature on AFNs is permeated with value judgements—sometimes explicit, more frequently implicit—on their desirability. Legitimate as they may be, they risk obscuring the analysis. For all their internal differences, the disciplines also have certain general attitudes, with anthropological, sociological, and geographical scholars most frequently tending to judge the existence and role of AFNs favourably while taking a generally critical view of the food system. For them, the risk is that of not considering the AFNs weaknesses and exaggerating their positive effects. Economists and environmental scientists are more attentive to objective facts and constraints and tend to have a more sceptical view. For them, the risk is the opposite, that of not considering the positive social and environmental effects of AFNs and hence of downplaying their importance and their prospects. The exchange of views between the disciplines was stimulating and, by smoothing out the differences in the emphasis given to positive and negative features, allowed for a more nuanced and balanced analysis.

The Future Prospects for AFNs

Our assessment of AFNs leads in the end to the question of their future. Will they scale up and shift from a niche sector to a larger share of the food market? Will they maintain their alternativeness? Will they be able to change the food system?

A short recapitulation of some of the main facts concerning AFNs will help put the issue in perspective. Participants in AFNs are a minority of consumers. This is particularly true for the most "committed" AFNs, like SPGs and CSAs. Pettenati and Dansero (2015) estimated that there are about 170 SPGs in Piedmont, and assuming, over-generously, that each has 200 participants gives 34,000 consumers out of a population of about 4.4 million. Patrons of FMs in the region are also relatively few, since 87 FMs take place periodically (typically once or twice a month) as against about 1000 open-air urban markets, most of which are held on a daily basis. The share of consumers who buy from farmers in district markets is relatively high (in our survey, one third of the respondents stated they bought predominantly from farmers), but this is also the channel that departs least from the conventional chain and where farmers sell side by side with conventional vendors. We are not aware of data on the weight of AFNs in other countries, but we can be reasonably certain that the numbers cannot be much higher. This fact in itself might simply be due to a lack of supply, so that one might argue that, if there were more FMs or SPGs, the share of consumers participating in AFNs would be much higher. Our data show that the preference for "alternative" quality conventions is widespread among consumers, even those who buy their food mainly in large-scale distribution. This continuum and the ubiquity of preferences for "non-standard" food could lead to two distinct possibilities: on the one hand, AFNs may expand and reach more consumers, since the preferences for "good, clean and fair" food are widespread and growing. On the other hand, conventional chains are exploiting the continuum to mimic some of AFNs' characteristics, and this trend could gain more ground.

In line with much of the literature, a second point that came to light is that consumers' motivations are heterogeneous, and different motivations can coexist in the same consumers. Motivations linked to the intrinsic attributes of food are dominant, which is consistent with the growing numbers of people who seek non-anonymous, tasty, safe, and environmentally friendly food. Frequently, stated motivations include intangible attributes, but a distinction should be made among them on the basis of whether or not they can be provided by the conventional chain. Product attributes such as low environmental impact or local origin can also be provided by food in supermarkets; a personal relationship with the farmer cannot. This distinction between those food attributes that could be provided by conventional chains and those that could not is crucial, because the former can simply be considered as a new demand that the conventional chain has not yet been able to meet, or to meet in full. This distinction is, for instance, at the core of the difficulties that the most politically committed AFNs, such as those discussed in Chap. 7, have in reconciling their opposition to supermarkets with the fact that some members' demand centres mainly on healthy food, so that they see no harm in buying it in supermarkets. In fact, the conventional chains are making efforts to meet the new demand. Walmart starting to sell local products and Carrefour creating a line of high-quality local products are examples in point, not to mention the organic food lines that virtually all supermarkets have introduced, scandalizing the purists of the original organic movement. And Eataly mimicking the atmosphere of popular markets (Chap. 5) is a further example of how certain intangible attributes can also be offered in conventional chains, precisely in order to satisfy particular consumer preferences.

The AFNs which resist this mimetic capability on the part of the conventional food system are those, like SPGs, that are most solidly based on the "value" of personal relationships in themselves. In such cases, what matters is not so much a preference for the intangible dimensions of food, but rather a shared feeling *against* the conventional food system, whose meaning is deeply intertwined with the interpersonal relationships within SPGs. Here we see a trade-off: to attract more consumers, AFNs must face the problem of better distribution and prices, which is a matter of spatial and economic scale. But this would appear to detract from the very value of AFNs, which are rooted in intrinsic motivations, political consumerism "against", and interpersonal ties.

Overall, the foregoing considerations lead us to conclude that the probability that growth in AFNs can bring about profound changes in the nature of food chains is rather low. It seems very unlikely that AFNs could compete with the conventional chains by scaling up, that is, growing in size and covering a larger share of total consumption, given these chains' superiority in logistics, economies of scale, and management skills. AFNs' current superiority in providing desired intrinsic attributes of food is threatened as the conventional chains make up for their delay in responding to new consumer demand. It is most likely a repetition of the process that affected organic farming, whose very success meant that it was subsumed into the mainstream economy, so that the movement lost its original oppositional and alternative nature (Guthman, 2014).

A different possibility for AFNs is scaling out, that is, increasing the network connecting AFNs to each other and to producers and consumers. Information and Communication Technologies (ICTs) provide great technical opportunities in this respect, and online orders are a common practice among SPGs. Online sales are also widely used by individual farmers. But online connections between consumers and producers are not equivalent to face-to-face relationships and cannot fully replicate the AFN experience (Bos & Owen, 2016). In addition, commercial firms are also mimicking SPGs. The Food Assembly (in French *La ruche qui dit oui*), a French firm that has now spread to several other European countries, provides an Internet platform where local organizers can manage sales by having consumers place orders with local farmers, who weekly bring their products for collection by buyers at a specified time and place. While the Food Assembly operates in the same way as an SPG, and also emphasizes local food and local farmers, it is an economic enterprise in which farmers pay a commission (16.7% in France, 20% in other countries) that is shared equally between the central firm and the local organizer. It is evident that such an organization follows a logic of instrumentalism (intrinsic characteristics of food and low prices for consumers, higher received prices for farmers compared to delivery to supermarkets) but, like supermarkets, cannot provide certain specific transaction characteristics that AFNs allow, namely, the personal producer-consumer relationship. Radical forms of AFN such as SPGs and the like will certainly survive, but more as spaces of radical civic participation than as economic competitors of the conventional food chains. As such, they might provide fertile ground for aspirations towards a "good life" in a "fair society", connecting everyday needs to large-scale aspirations and collective projects. Their effectiveness as food producers and distributors "for the masses" should not be taken for granted on normative basis.

Overall, the conclusion is that AFNs, if seen as food distribution organizations that consistently and openly aim to change the food system, will likely remain a niche. Their importance is more a matter of civic and political participation—a key problem indeed—than of offering a feasible alternative to the current food system. Radical AFNs are spaces for "activist citizens": "interested in challenging routine, understandings, and practices, which makes theirs a political project versus politics as usual" (Carolan, 2017, 198).

Much of the growth of the new chains as alternatives to the globalized food system stemmed from a combination of two factors: many consumers desired food having certain attributes and these attributes were not available in the food provided by the conventional chain. With this coincidence, the search for fresh, tasty, seasonal, and local food came to be associated with a critique of the existing food system. As supermarkets and the conventional distribution chains in general gradually cover this section of demand, the association between new food preferences and critical consumption is likely to fade. AFNs thus have the historic merit of pushing conventional chains to give more consideration to certain food attributes. Consequently, AFNs through their very existence have indirectly improved the intrinsic quality of food and its environmental impact by creating an incentive for the conventional chains to cover a further segment of the market. Nevertheless, conventional chains cannot hope to provide the personal relationships that are the crucial characteristic (though to differing extents) of AFNs, so there will still be room for AFNs to survive. Their survival and expansion is linked to the spread of conscious and explicit criticism of the food system and to the rejection of the impersonal and anonymous modalities of food provisioning that this entails.

A final note concerns the role of producers. Those who deliver to AFNs are a minority, and AFNs are often not the exclusive outlet for their products. The alternative chain is not automatically profitable for farmers, not necessarily even for small farmers, since it depends on the difference between the higher revenue and the higher costs normally entailed by AFNs. The growing demand for food with intrinsic quality characteristics and of local provenance will cause prices to rise, both in the direct sales channel and indirectly when large-scale retailers decide to address this demand segment. This may be followed by a shift in supply if other producers react to growing prices by entering these areas of production, so that the final outcome may be a larger quantity of quality products but not necessarily higher prices. In any case, AFNs may afford a segment of producers with an opportunity not only to increase their income but also to increase the satisfaction and pride in their product, through recognition from consumers they interact with personally, a recognition that anonymous and fungible delivery to conventional chains cannot provide.

References

Block, F. L. (1990). *Postindustrial Possibilities: A Critique of Economic Discourse.* Berkeley: University of California Press.

Bos, E., & Owen, L. (2016). Virtual Reconnection: The Online Spaces of Alternative Food Networks in England. *Journal of Rural Studies, 45*, 1–14.

Brunori, G., Galli, F., Barjolle, D., van Broekhuizen, R., Colombo, L., Giampietro, M., et al. (2016). Are Local Food Chains More Sustainable Than Global Food Chains? Considerations for Assessment. *Sustainability, 8*(5), 1–27.

Carolan, M. (2017). More-than-Active Food Citizens: A Longitudinal and Comparative Study of Alternative and Conventional Eaters. *Rural Sociology, 82*(2), 197–225.

Coley, D., Howard, M., & Winter, M. (2009). Local Food, Food Miles and Carbon Emissions: A Comparison of Farm Shop and Mass Distribution Approaches. *Food Policy, 34*(2), 150–155.

DEFRA. (2005). *The Validity of Food Miles as an Indicator of Sustainable Development.* Defra, Issue 7, 117 p.

Edwards-Jones, G., Milà i Canals, L., Hounsome, N., Truninger, M., Koerber, G., Hounsome, B., et al. (2008). Testing the Assertion That "Local Food Is

Best": The Challenges of an Evidence-Based Approach. *Trends in Food Science and Technology, 19*(5), 265–274.

Guthman, J. (2014). *Agrarian Dreams: The Paradox of Organic Farming in California*. Berkeley; Los Angeles: University of California Press.

Hinrichs, C. C. (2000). Embeddedness and Local Food Systems: Notes on Two Types of Direct Agricultural Market. *Journal of Rural Studies, 16*(3), 295–303.

Markussen, M. V., Kulak, M., Smith, L. G., Nemecek, T., & Østergård, H. (2014). Evaluating the Sustainability of a Small-Scale Low-Input Organic Vegetable Supply System in the United Kingdom. *Sustainability, 6*, 1913–1945.

Sage, C. (2003). Social Embeddedness and Relations of Regard: Alternative 'Good Food' Networks in South-West Ireland. *Journal of Rural Studies, 19*(1), 47–60.

Tregear, A. (2011). Progressing Knowledge in Alternative and Local Food Networks: Critical Reflections and a Research Agenda. *Journal of Rural Studies, 27*(4), 419–430.

Van Passel, S. (2013). Food Miles to Assess Sustainability: A Revision. *Sustainable Development, 21*(1), 1–17.

Index[1]

A

Attributes
- extrinsic, 127
- intangible, 61, 71, 77, 78, 166, 306, 309, 312–314, 317
- intrinsic, 59, 77, 78, 127, 171, 309, 313, 317, 318

C

Consumer
- behaviour, 7, 22, 36, 62, 120, 314
- choices, 51, 58–61, 66, 69, 78, 231, 253, 309, 315
- motivations, 6, 13, 36, 62, 177, 291, 307, 308, 311, 316
- participation, 36, 57–80, 200

Cost, 14–17, 26, 50, 51, 58–61, 64, 65, 69, 74, 81n5, 88, 124, 139, 147, 148, 153, 154, 167–169, 174–177, 179–183, 187, 189–192, 198–209, 210n1, 210n4, 211n6, 211n7, 216–222, 225, 228, 230, 232, 233, 237, 239, 251, 282, 291, 310, 313, 315, 320

D

Determinants
- altruistic, 313
- monetary, 311
- non-monetary, 311

Deterritorialization, 249, 281, 284

E

Economic viability, 5, 7, 197–210, 308

[1] Note: Page numbers followed by 'n' refer to notes.

A. Corsi et al. (eds.), *Alternative Food Networks*,
https://doi.org/10.1007/978-3-319-90409-2

Embeddedness, 11, 12, 33, 35, 216–220, 267, 306, 311, 313
Environmental impact, 4, 6, 7, 14, 17, 19, 22, 23, 34, 50, 51, 59, 79, 120, 127, 132, 132n3, 248–249, 253, 256–258, 260–266, 309, 317, 319

F
Farm structural characteristics, 188
Farmers' market (FM), 58, 59, 62–64, 66, 76–78, 93, 107, 122, 123, 127–129, 131, 166, 174–177, 180, 181, 193n1, 199, 275, 276, 289, 290, 295, 306, 311–313, 316
Farmers' personal characteristics, 68

G
Gruppi di Acquisto Solidale (GAS), 71, 178, 197–210, 275–280, 286, 289–292, 294, 295, 296n2, 297n6, 297n7

H
Hard quality, 21, 52, 54, 98–100, 104–107, 112, 113
Hybrid organizations, 21, 54, 107, 112–114, 200, 312

I
Income, 15, 16, 60, 61, 63, 66, 69, 73, 74, 77, 78, 95, 105, 115n8, 131, 142, 146, 167–171, 175, 176, 180–181, 197, 282, 308–310, 314, 320
Information, 7, 11, 12, 20, 24, 70, 72, 78, 98, 119–126, 128–132, 176, 178, 187, 192, 203, 205, 206, 217, 218, 240, 253, 275, 286
Innovation, 21, 33, 88–90, 113, 228, 229, 235, 265

L
Life Cycle Assessment (LCA), 248, 253–261, 265, 267
Local, 50, 59, 87, 121, 139, 180, 201, 221, 248, 252, 275, 306

M
Markets (sociology of), 5
Mimetic quality, 107–111

O
Off-farm sales, 92, 94, 183, 184, 187, 190, 191, 310
On-farm sales, 93, 175, 182–184, 187, 191, 199, 257, 310
Open-air market, 67

P
Packaging, 50, 127, 128, 130, 132n3, 174, 190, 201, 203, 248n3, 254, 256, 259–265, 309
Prices, 15, 50, 60, 90, 121, 138, 167, 174, 198, 215–241, 309
Producers
  behaviour, 188
  choices, 315
  motivations, 36, 188

participation, 7, 180, 292, 309
Proximity, 8, 22, 33, 54, 88, 106, 120, 168, 191, 249, 273–296

Q

Quality, 12, 50, 60, 87, 98–106, 119–132, 140, 166, 176, 199, 215–241, 267, 277, 306
Quality conventions, 7, 20, 21, 31, 53, 54, 87–114, 170, 216, 221, 222, 224–227, 232, 237, 306, 313, 316

R

Relationship
between consumers and producers, 72, 123, 125, 287, 307, 311, 318
personal, 7, 8, 12, 14, 16–18, 36n1, 51, 52, 69–71, 79, 109, 112, 113, 123, 171, 192, 217, 222, 234, 241, 312, 313, 317, 319
Reterritorialization, 8, 249, 273–296
Revenue, 15–17, 93, 168, 169, 174, 175, 177, 180, 181, 198, 203, 207, 210n4, 211n7, 219, 320

S

Soft quality, 21, 54, 55, 98–103, 106, 107, 112–114, 312
Solidarity Purchasing Group (SPG), *see* Gruppi di Acquisto Solidale
Space, 11, 21, 22, 30, 32, 33, 54, 106, 107, 111, 112, 114, 120, 141, 144, 146, 249, 266, 274, 277, 282, 284–286, 288, 289, 293, 318, 319
Spatial distribution, 35, 249, 274–281, 294
Supermarkets, 12, 16, 35, 49, 50, 52, 62, 68, 71–76, 80, 90, 92, 95, 96, 99, 106, 107, 109, 114, 114n4, 122–128, 130, 131, 138, 145, 146, 149–151, 156, 179, 227, 248, 254, 256, 257, 261, 265, 286, 306, 309, 312, 313, 317–319
Sustainability, 4, 7, 19, 23, 24, 35, 50, 53, 64, 87, 88, 91, 113, 119–121, 139, 197, 198, 201, 202, 209, 251–253, 256, 266, 267, 287, 291, 295, 297n6, 313

T

Territory, 21, 33, 247–249, 274, 281, 284
Trust, 12, 13, 20, 21, 50, 53, 54, 59, 66–72, 77, 78, 81n2, 90, 91, 98, 99, 112, 121–124, 128–131, 153, 189, 200, 201, 217, 218, 222, 223, 226, 227, 231, 234, 239–241, 285, 287

U

Urban food planning, 273–296

V

Value
of participation, 78, 209
of personal relationships, 317
of voluntary labour, 203–208

Kolibri 360 GmbH
Ferdinand-Jühlke-Straße 7
99095 Erfurt, Deutschland
produktsicherheit@kolibri360.de